WINES OF
BORDEAUX

FOREWORD BY HUGH JOHNSON

David Peppercorn

Wines of Bordeaux
by David Peppercorn

First published in Great Britain in 1986 as *David Peppercorn's Pocket Guide to The Wines of Bordeaux.* This edition, revised, updated and expanded, published in 1998 by Octopus Publishing Group Ltd., 2-4 Heron Quays, London E14 4JP.

A CIP catalogue record for this book is available from the British Library.

ISBN 1 84000 250 6

The author and publishers will be grateful for any information that will assist them in keeping future editions up to date. Although all reasonable care has been taken in the preparation of this book, neither the publishers nor the author can accept responsibility for any consequences arising from the use thereof or from the information contained therein.

Commissioning Editor: Rebecca Spry
Executive Art Editor: Tracy Killick
Senior Editor: Lucy Bridgers
Index: Anne Barrett
Production: Karen Farquhar

Typeset in Veljovic Book
Printed and bound in China

Contents

Introduction

Access to the personal files of a top professional is surely the most that any serious amateur of wine could ask. The new generation of wine books represented by David Peppercorn's guide to the wines of Bordeaux amounts almost to such a privileged snoop.

The situation reports and critical opinions that form the basis of buying decisions are normally classified information. But wine literature has moved with quite startling speed from the phase of enthusiastic generalisation to that of precise wine-by-wine commentary. In this book it drops at least its sixth, if not its seventh, veil. Now we are allowed to know as much as the most experienced professionals.

David Peppercorn is one of the most perceptive and respected of that ancient aristocracy of Anglo-Saxon merchants whose speciality is the wine of Bordeaux. He inherited both skill and passion from his father, one of the great 'claret men' of the previous generation. Indirectly, one might say, he inherited them from a long line of predecessors stretching right back to the *negotiator brittanicus* who was identified on the waterfront of Burdigala, Roman Bordeaux, 18 centuries ago.

Accumulated experience is a serious merchant's vital stock in trade. It allows him to watch the passing show with a sense of historical perspective, to interpret as well as to observe. But to keep up with such a complex scene as Bordeaux demands above all perpetual tastings and almost daily communication with the market-place. Thousands of properties vary from one vintage to another in their relative success or failure, while their older wines develop – not always in predictable ways.

David Peppercorn combines these two essential elements – a background of experience and a fund of knowledge constantly kept up to date – as well as any merchant-turned-author has ever done. It is a remarkable privilege to be able, as it were, to look over his shoulder at the enthralling pageant of Bordeaux.

Hugh Johnson

How to Use this Book

This book has three main sections: first, an introductory one giving a general picture of the Bordeaux wine region and how it works; second, a series of château profiles arranged by appellation with a short briefing on each appellation and third, an alphabetical listing of châteaux that do not feature in the profiles section, but whose product makes them worthy of a brief mention at least. Out of the 4,000 or so châteaux in the region, a careful selection has been made of some 1,000 properties, ranging from the most illustrious growths to many lesser-known *crus* that are worth seeking out. These include not only châteaux but also some domaines and cooperatives.

To look up a name, find the page reference in the full alphabetical index at the back of the book. If the reference leads to the Additional Châteaux section, the entry there will be followed by brief factual details such as appellation, ownership, vineyard area and production figures. A star beside one of these entries indicates that, although not profiled, the wine is above average in its class. If the château merits a profile, the index will refer you to the appropriate page in the body of the book – Château Profiles by Appellation. If the name is that of a second or other label, the index entry appears in italic and the page number refers to that of the parent château.

To save space, a number of abbreviations have been used. Vineyard areas are expressed in hectares (shortened to ha), and yields are given in hectolitres per hectare (hl/ha).

Where a company owns a property, the company name may be preceded by the following abbreviations. These indicate types of company as follows:

Éts	Établissement	**SARL**	Sociéte à Responsibilité Limité
GAEC	Groupement Agricole d'Exploitation en Commun	**SC**	Société Civile
		SCA	Société Civile Agricole
GFA	Groupement Foncier Agricole	**SCEA**	Société Civile d'Exploitation Agricole
SA	Société Anonyme	**SCI**	Société Civile Immobilière

The following abbreviations are used for grape varieties:

CF	Cabernet Franc	**Musc**	Muscadelle
Col	Colombard	**PV**	Petit Verdot
CS	Cabernet Sauvignon	**Sauv**	Sauvignon Blanc
Mal	Malbec	**Sém**	Sémillon
Mer	Merlot		

The Region and its Wines

Bordeaux occupies a pre-eminent place among the world's wine regions. Its special geographical situation enables it to produce more fine wines with more regularity than any other part of France, or any other country.

Nowhere else are the greatest wines made in such quantity (only Ausone and Pétrus are in really short supply). And if world-wide acclaim has driven the prices of the First Growths beyond the reach of most of us, there are a number of excellent wines at far more reasonable prices that can often rival them, especially when young. For if Bordeaux can claim nine Premiers Crus (eight red and one white), how many other remarkable and exceptional wines does it make? Tot up the best of the classified Médocs (and some of the unclassified ones) and the best of the Graves and St-Émilion classified growths, to say nothing of the best Pomerols, and you arrive at a figure of around 100 growths that can or do produce great bottles of wine. An impressive roll call. This covers only red wines, but there are also great sweet white wines and good dry whites.

Of course, this small elite is only the tip of the iceberg. The Bordeaux bible, *Bordeaux et Ses Vins*, by Edition Féret, lists over 4,800 property names in its 1995 edition, while just over 13,500 growers made wine in the *département* of Gironde in 1995 (this includes *vin de table*) and over 112,000 hectares of vineyards were dedicated to the growing of vines with the right to an *Appellation Contrôlée*. Bordeaux wines are indeed within the reach of all today and its most modest wines have never been better made.

Geography

Physically Bordeaux lies in the southwest of France, on the 45° latitude, with the often stormy waters of the Atlantic Ocean in the Bay of Biscay only a few miles to the west. Its vineyards spread out along the rivers Gironde, Garonne and Dordogne. Here the warming influence of the Gulf Stream is crucial – bear in mind that on the other side of the Atlantic the same latitude goes through Nova Scotia and Maine. The Gulf Stream and the Atlantic provide Bordeaux with hot summers, long mild autumns often extending to the end of October, relatively mild but wet winters, and mild springs. The consistency of the weather is emphasised by the way in which years of bitter cold (1709, 1740, 1820, 1956, 1985) or years of excessive rain (1930–32, 1965, 1968 and 1992) stand out.

The geology of the region is also important – not so much, it is now thought, for what the soils contain as for the drainage they provide. Going south from the Pointe de Grave and the ocean, the riverside land to the west of the Gironde and Garonne is basically gravel, that to the east predominantly sand, limestone and clay, in constantly changing patterns and proportions. There are exceptions, such as the outcrops of gravel found in parts of Pomerol and the part of St-Émilion that adjoins it, and the limestone and clay under the gravel which gives Sauternes its special character.

The flat, gravelly ridges of the Médoc and Graves are protected from Atlantic gales by the thick pine forests bordering the ocean which also buffer the rainfall. The hills and rivers in the Premières Côtes and Entre-Deux-Mers also provide important differences in microclimate between those vineyards to the west of the Gironde and Garonne (Médoc and Graves) and those to the east of the Dordogne (the Libournais). The distances involved are also significant. From the Pointe de Grave in the north to Langon in the south is 148 kilometres (92 miles); from the city of Bordeaux eastwards to Ste-Foy-la-Grande is 70 kilometres (44 miles), so important climatic variations are hardly surprising.

Historical Background

Three centuries of allegiance to the English crown (1152–1453) gave Bordeaux a sense of unity as a region set apart from the rest of France and helped to orientate it firmly towards the Atlantic and its associated seafaring trade routes.

During these centuries the relative strengths and weaknesses of the sides ebbed and flowed. In the long term the development of sea trade was to have the most far-reaching consequences of all. The evolution of the city of Bordeaux, both as the commercial centre of the region and as its principal port, was natural enough in view of its position. But the development of Libourne as the main port on the Dordogne resulted from a deliberate act of policy by the English to expand trade by creating in 1270 an entirely new town and port.

After the inevitable trading setback caused by the severance of the political ties between Bordeaux and England, it took some time for the region to recover but, as it did, the value of the sea routes and the trading links built up through them became clear. Not only was trade with England, and soon Scotland and Ireland, restored on a lesser scale, but trade with other maritime powers, such as Holland and the Hanseatic ports, was developed. Sea links were also important in establishing trade with Brittany, Normandy and Dunkirk. It was also quite logical that the lucrative West Indies business should have been built up and carried on through the port of Bordeaux. This brought considerable wealth to the city in the 18th century.

The 18th century also saw significant developments in the pattern of land ownership. The movement to build up important estates in the Médoc had begun in the previous century, but now it really began to take shape. This consolidation of land holdings in the hands of the so-called *noblesse de robe* (the legal and political aristocracy of Bordeaux) has had a vital influence in creating the château system which gives the Bordeaux vineyards their unique character. At the same time, a new and prosperous merchant class began to assert itself, first as *courtiers* (brokers) and *négociants*, and later as château proprietors.

This gave Bordeaux as a region a structure which was durable and resilient enough to withstand the vast social and political upheavals of the French revolutionary period (1789–96). Of course there were many important changes in ownership. One

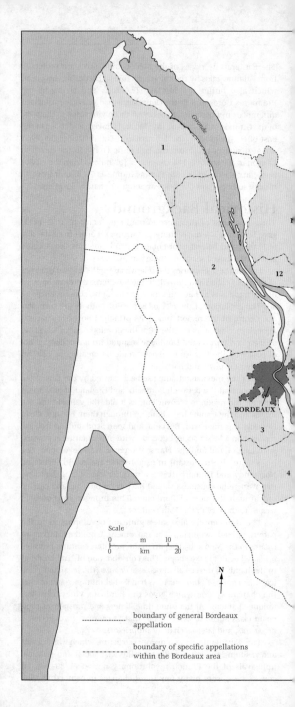

Scale
0   m   10
0   km   20

N

·········· boundary of general Bordeaux
appellation

– – – – – boundary of specific appellations
within the Bordeaux area

Gironde

1

2

12

BORDEAUX

3

4

The Bordeaux Region and its Wine Areas

British general even acquired a château and gave it his name, Palmer, after the final defeat of Napoleon in 1815. But many châteaux changed ownership in name only, having been bought by relatives of exiles whose absence abroad led to their lands being forfeited, and the eventual return of these exiles, in many cases, saw a restoration of the status quo.

In the post-Napoleonic era the importance of the new merchant class, often enriched by commerce with the West Indies, greatly increased. Families such as Barton, Guestier, and Johnston became château proprietors as well as *négociants*. The growing success of the Médoc was crowned by the Paris Exhibition of 1855 for which the famous classification was prepared, covering the red wines of the Médoc (with the exception of Haut-Brion) and the great sweet wines of Sauternes and Barsac.

In 1853 the Paris-Bordeaux railway was opened. This was to have a vital impact on the opening of much of the French market to Bordeaux wines at a period of increasing prosperity. It was especially important for the development of St-Émilion, which had lagged behind Médoc until this time. Napoleon III had ushered in the Second Empire in 1851, and a period of new buoyancy enabled France increasingly to share in the fruits of the industrial revolution, which had been launched in Britain.

Parisian bankers such as the Rothschilds (Lafite and Mouton) and the Péreires (Palmer) invested in properties in the Médoc. Even more important in the long run, the Libournais (St-Émilion, Pomerol and Fronsac) began to emerge from their long obscurity and make their mark. But just as the whole region seemed set on the greatest period of expansion and prosperity in its history, disaster struck. The period often called the *Grande Belle Époque* was effectively ended in 1878 by the devastations of phylloxera. Not until 1893 was there a large vintage of fine quality again.

It said much for the resources built up during the previous years, as well as the energy and determination of the large landowners who led the way in combating the disease, that Bordeaux recovered in the way it did. Once it was discovered that grafting the original French vines onto disease-resistant American rootstock was the only sure remedy, the reconstitution of the vineyards began. But an undertaking of this magnitude could not be accomplished overnight, nor without a great deal of cost and much experimentation.

The picture of what actually happened during these years is a complex one. The need to produce large quantities of serviceable wines quickly was met by planting on marginal lands not previously used for vines and on the *palus* (riverside plain) where treatment by flooding and the sandy soil inhibited the spread of the disease. At the same time, the owners of quality vineyards fought, with a good deal of success, to preserve their ungrafted vines, realising that fine wines needed mature vines. That is why many of the great vineyards of the Médoc, as well as some in St-Émilion and Pomerol such as Cheval-Blanc, Figeac and La Conseillante, were able to continue making great wines during the years of transition.

But a new *Belle Époque* was not yet in sight. After two great years in 1899 and 1900, there was to be no outstanding vintage again until 1920. Economically the years leading up to the First World War were depressed in Europe as a whole, and the Bordeaux trade did not experience the same degree of prosperity it had known in the 1850s, 1860s and 1870s. Although the 1920s produced some splendid vintages, economic conditions became steadily worse. The price of the 1926 vintage collapsed, and the world slump soon followed. Poor vintages and a disastrous economic climate spelt ruin for many growers and merchants during the 1930s.

Bordeaux Since 1945

It was against this background that Bordeaux celebrated peace in 1945 with a series of wonderful vintages, but it took some time for the region to repair the years of neglect and begin to rebuild its prosperity. It was not until the late 1950s that one could say with confidence that a new age was dawning. Prices, and with them investment in vineyards and buildings, began to rise. The real prosperity of the 1960s culminated in the speculation and spiralling prices of 1971–73, which ended in disaster precipitated by the oil crisis of 1974 and was exacerbated by a thoroughly unhealthy market situation in Bordeaux itself. But after only two years of disorder the Bordeaux market recovered, and progress, prosperity and good vintages were the region's hallmarks until the combination of the world recession, high stocks following the exceptional and plentiful vintages of the 1980s, and the difficult vintages of '91 and '92 led to a sharp fall in prices. The *primeur* campaigns for '95, '96 and '97 saw a spiralling of prices similar to that of '70/'71, taking them to a new level for the leading *crus*. The '88 vintage marked the peak of prices in the 1980s: they did not attain this level again until '95.

The revival of prosperity, especially in the Médoc, owed not a little to the enterprise and hard work of an important group of newcomers, colloquially known as *pieds noirs*. These were Frenchmen who had owned estates in Algeria prior to 1960. Many of them bought properties especially in the northern Médoc where prices were low and much of the land was lying fallow.

Technical Progress and Innovation

The 1960s and 1970s were years of enormous technical progress. In the vineyards, the success of sprays in preventing rot have meant that a Bordeaux vintage has not been harvested in an unhealthy condition since 1968. The vinification of these healthy grapes has also seen important improvements. The temperature at which wine is fermented is now much more carefully controlled so that even in hot years, such as 1982, 1983, 1985, 1989 and 1990, few wines become acetic, whereas in 1947 this misfortune was commonplace. The quality of dry white wines has improved almost beyond recognition now that fermentation is carried out at around 18°C (64°F) and the wine is aged in steel rather than wooden barrels. But in recent years there has been a widespread return to cask-fermentation for quality wines.

Great improvements have been made among top growths, especially in the Médoc where the properties are large, by taking much more care over the selection of grapes before the final *assemblage* for the *grand vin*. This has been one of Professor Émile Peynaud's many contributions to the improvements in quality which have been so widely achieved over the past 30 years.

Bordeaux tends to be rather ambivalent about modernisation, so not everyone would hail the introduction of mechanical harvesters as an improvement. Nowhere in France has their use spread more rapidly, and today more machines are employed in the Gironde than in any other *vignoble* of France – 1,050 were in use by 1983 and 1,500 by 1986, harvesting more than half the area under vine. Today the figure is nearer two-thirds. The large estates in Médoc and Entre-Deux-Mers are especially well adapted to their use as the land is rather flat and the *cuviers* where the wine is vinified are usually adjacent to the vineyards. The major advantage of mechanical harvesting is its speed, enabling a much more precise decision to be made as to when the picking should take place, permitting all the grapes to be harvested when perfectly ripe and minimising the risk of part of the harvest being overripe or the weather breaking mid-harvest.

Many of the Crus Classés are still resisting the introduction of machines on the grounds that it would be detrimental to quality. One suspects that they are also concerned about the image created by the machine in the context of an expensive, high-quality product.

The present indications are that, with the progress that has been made in adapting these machines to French vineyards, excellent results can be obtained. For white wines, the cylindrical presses now in use in the winery – the horizontal screw press and, especially in recent years, the pneumatic press – can press the white grapes. Machines also leave unripe grapes unpicked, and in this respect make a better selection 'on the vine' than would most pickers. In recent vintages, the use of the 'Vendange Vert', a severe cutting off of grapes in July, has become widespread in the best vineyards in an effort to control excessive yields, and so improve quality.

The Appellations

The concept of appellations, developed in France immediately after the First World War, and the final legislation giving effect to the system we now know, was enacted in 1935. It meant that any wine of more than purely local fame was given the designation *Appellation d'Origine Contrôlée* (AOC), usually shortened to *Appellation Contrôlée* (AC). The original purpose was to protect the famous wine names of France from cheap imitations at a time of surplus production and low prices. It also spearheaded an important campaign to remove hybrid vines from French appellation vineyards. These are crosses between European vines and phylloxera-resistant American vines, as distinct from grafted vines or crosses between different European vines (such as Müller-Thurgau). These hybrids, which often carry over something of the odd 'foxy' flavour to be found in American vines, were planted in many vineyards after the phylloxera epidemic as an alternative to grafting.

The principal functions of an appellation regulation are:

1 to define the area entitled to a name (eg Médoc);
2 to list what grape varieties may be planted;
3 to specify the density per hectare of vines to be planted, and how they shall be pruned;
4 to set maximum yields per hectare;
5 to set minimum degrees of alcohol (and sometimes for white wines, maximum degrees) and regulate chaptalization (addition of sugar to must to increase alcoholic degree in years of deficient ripeness);
6 since 1974, to insist on analyses and tastings before finished wines may receive their appellation documents;
7 to require growers to make a declaration of their production after each vintage, and a declaration of the stocks they hold as at August 31 each year.

To administer this system and liaise with the syndicates of growers in each appellation, the Institut National des Appellations d'Origine (INAO) was formed, and remains the key body for watching over and reforming the system.

In the Bordeaux region the definition of a particular area entitled to an appellation of its own caused fewer problems than in some other parts of France. But in the Libournais there was much local controversy as to the use of the name St-Émilion. In the 19th century its use was widespread, as old copies of Cocks & Féret's *Bordeaux et ses Vins* bear witness. St-Émilion at this time included not only Pomerol and the communes to the north but also the area to the east now known as the Côtes de Castillon. In 1921, the situation was finally resolved when the Tribunal of Libourne judged that the name of St-Émilion should refer only to those parishes contained within the ancient jurisdiction of the Jurade de St-Émilion. But in 1936 the communes that had been refused the right to sell their wines as St-Émilion were permitted to add the name to their own, thus Montagne-St-Émilion, etc. These are now known as the St-Émilion Satellites.

In the Médoc, the area north of St-Estèphe known as Bas-Médoc received the AC Médoc, while the best part southwards as far as Blanquefort was made Haut-Médoc. However, within the Haut-Médoc, the growers of the most renowned villages sought, and eventually received, their own appellations. A similar situation arose in Graves where the growers in the best northern parts sought to use the names of Pessac and Léognan instead of Graves. A compromise was agreed in 1984, each château concerned adding one of the two names to that of Graves. In 1987 however, after a long campaign, the new appellation Pessac-Léognan was granted. A rather odd anomaly exists in Sauternes, where the commune of Barsac, one of five within the appellation, also has its own AC, and growers may choose to call their wines either Barsac or Sauternes.

The control of what grape varieties may be planted ensures that the traditional character of each wine is preserved and prevents the use of inferior, and possibly higher-yielding, varieties. At the same time, of course, it prevents experimentation, not that this is something much sought after in Bordeaux.

The significance of the density with which vines are planted may not at first be obvious. However, it has been shown that if vines are planted more widely apart than is traditional in Bordeaux they produce higher yields, and the character and quality of the wine changes. A decree in 1974 fixed 2,000 vines per hectare for the Bordeaux AC, as opposed to 5,000 to 10,000 for the Médoc ACs. Traditionally between 8,000 and 9,000 vines are planted per hectare in the Médoc, the figure being closer to 6,000 per hectare in St-Émilion.

The relationship between quantity and quality has long been a vexed one. While it is clear that high yields normally lead to lower quality, at what stage this occurs is not always easy to determine. Several points need to be made. The more effective control of disease, more extensive use of fertilizers and the cloning of the most successful vines have all produced higher yields. The vintage of '53 produced an average yield of 40·8 hectolitres per hectare, and '55 yielded 41·1, compared to 24 in '49 and 25·7 in '61. But '70 produced 52·6, and '73 achieved 55·3, which seemed remarkable by all historic standards. However, '79 saw a figure of 62·9 hectolitres per hectare reached, and the great '82 vintage yielded 60, as did '89. With its disastrous flowering of the Merlot, '84 achieved only 36·9, but that should be compared with the figure of 17 in '56 after the infamous frost, while the spring frost of 1991 reduced the figure that year to 24.

It is clear then that the red grape varieties planted in Bordeaux are capable of producing fine wines from relatively high yields, certainly much higher than would have been thought possible a few years ago. In Burgundy, by contrast, the Pinot Noir's quality falls significantly when yields rise over 50 hectolitres per hectare in hillside vineyards. There were many examples of this in '82. But in the same vintage in Bordeaux both the Merlot and Cabernet Sauvignon produced magnificent wines of real concentration at this level of yield and higher. White wines are less susceptible to loss of quality from high yields, and in Bordeaux the best growths for dry wines tend to combine the more dependable Sémillon and the more irregular Sauvignon.

The minimum of degrees of alcohol are supposed to provide some guarantee of quality and, unless they are achieved, chaptalization (the addition of sugar) is illegal. But it is interesting to note that the great clarets of the past were low in alcohol, often between nine and ten per cent by volume, and many have lasted superbly. Even as recently as the 1940s some great wines scarcely reached 11 per cent. Certainly, there is no call for a Médoc to be more than 12 per cent alcohol if it has to be chaptalized, or for a St-Émilion to be more than 12·5 per cent. In exceptional vintages it is, of course, possible to produce wines of over 13 per cent quite naturally in St-Émilion.

Bordeaux was the first major wine region in France to institute tastings before the granting of an appellation. St-Émilion had made this part of its new classification system, in itself the first classification to be tied to AC regulations, in 1955. In the Médoc tasting was introduced on a voluntary basis. After the major overhaul of the whole AC system in 1974, tastings became compulsory throughout the whole of France in the awarding of appellations. There is a certain cynicism about the tastings because it is said that wines are rarely turned down. The panels consist of growers, *courtiers* (brokers) and *négociants* (merchants). The cask or vat samples must represent an *assemblage* of all wines at a given property (including *vin de presse* and second-label wines) for which the appellation is required. So the quality of a sample is usually inferior to the that of the wine that will go out under the château label, especially at the larger properties. Proprietors are often requested to resubmit samples because, in the early stages, wines often show minor faults which subsequently disappear. My own experience of these tastings is that they are serious affairs.

The declaration of stocks, which is another stipulation of the AC system, is more or less self-explanatory. It enables the authorities and the trade to know precisely how the last year's sales have gone and thus what there is to sell in the coming year. By adding together the stocks at August 31 with the declarations for the new vintage, the amount available for the coming sales campaign becomes clear. A comparison of the level of stocks from year to year also provides a valuable barometer of the health of the market and has an influence on price levels.

The overhaul of the AC system in 1974 did much to remove the inflexibility of the old system and its insensitivity towards vintage variations. The new system revolves around three concepts:

rendement de base (basic permitted yield). This corresponds to the old maximum yields which had changed little since being established in 1935. For Bordeaux they were revised in 1984 (backdated to apply to the '83 vintage), and most appellations were given higher allowances, sometimes by as much as five hectolitres per hectare. But under the new system this simply represents a norm and has less significance than previously.

rendement annuel (annual yield). Each year the growers in each appellation, through their syndicate, make a proposal to the INAO as to what normal production levels should be, bearing in mind the actual conditions of the year. This figure may be above or below the *rendement de base*.

plafond limite de classement (PLC). This is a fixed proportion (usually 20 per cent) given in the decrees governing each appellation which, when applied to the *rendement annuel*, gives the maximum permitted yield for that year. If the *rendement annuel* allows a flexibility for the conditions of a particular year, the PLC allows flexibility between different vineyards and growers. To apply for this extra allowance, all the property's wines must be offered for tasting: anything over this limit has to be used for distillation.

Grape Varieties

Today five grape varieties, three red and two white, dominate the vineyards of Bordeaux, but it was not always so. At the end of the 18th century, nine red and four white varieties were recorded in the Médoc, but this was nothing compared with the 34 red and 29 white varieties in the Libournais. The process of selection made rapid progress in the 19th century and its completion was finally precipitated by the phylloxera crisis which, over a period of years, led to the replanting of all vineyards. Today the most important varieties are as follows.

RED

Cabernet Sauvignon This is the most important variety in Médoc and Graves, especially for the Grands Crus. It produces wine with a deep, brilliant colour, a marked bouquet, often reminiscent of blackcurrants, and a flavour which is markedly tannic when young but which develops great finesse and complexity. This is a hardy variety and it is notably resistant to *coulure* at flowering and to grey rot before the harvest. It has a thick skin and is a late ripener. It does best on gravelly soils and has a relatively low yield.

Cabernet Franc This is an important secondary variety in both St-Émilion and Médoc. In St-Émilion it is known generally as Bouchet. It produces perfumed wines with less colour and tannin than Cabernet Sauvignon, but in other respects it is similar.

Merlot The most important variety in St-Émilion and Pomerol, but also important in Médoc and Graves since it harmonises so well with Cabernet Sauvignon. It produces wines that are deep in colour, less tannic and higher in alcohol than Cabernet Sauvignon, supple and full-flavoured. It does well in the presence of clay, precisely where the Cabernet Sauvignon does less well. It is an early ripener and generous yielder, but it is susceptible to *coulure* during the flowering and to rot in wet weather. However, new sprays have helped to overcome this last deficiency.

Malbec Also known as Pressac in the Libournais and as Cot in Cahors. This variety used to be particularly important in Fronsac, Pomerol and the Côtes de Bourg, as well as having a minor role in most Médoc vineyards. Today, because of its flowering problems, its importance has seriously declined, and only in Bourg and Blaye does it remain a significant element, although many châteaux in the Médoc, St-Émilion and Pomerol still have a few old Malbec vines left. This is a high-yielding, early-ripening variety, producing soft, delicate wines with good colour. It is especially useful for blending with more tannic varieties such as Cabernet Sauvignon.

Petit Verdot This is used in small quantities in the Médoc, especially on the lighter soils of Margaux, but is of declining importance. It is late in ripening and produces highly coloured wines, high in alcohol and tannin, and adds complexity to wines for long ageing.

WHITE

Sémillon This is the most distinctively Bordelais of the white
varieties. It has suffered as a result of the popularity of the
Sauvignon, but it is now making something of a comeback. It
is the most important component of all the great sweet wines,
and provides complexity and aging potential in dry Graves.
Its distinctive and complex bouquet requires bottle-age to
develop in dry wines, and becomes richer and more honeyed.
The wine is taut and firm, before becoming increasingly full-
flavoured and complex with ageing. It blends well with
Sauvignon. Its susceptibility to *pourriture noble* (noble rot) is
responsible for its success in making great dessert wines.

Sauvignon Blanc This has been traditionally planted as a minor
partner to the Sémillon in the sweet wine areas and as an
equal component of the dry wines. In recent years it has been
increasingly used on its own, especially in Entre-Deux-Mers,
to produce wines sold as Bordeaux Blanc Sauvignon. This variety, also widely planted in other parts of France, tends when
unblended to have a character so strong that it obliterates
regional characteristics, especially when complete ripeness is
not obtained. However, in Bordeaux it can produce wines high
in natural sugar and therefore in alcohol, with more finesse
and style, especially when aged in oak. The Pavillon Blanc of
Château Margaux is an outstanding example of this.
Sauvignon tends to be a lower and more erratic yielder than
Sémillon, so that where a vineyard is planted half-and-half
with Sémillon, there will always be more Sémillon in the
resulting blend.

Muscadelle An extremely perfumed and aromatic variety that
can be useful in small doses. It is particularly favoured in the
Premières Côtes for producing sweet wines for early drinking,
and as an adjunct to Sémillon and Sauvignon.

The essence of winemaking in Bordeaux is to mix the different
varieties in the right proportions for the soil in each particular
vineyard and the style of wine the proprietor is trying to make.
The small but important variations from château to château, cou-
pled with soil and microclimatic differences, are what give
Bordeaux wines their remarkable variations and individuality.
Thus, in the Médoc, where the Cabernet Sauvignon dominates,
some proprietors use Merlot as their second variety, with little
Cabernet Franc; others use less Merlot and more Cabernet Franc.
In St-Émilion and Pomerol, where Merlot is dominant, some proprietors have 80 per cent Merlot, while others plant it
half-and-half with Cabernet Franc or mix it with Cabernet Franc
and Cabernet Sauvignon in a ratio of one third each – in fact you
can find every conceivable variation in the proportions.

Châteaux

The château system has been a crucial factor in building the prestige of the great Bordeaux wines. In the Médoc in the 18th
century, many small farms came together to form large estates,

capable of producing sufficient quantities of wine to create a wide reputation on many markets. The First Growths led the way in England in the early years of the 18th century; the others followed, creating a unique image of excellence for Bordeaux.

In the Médoc, the château names have in effect become *marques*, whose proprietors can increase the size of their vineyards at will, provided they remain in the same appellation. Nobody controls the extent of an individual vineyard now. Only the reputation of the wine and its consistent quality counts.

In St-Émilion, however, where the 1954 classification system is under the control of the INAO, vineyards of classified wines cannot be expanded at will, and when Beau-Séjour-Bécot took over two other properties and incorporated their production into its Premier Grand Cru Classé wine, it lost its status in the 1985 revision of the classification. It worked its passage back, however, and was reinstated in the 1995 version.

The success of the château system, however, has produced its own problems. It is difficult for the consumer to remember the names of more than a handful of châteaux, let alone the thousands that exist in the whole region. But because the consumer knows that good Bordeaux wines come from châteaux it is hard to create successful brands which cannot of their nature have a château name. It is not without significance that the most successful brand of claret by far is Mouton-Cadet, precisely because many consumers believe, erroneously, that the wine is directly connected with the famous Château Mouton-Rothschild. Even the *caves coopératives* now sell many of their wines under château names.

Cooperatives

Cooperatives are of increasing importance in Bordeaux, and their role is changing. In the '92 vintage, their members accounted for 38 per cent of the declarants in the Gironde and produced 24 per cent of the AC wine made from 23 per cent of the surface area.

Initially much of the wine sold by cooperatives went to *négociants* for their generic blends and brands. Increasingly however, they are vinifying the wines of their best members separately and marketing them under their château labels, on which they have the right to put *'mis à la propriété'*. In addition cooperatives are creating their own brands and selling these and some of their château wines directly to wholesalers in France and to importers in foreign markets, rather than selling them through the traditional Bordeaux trade, although the latter remains a significant part of their business.

The most important cooperative in Médoc is at Bégadan, with 170 members producing some 25,000 hectolitres of Médoc AC. In St-Émilion the Union des Producteurs has 360 members producing some 45,000 hectolitres, including over 16,000 hectolitres of St-Émilion Grand Cru, the best of it aged in casks. In the Haut-Médoc, the most important cooperative is at St-Estèphe. It has 200 members and produces some 18,000 hectolitres of this important AC, nearly one third of the appellation's total production.

Négociants

Traditionally, the Bordeaux trade has been carried out by the *négociants*. In Bordeaux itself this used to centre on the Quai des Chartrons, conveniently placed for the docks. *Négociants* not only distributed Bordeaux wines in France and on export markets, they also effectively acted as bankers for the château proprietors, buying their wines when they were a few months old, then either taking them into their own cellars, where they would be looked after until ready for bottling, or keeping them at the château for château-bottling. They also kept substantial bottle stocks and could always supply mature wines ready for drinking or old vintages for special occasions.

Inflation and high interest rates, however, have provided a challenge to which the *négociants* have found no answer. None has been able to achieve the size and financial muscle to meet the new problems while retaining its traditional role, which has inevitably contracted. Far more wines are now château-bottled, and far more stock is now held and financed at the property than ever before. Many firms now work on minimum stocks or act purely as brokers, not buying wines until they have sold them, which puts them at the mercy of the notoriously volatile Bordeaux market. The *courtiers* themselves still have an important role as the link between the growers and the *négociants*; largely because there are so many growers – the bigger merchants simply could not select from the huge range of wines.

The following list describes today's leading *négociant* houses.

B d'Arfeuille A small, respected family firm in Libourne; also proprietor of St-Émilion Grand Cru Classé Château La Serre and Pomerol La Pointe. D'Arfeuille specialises in Libournais wines, but covers the full range of other Bordeaux districts.

Baron Philippe de Rothschild SA (formerly La Bergerie and then La Baronnie) After the legendary Baron's death in 1987 it was decided to perpetuate his name in this, the commercial arm of his enterprise. Apart from selling its property wines, d'Armailhac and Clerc-Milon, the principal business is Mouton Cadet and its associated brands. (Mouton-Rothschild is sold via the Bordeaux market, and not exclusively through this house.) The firm is strong on export markets.

Barton & Guestier This famous old concern is now part of Seagrams and is only a pale reflection of the firm it used to be, largely concentrating on brands sold on the US market. In 1995 it sold its bottling and warehousing operation to Cordier and entered into a contract with them to bottle their requirements. Nevertheless the quality of the wines remains good.

Borie-Manoux This is a dynamic family firm with some important properties which include Châteaux Batailley, Trottevieille and Beau-Site as a basis for its quality business. Its wines are well distributed on export markets as well as in France.

Calvet Once one of the great names of Bordeaux, now only a shadow of its former self. Calvet is strong on brands and exclusive *petits châteaux* and specialises in the Far East market.

Castel Frères A large firm specialising in cheap wines, especially its *vin de table marque*, Castelvin. Only 55 per cent of its business is in Bordeaux wines. Main export markets are Holland, Germany, UK, US and the Far East.

Cheval Quancard A family firm formerly known as Les Fils de Marcel Quancard based at La Grave-d'Ambarès in Entre-Deux-Mers, which has grown considerably in the past 25 years. It owns several properties, including Château Terrefort, and offers a wide range of Petits Châteaux and brands.

Cordier One of the leading firms in Bordeaux, which also owns Meyney, Lafaurie-Peyraguey and Clos-des-Jacobins – as well as managing Cantemerle. The Cordier family sold control of the company in 1984 to an important financial group whose other interests include the Domaines des Salins du Midi. The Cordier properties are sold on an exclusive basis and not through the market, so it specialises in selling a limited range of its own exclusivities and generic brands. Two-thirds of its business is export.

Crus et Domaines de France A subsidiary of Pernot-Ricard owning Cruse and Alexis Lichine.

CVBG (Consortium Vinicole Bordeaux-Gironde) This group includes Dourthe and Kressmann, and the wines are marketed under these old company names. In 1983 the families sold to a Dutch firm but since 1998 belongs to its managers. These companies have a good reputation and sell a wide range of wines, many on an exclusive basis. Château Maucaillou, for a long time a Dourthe flagship, has now been put on the Bordeaux market, and is no longer an exclusivity. The Kressmanns own the classified Graves Château La Tour-Martillac.

Dulong Frères & Fils A family business situated at Floirac just across the bridge from Bordeaux. It enjoys a good reputation for its Petits Châteaux and Cru Bourgeois exported to the UK and the US.

Ginestet Now part of the Bernard Taillan Group, this is now one of the leading Bordeaux merchants, with a large portfolio of managed and exclusive properties, as well as developing brands – over 40 per cent of its turnover in exports.

GVG (Grands Vins de Gironde) Formerly owned by Rémy-Cointreau, but subject to a management buy-out in 1999. It now includes de Luze, De Rivoyre & Diprovin, SDFV and Chantecaille. Combined, it now forms the region's largest group, commercialising some ten per cent of the region's production.

Nathaniel Johnston Formed in 1734, it is still run by the same family. Even if it no longer owns great châteaux such as Ducru-Beaucaillou, it still specialises in selling a wide range of Bordeaux's leading growths, especially for export.

J Lebègue & Cie The company has a Libournais base since 1971 and the participation of the new owner of Château de la Rivière has given it fresh impetus.

Alexis Lichine & Cie There is now no connection between the Lichine family and the company that bears its name: the latter belonged to the British brewery Bass Charrington before being sold to Pernod-Ricard. An important company selling a wide range of wines and operating widely in export markets.

A de Luze & Fils This old family firm was sold to a British paper group during the oil crisis but now forms part of GVG.

Mähler-Besse A family firm still firmly rooted in its Dutch origins. Part-owner of Château Palmer.

Yvon Mau & Fils A family firm specialising in middle-price range wines, situated near La Réole in Entre-Deux-Mers. Now one of the leading exporters.

Mestrezat & Domaines SA This is a house specialising in a wide range of wines, mostly château-bottled. It manages Grand-Puy-Ducasse and Rayne-Vigneau, as well as several lesser *crus*.

Antoine Moueix This may not have the glamour of the cousin's firm in Libourne, but this is a serious quality house nevertheless. It is also firmly based on properties, of which the two Grands Crus Classés of St-Émilion, Châteaux La-Tour-du-Pin-Figeac and Fonplégade, are the best.

J-P Moueix Jean-Pierre Moueix is a legend in his own lifetime. No one has done more to carry the fame of Libournais wines into the US and UK markets and to raise their prestige worldwide. Now Christian, his son, and Jean-Jacques, his nephew, are there to carry on the tradition, and the old Bordeaux house of Duclot compliments this, with a classic range of Médocs, Graves and Sauternes to complement the St-Émilions and Pomerols. This firm has the ownership or exclusive distribution of many châteaux, headed by Pétrus, Trotanoy, La Fleur-Pétrus and Magdelaine.

De Rivoyre & Diprovin *See under* GVG.

Schröder & Schÿler This famous old business was founded in 1739: there are still Schÿlers working in the company. The main markets are Scandinavia and Holland. Owns Château Kirwan.

SDVF (Société de Distribution des Vins Fins) This firm was founded in 1973 by M Hernandez at a time when many firms were in financial trouble. He bought large stocks of Crus Classés at low prices when no one else wanted them. The firm ran into difficulties during the recession of the early 1990s, and in 1994 was acquired by the GVG group (*see above*).

Maison Sichel Following the death of Peter Sichel in 1998, his son Allan is new president and managing director, three of his brothers share the responsibilities for exports, while Benjamin runs the family property at d'Angludet. Since it separated from H Sichel of Mainz and London, all Sichel brands in Germany, the UK, Eire and the US (where Shieffelin owns the rights) have passed out of its hands. In the UK Peter A Sichel trades under his own name. In 1992 Peter A Sichel acquired the business of Édmond Coste at Langon. In France, Coste's wines continue to be sold from the Langon office, but the Peter A Sichel company looks after all the export business for Coste's selections. H Sichel has its own company in Bordeaux which furnishes the wines for the Sichel brands in Germany, the UK, Eire and the US.

Understanding a Bordeaux Label

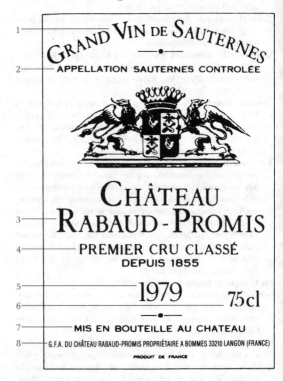

1   Almost every Bordeaux wine describes itself as a *grand vin*, whether it is a Cru Classé or a simple Bordeaux rouge.
2   It is a legal requirement that the appellation be indicated, the name shown between the words 'Appellation' and 'Contrôlée'.
3   Most Bordeaux wines are sold under a château name. In addition, many wines that are sent to be vinified at *caves coopératives*, but kept separate, are allowed to use the name of their property on the label.

4 Classification. The wines of Sauternes and Barsac were classified in 1855 at the same time as those of the Médoc. More
recently there have been classifications for St-Émilion and
Graves.
5 Year of vintage.
6 This is the standard bottle-size in the EU.
7 'Bottled at the château'. Until the 1970s the majority of
Bordeaux wines were bottled either in the Bordeaux cellars
of *négociants* or abroad in such places as London and Brussels.
Château-bottling became obligatory for all Crus Classés in
the early 1970s. The words '*mis en bouteille à la propriété*' indicate that the wine has been bottled by the *cave coopérative*
where it was made.
8 Name and address of producer.

Classifications

1855 CLASSIFICATION OF THE MÉDOC

The Médoc First Growths had emerged as such in the 18th century and, by the early 19th century, classifications were being
made covering a range of Médocs and some Graves. They were
essentially based on market prices and were produced by *courtiers*
and *négociants* as guides for their customers.

When the newly fledged Second Empire was preparing its
answer to London's Great Exhibition of 1851, it was decided to
show a range of Bordeaux wines, and the question arose as to
which châteaux should represent the region. A commission of
courtiers was given the task, and the result was the Classification
of 1855 encompassing the red wines of Médoc plus Château Haut-
Brion and the great sweet wines of Sauternes. It was rather an
accident of history that this particular list should have become
enshrined as an immutable and permanent order of merit, something its authors certainly never intended. When, in 1867, a group
of St-Émilions was shown at a subsequent Paris Exhibition, no
such permanent value was accorded to the list.

There have been various attempts to update the 1855 classification, but the vested interests opposed to it seem more powerful
than those who would like to see change. I have indicated under
the individual entries which growth I consider to be superior or
otherwise to their classification. The only official change was the
elevation of Mouton-Rothschild to the status of First Growth in
1973, recognising a position it had in reality long held.

It is important to remember that there is no control over the
vineyards of any of the listed châteaux. Some have remained virtually unchanged since 1855, while others have expanded or
contracted.

The list that follows is essentially the original 1855 list. Apart
from the promotion of Mouton-Rothschild to Premier Cru in 1973
there have been no fundamental changes, except that certain *crus*
have disappeared and others have been divided or changed their
names. The list encompasses the great red wines of the Médoc,
the sole exception being the inclusion of Haut-Brion in the Graves.

1855 Classification of the Médoc

The château name is followed by that of the commune.

Premiers Crus

Lafite-Rothschild	Pauillac
Margaux	Margaux
Latour	Pauillac
Haut-Brion	Pessac (Graves)
Mouton-Rothschild	Pauillac

Deuxièmes Crus

Rauzan-Ségla	Margaux
Rauzan-Gassies	Margaux
Léoville-Las-Cases	St-Julien
Léoville-Poyferré	St-Julien
Léoville-Barton	St-Julien
Durfort-Vivens	Margaux
Gruaud-Larose	St-Julien
Lascombes	Margaux
Brane-Cantenac	Cantenac
Pichon-Longueville Baron	Pauillac
Pichon-Longueville Comtesse	Pauillac
Ducru-Beaucaillou	St-Julien
Cos-d'Estournel	St-Estèphe
Montrose	St-Estèphe

Troisièmes Crus

Kirwan	Cantenac
d'Issan	Cantenac
Lagrange	St-Julien
Langoa-Barton	St-Julien
Giscours	Labarde
Malescot-St-Exupéry	Margaux
Boyd-Cantenac	Cantenac
Cantenac-Brown	Cantenac
Palmer	Cantenac
La Lagune	Ludon
Desmirail	Margaux
Calon-Ségur	St-Estèphe
Ferrière	Margaux
Marquis-d'Alesme-Becker	Margaux

Quatrièmes Crus

St-Pierre	St-Julien
Talbot	St-Julien
Branaire-Ducru	St-Julien
Duhart-Milon	Pauillac
Pouget	Cantenac
La Tour-Carnet	St-Laurent
Lafon-Rochet	St-Estèphe
Beychevelle	St-Julien
Prieuré-Lichine	Cantenac
Marquis-de-Terme	Margaux

Cinquièmes Crus

Pontet-Canet	Pauillac
Batailley	Pauillac
Haut-Batailley	Pauillac
Grand-Puy-Lacoste	Pauillac
Grand-Puy-Ducasse	Pauillac
Lynch-Bages	Pauillac
Lynch-Moussas	Pauillac
Dauzac	Labarde
d'Armailhac	Pauillac
du Tertre	Arsac
Haut-Bages-Libéral	Pauillac
Pédesclaux	Pauillac
Belgrave	St-Laurent
Camensac	St-Laurent
Cos-Labory	St-Estèphe
Clerc-Milon	Pauillac
Croizet-Bages	Pauillac
Cantemerle	Macau

1855 CLASSIFICATION OF THE SAUTERNES

Again the original list, apart from divisions and changes of name. The château name is followed by that of the commune.

Grand Premier Cru

d'Yquem	Sauternes

Premiers Crus

La Tour-Blanche	Bommes
Lafaurie-Peyraguey	Bommes
Clos Haut-Peyraguey	Bommes
Rayne-Vigneau	Bommes
Suduiraut	Preignac
Coutet	Barsac
Climens	Barsac
Guiraud	Sauternes

Rieussec	Fargues	d'Arche	Sauternes
Rabaud-Promis	Bommes	Filhot	Sauternes
Sigalas-Rabaud	Bommes	Broustet	Barsac
		Nairac	Barsac
Deuxièmes Crus		Caillou	Barsac
de Myrat	Barsac	Suau	Barsac
Doisy-Daëne	Barsac	de Malle	Preignac
Doisy-Dubroca	Barsac	Romer-du-Hayot	Farques
Doisy-Védrines	Barsac	Lamothe	Sauternes

CLASSED GROWTHS OF THE GRAVES

After the Second World War, interest in classification revived, and both Graves and St-Émilion began to negotiate with the INAO for their own. The Graves classification, which was a great deal simpler to agree, emerged first in 1953, encompassing only red wines. It was revised in 1959 to include whites. With such a small number of wines actually classified, there is not surprisingly no attempt to place the wines in different categories, with the result that the wines vary in quality considerably from Haut-Brion with its Premier Cru status to wines that sell at prices of Médoc Fifth Growths or top Crus Bourgeois. Again, I have assessed the standing of each wine under its individual entry.

Red Wines

Bouscaut	Cadaujac
Haut-Bailly	Léognan
Carbonnieux	Léognan
Domaine de Chevalier	Léognan
Fieuzal	Léognan
Olivier	Léognan
Malartic-Lagravière	Léognan
La Tour-Martillac	Martillac
Smith-Haut-Lafitte	Martillac
Haut-Brion	Pessac
La Mission-Haut-Brion	Talence
Pape-Clément	Pessac
Latour-Haut-Brion	Talence

White Wines

Bouscaut	Cadaujac
Carbonnieux	Léognan
Domaine de Chevalier	Léognan
Olivier	Léognan
Malartic-Lagravière	Léognan
La Tour-Martillac	Martillac
Laville-Haut-Brion	Talence
Couhins	Villenave d'Ornon

THE 1996 ST-ÉMILION CLASSIFICATION

St-Émilion had long been in a chaotic state, posing special problems for the consumer. Many *crus* described themselves as Premiers, and the properties, mostly small and many with similar names, change more often than elsewhere. Although there are over 5,000 hectares under vine in the appellation, only 14 domaines are of more than 25 hectares, and only 34 properties have between 12 and 25 hectares, the total area of these covering 589 hectares. The classification divides the châteaux into two categories, Premiers Grands Crus Classés and Grands Crus Classés, with the Premiers Ausone and Cheval Blanc singled out as category A, the rest as B. The first list, published in 1955, comprised 12 Premiers Grands Crus and 63 Grands Crus. At the first revision (1969), the Grands Crus were increased to 71; a second (1985) reduced the Premiers Crus to 11 and the Grands Crus to 62. A third (1996) increased the Premiers Crus to 13 and reduced the Grands Crus to 55, its smallest numbers yet. Three *crus* demoted in 1985 were restored, while Laroque was classified for the first time.

The 1996 St-Émilion Classification

Premiers Grands Crus Classés

(A) Ausone
    Cheval-Blanc
(B) L'Angélus
    Beauséjour (Duffau-
        Lagrosse)
    Beau-Séjour-Bécot
    Belair
    Canon
    Clos Fourtet
    Figeac
    La Gaffelière
    Magdelaine
    Pavie
    Trottevieille

Grands Crus Classés

L'Arrosée
Balestard-la-Tonnelle
Bellevue
Bergat
Berliquet
Cadet Bon
Cadet-Piola
Canon-la-Gaffelière
Cap-de-Mourlin
Chauvin
Clos des Jacobins
Clos de l'Oratoire
Clos St-Martin
La Clotte
La Clusière
La Couspaude
Corbin
Corbin-Michotte
Couvent des Jacobins

Curé-Bon-La-Madeleine
Dassault
La Dominique
Faurie-de-Souchard
Fonplégade
Fonroque
Franc-Mayne
Grand-Mayne
Grand-Pontet
Guadet-St-Julien
Grandes Murailles
Haut-Corbin
Haut-Sarpe
Laniote
Larcis-Ducasse
Lamarzelle
Larmande
Laroque
Laroze
Matras
Moulin-du-Cadet
Pavie-Decesse
Pavie-Macquin
Petit-Faurie de Soutard
Le Prieuré
Ripeau
St-Georges-Côte-Pavie
La Serre
Soutard
Tertre-Daugay
La Tour-du-Pin-Figeac
    (Giraud-Bélivier)
La Tour-du-Pin-Figeac (Moueix)
La Tour-Figeac
Troplong-Mondot
Villemaurine
Yon-Figeac

1978 CLASSIFICATION OF THE CRUS BOURGEOIS OF THE MÉDOC AND HAUT-MÉDOC

The Crus Bourgeois of the Médoc were originally classified in 1920, but by 1962 there were only 94 members compared with the 444 properties that existed in 1932. Today there are over 200 *crus* claiming to be Crus Bourgeois, and of these 150 belong to the Syndicat. The first *classement* was issued in 1966, and a revision in 1978 divided the members into Grands Bourgeois Exceptionnels, Grands Bourgeois, and Bourgeois. But unfortunately EU regulations permit only the words 'Cru Bourgeois' to appear on a label. The distinctions made in 1978 are useful, however, because of the criteria used.

Cru Bourgeois There are 68 properties in this category, each of which must have a minimum of seven hectares, the wine must be made on the property (not at a cooperative) and the Syndicat must be satisfied that the wine is of good quality.

Cru Grand Bourgeois In addition to meeting the Cru Bourgeois criteria the wine must be wood-matured in cask. There are 41 such *crus*.

Cru Grand Bourgeois Exceptionnel This category has the most stringent criteria. In addition to the requirements for the above categories, these *crus* must be in the communes of the Haut-Médoc, the area covered by the Crus Classés, and the wine must be château-bottled. There are 18 of these (indicated by *).

The château name is followed by that of the commune.

Grand Bourgeois

Agassac*	Ludon	Greysac	Bégadan
Andron-Blanquet*	St-Estèphe	Hanteillan	Cissac
Beaumont	Cussac	Haut-Marbuzet*	St-Estèphe
Beau-Site*	St-Estèphe	Lafon	Listrac
Bel-Orme	St-Seurin-de-Cadourne	de Lamarque	Lamarque
		Lamothe-Cissac	Cissac
Brillette	Moulis	Larose-Trintaudon	St-Laurent
Capbern*	St-Estèphe	Laujac	Bégadan
La Cardonne	Blaignan	Liversan	St-Sauveur
Caronne-Ste-Gemme*	St-Laurent	Loudenne	St-Yzans
		MacCarthy	St-Estèphe
Chasse-Spleen*	Moulis	Malleret	Le-Pian
Cissac*	Cissac	Marbuzet*	St-Estèphe
Citran*	Avensan	Martinens	Margaux
Colombier-Monpelou	Pauillac	Meyney*	St-Estèphe
		Le Meynieu	Vertheuil
Coufran	St-Seurin-de-Cadourne	Morin	St-Estèphe
		Moulin-à-Vent	Moulis
Coutelin-Merville	St-Estèphe	les Ormes-de-Pez	St-Estèphe
Le Crock*	St-Estèphe	les Ormes-Sorbet	Couquèques
Duplessis (Hauchecorne)	Moulis	Patache d'Aux	Bégadan
		Paveil-de-Luze	Soussans
Dutruch Grand Poujeaux*	Moulis	Peyrabon	St-Saveur
		Phélan-Ségur*	St-Estèphe
La Fleur-Milon	Pauillac	Pontoise-Cabarrus	St-Seurin-de-Cadourne
Fontesteau	St-Sauveur		
Fourcas-Dupré*	Listrac	Potensac	Potensac
Fourcas-Hosten*	Listrac	Poujeaux*	Moulis
du Glana*	St-Julien	Reysson	Vertheuil
		Sigognac	St-Yzans

Sociando-Mallet	St-Seurin-de-Cadourne	Haut-Bages-Monpelou	Pauillac
du Taillan	Le Taillan	Haut-Canteloup	Couquèques
La Tour-de-By	Bégadan	Haut-Garin	Bégadan
Tour-du-Haut-Moulin	Cussac	Haut-Padarnac	Pauillac
Tronquoy-Lalande	St-Estèphe	Houbanon	Prignac
Verdignan	St-Seurin-de-Cadourne	Hourtin-Ducasse	St-Saveur
		de Labat	St-Laurent
		Lamothe-Bergeron	Cussac
Bourgeois		Le Landat	Cissac
Aney	Cussac	Landon	Bégadan
Balac	St-Laurent	Lartigue-de-Brochon	St-Seurin-de-Cadourne
La Bécade	Listrac	Cru Lassalle	Potensac
Bellerive	Valeyrac	Lestage	Listrac
Belle-Rose	Pauillac	MacCarthy-Moula	St-Estèphe
Bonneau-Livran	St-Seurin-de-Cadourne	de Monthil	Bégadan
Le Boscq	St-Christoly	Moulin Rouge	Cussac
du Breuil	Cissac	Panigon	Civrac
La Bridane	St-Julien	Pibran	Pauillac
de By	Bégadan	Plantey-de-la-Croix	St-Seurin-de-Cadourne
Castéra	St-Germain-d'Esteuil	Pontet	Blaignan
Cap-Léon-Veyrin	Listrac	Ramage-la-Bâtisse	St-Sauveur
Carcanieux	Queyrac	La Roque-de-By	Bégadan
Chambert-Marbuzet	St-Estèphe	La Rose-Maréchale	St-Seurin-de-Cadourne
La Clare	Bégadan	St-Bonnet	St-Christoly
la Closerie	Moulis	Saransot	Listrac
Duplessis-Fabre	Moulis	Soudars	Avensan
Fonréaud	Listrac	Tayac	Soussans
Fonpiqueyre	St-Saveur	La Tour Blanche	St-Christoly
Fort Vauban	Cussac	La Tour-Haut-Caussan	Blaignan
La France	Blaignan	Tour-du-Mirail	Cissac
Gallais Bellevue	Potensac	La Tour-St-Bonnet	St-Christoly
Grand-Duroc-Milon	Pauillac	La Tour-St-Joseph	Cissac
		des Tourelles	Blaignan
Grand-Moulin	St-Seurin-de-Cadourne	Vieux Robin	Bégadan

Vineyards at present being reconstituted

les Bertins	Valeyrac	Lavalière	St-Christoly
Clarke	Listrac	Romefort	Cussac
Larivière	Blaignan	Vernous	Lesparre

The properties listed opposite (alongside their communes) have joined the Syndicate of Bourgeois Growths of the Médoc since 1978 but at present are not classified because of EU regulations.

Anthonic	Moulis	Monbrison	Arsac
Beau-Site	St-Estèphe	Moulin-de-Castillon	St-Christoly
Bellevue	Valeyrac	Moulin-de-Laborde	Listrac
Les Bertins	Valeyrac	Moulin-de-la-Roque	Bégadan
Blaignan	Blaignan	Moulin-Riche	St-Julien
Bonneau	Avensan	Moulin-de-St-Vincent	Moulis
Bourdieu	Vertheuil	Moulis	Moulis
Bournac	Civrac St-Julien	Pey-Martin	Ordonnac
Cailloux-de-By	Bégadan	Peyredon-Lagravette	Medrac-Listrac
Canuet	Margaux	Le Plantey	St-Yzans
Charmail	St-Seurin	Pomys	St-Estèphe
La Commanderie de Conques	Couquèques	Preuilhac	Lesparre
Domaine de la Croix	Ordonnac	Puy-Castéra	Cissac
L'Estruelle	St-Yzans	Domaine de la Ronceray	St-Estèphe
Goudy-la-Cardonne	Ordonnac	St-Ahon	Caychac
Grivière	Blaignan	St-Aubin	Jau
Hauterive	St-Germain-d'Esteuil	St-Estèphe	St-Estèphe
Haut Logat	Cissac	St-Paul	St-Seurin
Lalande	Listrac	St-Roch	St-Estèphe
Lacombe–Noaillac	Jau	Sestignan	Jau Dignac-Loirac
Lagorce	Blaignan		
Lagrave	St-Sauveur	Terrey-Gros-Cailloux	St-Julien
Lestage Simon	St-Seurin	La Tour-de-Mons	Margaux
Lieujan	St-Sauveur	Tour-du-Roc	Arcins
Liouner	Listrac	Tourteran	St-Saveur
Marsac-Séguineau	Soussans	Troupian	St-Seurin-de-Cadourne
Martinens	Cantenac		
Maucaillou	Moulis	Les Tuileries	St-Yzans
Maucamps	Macau	Vieux-Robin	Bégadan

What Happens in the Vineyard

Good wine begins with good grapes, and good grapes in turn depend on good viticulture and the weather. After the enormous progress made in winemaking in the past 30 years, some say there is little more to be done in this respect, but there are certainly still improvements possible in viticulture.

Starting with a new vine, the first decision concerns what American rootstock to use and which clone of the European vine to select. Different varieties perform better in different soils. Much work has been done by the Station de Recherches Viticoles du Sud-Ouest to discover rootstocks that are resistant to chlorosis in limestone soils. Some varieties do better than others in poorly-drained, humid soils as against dry, well-drained ones. Less work has been done on the cloning of vines here than in Burgundy, to say nothing of Germany. Recently there has been a steady move in favour of more natural methods, reducing sprays and looking to natural predators to counter pests such as red spider.

The yearly pattern of work in the vineyards proceeds along the following lines.

January The work of the *taille* (pruning), begun in December, continues. New stakes are put in place and secured, and the pruned canes are attached to the vines.

February The pruning continues, together with the clearing of the vineyard, gathering of the bundled canes and so on. The vines are given their first treatment against excoriose (a fungus which attacks the wood), esca (another fungus, also called black measles), and red and yellow spider (which later attack the young leaves).

March The first buds normally break in late March, between the 20th and 30th of the month. The first ploughing removes the earth from around the foot of the vine in order to aerate it after the winter.

April Spring begins. Any dead vines are replaced and the first hoeing takes place. The vines may be dusted with sulphur against oidium and sprayed with a copper sulphate solution against mildew.

May The work begun in April continues according to weather conditions, as do the treatments against disease. The first pinching back of the young shoots is carried out at this stage to limit the growth of the vine and direct it towards the production of grapes. Stray shoots from the base of the vine are cut back.

June This is classically the month of the flowering. Most typically it happens between the 2nd and 10th of the month. This gives the approximate timing for the vintage, which normally occurs 100 to 110 days after the flowering. Ploughing continues, the new shoots are tied up, and the length of the new growth permits it to be trained between the second and third row of wires, though not attached to them.

July The soil is now ploughed away from the vines again so there is a mound of soil running between each row of vines, and weeds are hoed. Treatment continues according to the conditions. The *véraison* (the changing of the colour of the grapes, the most important indication of ripening between the flowering and the vintage) can begin in late July. If the potential crop looks too large, this is the usual time to thin out (Vendange Vert).

August A quiet period when many *vignerons* go on holiday, this can nevertheless be a crucial time for treating the vines, especially against premature rot if the weather is damp and humid. If the *véraison* has not occurred in July it usually happens in the first week of August.

September The preferred month for beginning the harvest. From '85 to '96 all vintages began in this month. In the weeks before the harvest the last preventative treatments are carried out, but at this time the *vigneron* hopes to be able to concentrate his efforts on preparing for the vintage in the *cuvier*.

October The month of the harvest (vintage or *récolte*) and hence the key month in the viticultural calendar. Even if the vintage began in September, much of it will take place and be completed in October. Sometimes the vintage in Sauternes will go on until the end of the month, or beyond.

November The harvest is over and the plough returns to the vineyard to earth up the vines for the winter. The manuring also takes place.

December The pruning begins. First the foliage is cut back to make the work of pruning easier. The cuttings are bundled up and burnt. Any vines that have been damaged or have died during the year are noted for replacement next year. The work goes on.

Making Wine

RED WINE

Forty years ago it was almost true to say that in most years the great red Bordeaux made themselves. They are still not complicated wines to make, but the art has been refined, at least at most properties.

The process is as follows.

1 The grapes arrive in the *cuvier* and are moved via an Archimedean screw mechanism to the *fouloir-égrappoir*, which crushes and destalks the grapes. The word 'crush' is perhaps an exaggeration of what actually happens; this machine breaks the skins rather than crushing the grapes, as can be clearly seen when the pulp is then pumped into the fermenting vat. Mechanically-harvested grapes do not usually need to be de-stemmed. There has been much refinement of the basic *fouloir-égrappoir* in recent years to make the process gentler and to ensure that no tannins from the stalks are released into the pulp.

2 The traditional Bordeaux fermentation *cuve* (vat) is wooden, and the top is often reached by a wooden gallery. Many of these old *cuves* are still in use, but they are steadily being replaced by vats of stainless steel, metal lined with enamel, or concrete lined with enamel. The advantages of the new *cuves* are that (a) they are easier to clean; (b) the temperature at which fermentation takes place is easier to control; (c) they are often of smaller size to assist selection and temperature control. But recent research suggests that the advantages are not all in one direction and that wooden *cuves* may produce better results. Fermentation usually lasts from five to ten days, and the object is to ferment at 28–30°C (82–86°F), instead of allowing the temperature to rise to 34°C (93°F) as formerly.

3 After the fermentation has been in progress for a few hours, the solid matter, mostly skins, rises to the top of the vat to form what is known as the cap. At regular intervals the

fermenting must is pumped over the top of the cap to keep it moist, keep its temperature down, and extract colour. A variation on this classic system is that in which the cap is submerged. In this method the cap is prevented by a mesh from rising to the top of the *cuve*.

4   In Bordeaux natural yeasts are usually allowed to bring about and sustain the fermentation. Normally there is an abundance of them, and the results they give usually prove satisfactory. Only when the grapes are unhealthy (affected by rot) can problems arise with this approach, and this is now rare.

5   The temperature is controlled by a variety of means. The most traditional in Bordeaux is a contraption that looks like a milk cooler. The must passes through a coil while cold water runs over the outside. With stainless steel vats, either the cold water runs down their exterior sides, or interior cooling coils are used, as they can be for other types of vat. All this is a long way from throwing blocks of ice into vats, a system that was still in use in many cellars in 1961. Many of the most recent installations have computer-controlled cooling systems.

6   Chaptalization (the addition of sugar to fermenting must to increase its potential alcohol) is now much more common in Bordeaux where, prior to 1962, it was almost unknown and illegal. Most Médocs are now chaptalized to 12 per cent and St-Émilions and Pomerols to 12·5 per cent, except in the best years when the natural degrees are quite sufficient. The sugar is normally added at the beginning of fermentation after the composition of the must has been carefully checked.

7   The progress of the fermentation, the fall in density and the temperature, is normally shown in chart form on each vat and checked every few hours. When no sugar remains, the wine (as it has now become) is either drawn off or left to macerate for some days with the skins. In the past this often continued for several weeks, but now the view is that most of the colour extraction takes place during fermentation, owing to the high temperatures, and that afterwards any improvement in the colour is minimal but tannins are still extracted, and these may not always be desirable. Bacterial infections may also be caused by prolonged skin contact and many winemakers like to draw the wine off immediately it has finished to avoid this.

8   After the new wine has been drawn off, the remaining solid matter (mostly that which was contained in the cap) is removed from the vat and pressed. The result is what is known as *vin de presse*. The first *vin de presse* is usually of superior quality and will later be put back into the finished wine at the *assemblage*. The result of the second pressing is not normally of sufficiently high quality to be included. These two *vins de presse* between them account for about 15 per cent of the wine produced. While *vin de presse* is not usually a desirable element in ordinary wines made for early consumption, it is richer in all its elements than the free-run wine, except in alcoholic degree, and so adds an important element in fine wines intended for long maturation and keeping.

9   The next stage is known as malolactic fermentation. Ideally,
    this should follow immediately after the alcoholic fermenta-
    tion. It is the process by which the astringent malic acid is
    converted into the more supple lactic acid, and in the process
    the total acidity is also diminished. Some winemakers like this
    to take place in *cuve*, others put the wine straight into cask. This
    secondary fermentation occurs most easily at 20–25°C
    (68–77°F), so much emphasis is placed on completing it
    before the weather turns too cold as the large *cuviers* of
    Bordeaux are hard to heat, particularly in comparison with
    the small cellars of Burgundy. If vats are equipped with an
    internal cooling system this can also be used, if necessary, for
    warming, thus facilitating the onset of malolactic fermenta-
    tion. Until this process is finished the wine is not truly stable
    and it is also vulnerable to bacterial infections. In the past it
    was often observed that the wine would begin 'working' in the
    spring, at the time when the vine began to push out its first
    buds; this was, in reality, carbon dioxide released when the
    malolactic fermentation began again, the warm weather per-
    mitting the bacteria to become active once more. It is
    preferable, however, to finish the process in the autumn
    rather than leaving the wine unstable through the winter.

10 Most, but not all, properties leave the new wine in *cuve* until
    the final selection or *assemblage* (blending) has been com-
    pleted. This usually happens in January, sometimes later,
    depending on the year. All the *cuves* are tasted and decisions
    taken as to what will go into the *grand vin* (the main château
    label) and what should be eliminated in order to maintain the
    quality and reputation of the château wine. Increasingly there
    is a second label (such as Pavillon Rouge of Château Margaux,
    Réserve de la Comtesse of Pichon-Lalande, Clos du Marquis of
    Léoville-Las-Cases), but most of the rejected wine is usually
    sold under a simple generic label. This applies mostly to large
    properties and therefore mostly to the Médoc.

    One of the less publicised but important decisions taken at
    this time is the addition of *vin de presse*. This gives the wine
    more tannin and extracts, and provides an important element
    in wines of quality that are intended for ageing.

11 The best Bordeaux châteaux mature their wines in 225-litre
    oak casks, the finest using 100 per cent new casks each year.
    But the wine has to have the power and composition to with-
    stand such handling and, apart from the First Growths, most
    Crus Classés use around one third new wood each year.
    Wooden barrels are important in giving complexity and 'fin-
    ish' to a wine but they must be in good condition and not more
    than about five years old. In the past many lesser *crus*, not
    being able to afford to buy new casks regularly, spoilt their
    wines by keeping them in old casks; these can easily taint the
    wine, making it seem mouldy or just not clean. It is better to
    keep the wine in vat rather than do this, and this is the policy
    of many lesser *crus* today, with resulting benefit to the
    wine. Bottling dates vary according to style and quality. The

old system for the First Growths was to bottle only after the third winter in cask, that is in the spring of the third year. Now most are bottled either after the vintage in the second year (at the latest) or several months earlier in the late spring or (most commonly) in the summer of the second year.

DRY WHITE WINES

Over the past few years in Bordeaux the preparation of these has changed much more radically than winemaking techniques for the reds. The use of stainless steel horizontal presses, pneumatic presses and low-temperature fermentation has revolutionised the style and quality of dry wines. In the past, Bordeaux made a few superb white Graves, but much of its white wine production was over-sulphured, heavy and dull. Now the wines are fruity and perfumed, fresh and clean.

The basic process is as follows.

1   The grapes are fed into a horizontal or pneumatic press as they come from the vineyard. The pressing must be gentle, and the *marc* (solid cake or pomace of skins and other solid matter left after pressing) is continuously broken up by chains inside the horizontal presses, which rotate at the same time as the grapes are squeezed.

2   Juice runs from the press and is collected in a stainless steel *cuve*. This is often nowadays chilled and held as grape juice over a period of 12 to 24 hours in order to precipitate its solids. This process is known as *débourbage*. An increasing number of Graves *vignerons*, and even some in Entre-Deux-Mers have now reverted to barrel fermentation in place of stainless steel. In this case, the must is run straight into new or used barrels, which are often kept in an air-conditioned *chai*. The must is lightly sulphured to guard against oxidation.

3   Fermentation then takes place once the must has been racked off its solids after the *débourbage*, either into another *cuve* or into barrel. Fermentation is now usually controlled at 15–20°C (59–68°F).

4   As with reds, white wines in Bordeaux normally undergo a malolactic fermentation.

5   As soon as the second fermentation is finished, the wine is clarified to prevent it from picking up any undesirable odours. This is usually done by filtration, or in large cellars by centrifuge.

6   Since the object nowadays is to prevent oxidation, wines spend much less time in pre-bottle maturation. Only the finest Graves spend more than a few months in cask; most wines are kept in *cuve* and bottled in the spring, some six months after the vintage, to conserve their freshness and fruit.

SWEET WHITE WINES

Because of the state of grapes affected by *pourriture noble* (noble rot or *Botrytis cinerea*, to give the scientific name), both the harvesting and vinifying of grapes for sweet wines pose special problems. The grapes cannot be picked as for dry wines, because the infection by *Botrytis cinerea* does not occur uniformly, either in the vineyard or even in single bunches. This means that the workers must go through a vineyard several times (four to six times at the best properties) selecting the best grapes from each bunch, a method requiring a certain amount of skill. Such grapes obviously cannot be mechanically harvested.

Botrytis cinerea itself is a fungus which, when it attacks over-ripe grapes, dehydrates them thus concentrating their sugar content. Mild humid conditions, typical of a Bordeaux autumn, are required for this infection to thrive. If conditions are too dry, the fungus will not attack even ripe grapes. This happened in 1978. On the other hand, if it rains at the wrong moment the vintage can be ruined, or only a small part of it will be useable. For these reasons there are far fewer successful vintages in Sauternes than in neighbouring Graves.

The process of vinification is as follows.

1   Because of the condition of the grapes they are not crushed in a separate operation but go straight into the press. The pressing is difficult because the grapes are so rich in sugar (20–25° Baumé – 360–450 grams per litre) and the juice so viscous. Three pressings are usual for Sauternes.

2   A *débourbage* is not usual because of the danger of sulphur dioxide binding the yeast cells and thus inhibiting their activity, and because a must so rich in sugar and bacteria is susceptible to oxidation at this stage. The best method of clarification is to centrifuge and then chill the must before beginning the fermentation, which can still be in barrel, but is now more usually and safely effected in *cuve*.

3   The fermentation is slow and often continues for many weeks. It must be controlled carefully in order to obtain a balanced wine. Thus, a wine with 12·5 per cent alcohol is well balanced with 30–35 grams of sugar per litre but not with 50. This sort of result would be typical of wines made in the Premières Côtes. A wine with 14 per cent alcohol however needs 60–70 grams to be balanced. Although the yeast becomes tired and 'blocked' when the level of alcohol rises to around 14 per cent, the wine will still not be permanently stable, and must therefore be stabilised by the addition of sulphur dioxide. Stabilisation is often assisted by filtration and chilling. Wines with less sugar must, in any case, be stopped from further fermentation in this way in order to ensure a balance.

4   The *élevage* (literally 'raising' the wine, as one would children or livestock) then proceeds in much the same way as for dry wines, except that the best sweet wines seem to benefit from maturing in cask, and the process is more lengthy, as much as two to two-and-a-half years before bottling takes place. Selection between *cuves* and even casks is also important when seeking to obtain really fine Sauternes, or indeed Loupiac or Ste-Croix-du-Mont.

Vintages

In temperate climates vintages are always important. Although there are fewer poor vintages than there used to be in Bordeaux, it is still important to know how the vintages vary, because this can tell you broadly which wines should be laid down and which can be drunk early. But each year has its distinctive character. Indeed the finer the year, the stronger the vintage character, and the more pronounced the character of each *cru*.

'98

Weather and General Assessment The special character of this vintage is due to the exceptional heat of August, after a good flowering and cool weather in June and July. This meant that when rain came in September, just before the harvest, and then more seriously at the end of the month, the effect was much less than expected. Although the chance to make a great vintage may have slipped by, some great wines were undoubtedly made. The wines have exceptional colour and powerful rich tannins. Initially heralded as a Merlot year, the evaluation of the Cabernets has surprised many tasters. The dry whites and sweet wines are excellent.

Médoc and Graves The favourable evolution of the Cabernets, together with the outstanding Merlots, have surprised many early pessimists. Great wines have been made on the great terroirs. Pessac-Léognan is especially successful, St-Estèphe perhaps less so than the communes to the south.

St-Emilion and Pomerol This is undoubtedly a great year for Pomerol but St-Emilion is more mixed. There are dense, textured, opulent wines, but some St-Emilions seem over-extracted.

Dry whites Lovely wines of intense fruit, reminiscent of '96, but with less acidity.

Sauternes Very rich, concentrated wines which seem to resemble the '96s but have less elegance than '97.

'97

Weather and General Assessment A year marked by a most unusual weather pattern. A warm spring resulting in a flowering which began in early May, but which then continued throughout the month as the weather turned cold. This resulted in an unevenness of maturity of the grapes which continued through to the vintage. Four weeks of hot, humid weather from 25 July to 28 August, followed by a week's stormy weather led into September, when from 2nd to 5th no rain fell. Vintaging was very spread out and difficult. At their best the wines have elegance and charm, but are less concentrated than '95 and '96.

Médoc and Graves The more careful growers have produced delicious, early drinking wines in all areas, but the public perception has been damaged by the excessive primeur prices. They have breed and style.

St-Emilion and Pomerol Many wines developed much better than at first seemed likely. In some cases the wines rival the rather variable '96s.

Dry whites While quantities are small due to problems at the time of harvesting, the top properties made delightful wines.

Sauternes The one region to produce indisputably great wines of remarkable elegance and style this year, although less rich than the '96s.

'96

Weather and General Assessment The unusual weather pattern produced wines of marked character. Often above-average temperatures in June and July, but those of August were below average and there was more rain than usual. Then came three weeks of dry sunny weather, but less heat than expected in early September. This surprisingly caused a rapid rise in sugar levels while the cold nights left acidity levels high. The result was exceptional Cabernet Sauvignon, higher in sugar content than in '89 or '82; Merlot higher than '85 but lower than '89, exceptional dry white wines and sweet wines.

Médoc and Graves The best wines are in St-Julien and points north where they resemble '89s, with great depth of flavour and power. In Margaux, southern Médoc and Graves, where there was more rain, the wines are similar to '85 and elegant.

St-Émilion and Pomerol The quality is not as uniformly high as in '95, and some wines are noticeably lighter, but the best are still rich and fine.

Dry Whites With the richness of '89 and '90 but an exceptional acidity balance, the wines are extremely good with the top Pessac-Léognan reaching heights seldom seen.

Sauternes Undoubtedly a great year. The wines have the richness of '89 but the higher acidities give them the elegance of '88.

'95

Weather and General Assessment At last the vintage Bordeaux was waiting for after the disappointment of '94 and '93. The growing season was dry and hot and the vines were as forward as they had been in '94 and '93. But this time the usual September rainfall was much less serious, and perfect weather from September 20 until October enabled ripe grapes to be harvested without the anxieties of '94. The feature of the year is the regularity of the quality at all levels.

Médoc and Graves Classic fruity Cabernet wines with breed and style, resembling '85 with a touch more firmness. All districts did well, but the St-Estèphes were especially rewarding.

St-Émilion and Pomerol A superb vintage. The wines have richness and beauty of flavour. Some great wines were made.

Dry Whites Well-balanced, fruity and elegant wines.

Sauternes The best vintage since '90. Perfumed wines with good botrytis concentration and fruit. A fine if not a great year.

'94

Weather and General Assessment Once more a great vintage was dashed from our lips at the last moment. An early flowering and excellent growing and ripening conditions had produced grapes which in the first week in September were in line with '82 and '90. But heavy rain between 14 and

17 September, followed by intermittent showers, often heavy, until the end of the month, detracted from the quality of the vintage. However, the ripeness and excellent condition of the grapes resulted in significantly better wines than in '93. The top *crus* produced firm fine wines with style and richness. Yields were as much as 20 per cent below those of '93 in many vineyards.

Médoc and Graves The best wines came from vineyards with the earliest ripening Cabernet Sauvignon, which was of excellent quality. The AC Médoc and those Haut-Médocs furthest from the river did less well. Pessac-Léognan was uniformly good, and St-Julien was of a high overall standard.

St-Émilion and Pomerol A good overall level of quality, with juicy ripe wines that show generous fruit and good structure.

Dry Whites Mostly gathered in before the rains; fruity, well-balanced stylish wines were made.

Sauternes Another traumatic vintage for producers. The weather changed at the beginning of October but there was little left to save. A handful of decent wines were made in tiny quantities.

'93

Weather and General Assessment A much better growing and ripening season: conditions were almost a re-run of '92, much to the frustration of producers. The yields were a little below the record of the previous year, but still high, and while the rain seemed more intermittent, this was still a wet September. Many of the lesser wines which seemed fruity and charming in vat are now mean in bottle and only the top *crus* succeeded in making significantly better wines than in '92.

Médoc and Graves After a dull patch most wines are now drinking well. Pessac-Léognan, St-Julien, Pauillac and St-Estèphe produced the best results, with a handful of really good attractive wines.

St-Émilion and Pomerol The Merlot did much better than '92, but Cabernet Franc still had problems. The wines are less dilute and plenty of pleasing examples were the result.

Dry Whites Because most of the grapes were brought in before the rain affected them, this is a good year for Entre-Deux-Mers and Graves, with fruity stylish wines.

Sauternes Only marginally less awful than in '92, with a handful of usable wines.

'92

Weather and General Assessment These were probably the most difficult weather conditions for *vignerons* since '74. The growing season was exceptionally wet, with the August rainfall three times its normal level, while temperatures fluctuated between warm (during May, July and August) and cool (in June and first three weeks of September). To crown it all, it rained right through the harvest. As far as volume is concerned, this was the largest crop of the AC wines recorded, beating the '90 total by over 260,000 hectolitres, the first AC red wine harvest of over five million hectolitres and the largest AC white wine crop since '73. Well-run properties were able to make severe selections resulting in pleasant commercial wines for early drinking for the red – but the whites are generally more successful.

Médoc and Graves Rather dilute Cabernets result in a wide variation in quality. Wines with a good proportion of Merlot did best and strict selection was vital. The best wines are light, fruity and charming for early drinking, but some producers have been tempted to over-concentrate and over-oak. In style, the wines resemble the '87s.

St-Émilion and Pomerol Merlots did well but Cabernet Franc posed problems at many properties. The best wines show attractive supple fruit, but some are over-oaked for their structure.

Dry Whites Some fine Graves and plenty of attractive wines from Entre-Deux-Mers, but a wide range of qualities.

Sauternes A few good wines were made from grapes gathered before the rain washed away hope of any quantity of reasonable quality, but these wines are light.

'91

Weather and General Assessment The frost on the night of April 20/21 was the most serious to strike Bordeaux since that of 1945. Then cold weather hampered the development of secondary shoots, resulting in big ripening differences at harvest time. Poor weather in September and rain during the vintage dashed any hopes of reasonable quality. Only a few exceptional sites, mostly in Médoc, were able to make wines solely from first-generation grapes – and only the first-generation grapes produced any real quality.

Médoc and Graves A few vineyards close to the Gironde were spared the worst of the frost, and châteaux such as La Tour de By, Montrose, Cos-d'Estournel, Latour and Léoville-Las-Cases produced surprisingly attractive supple wines of real substance. However, in general, the wines are pretty but insubstantial.

St-Émilion and Pomerol The story here is bleak. Only part of the Côte de Pavie escaped the full ravages of the frost, and then the poor weather conditions were not kind to the remaining second-generation Merlots.

Dry Whites The smallest crop recorded in Bordeaux! Yields in Pessac-Léognan were only 12·9 hl/ha. But the wines that were made were fruity and attractive.

Sauternes Disastrous yields between ten and 11 hectolitres per hectare but one or two good selections resulted in tiny quantities of wine which are finer and richer than the '92s.

'90

Weather and General Assessment The pattern of '89 was followed to a degree that is rare. The flowering was in May and but for a combination of heat and drought in July, which simply stopped the vines in their tracks, the vintage would have been even earlier than in '89. As it was the vintage for the Merlots began around September 10, while the Cabernet Sauvignons in the Médoc needed to wait until the beginning of October.

The wines have outstanding fruit and good structure, in the mould of '82 and '89 – the crop was marginally larger than '89, but with slightly lower yields.

Médoc and Graves The more northerly regions of the Médoc, with their heavier soils, did especially well. There are many outstanding successes among the Crus Bourgeois, and many exceptional wines in St-Estèphe, Pauillac and St-Julien, but Margaux is more varied. Graves are often opulent but also have elegance and great individuality.

St-Émilion and Pomerol St-Émilions are characterised by an attractive combination of rich, luscious fruit and good structure, while Pomerols are notable for the concentration of the wines.

Dry Whites Outstandingly aromatic fruit. Many producers achieved better balance and acidity than they did with the '89.

Sweet Whites The *annus mirabilis* for Sauternes, with the richest wines seen since '29, even surpassing the wonderful '89s. The wines are remarkably exotic in character.

'89

Weather and General Assessment The warmest, sunniest and driest summer, on average, in 30 years, with a flowering that began on May 20, and the earliest vintage since 1893, beginning on August 28. The wines are high in alcohol, with luscious fruit and soft ripe tannins reminiscent of '82. The yields for red AC wines set a new record, surpassing that of the '86 vintage by over 350,000 hectolitres.

Médoc and Graves The St-Juliens are a stunning group, but there are lovely wines in all the main communes. Selection of the best fruit, due to high yields, has meant that the leading growths have done correspondingly better than the lesser *crus*. There are some gloriously rich fruity wines. The Graves are lighter and more elegant in structure.

St-Émilion and Pomerol Amazingly dense-textured and forceful wines, with exceptional structure to add to the opulence of a great Merlot vintage.

Dry Whites Big fat fruity wines, but many suffer from shortage of acidity and could with advantage have been harvested even earlier. For early drinking.

Sweet Whites This is an exceptional year, comparable with '47 but with more of everything. The '89 and '90 must be the greatest pair of Sauternes since '28 and '29, coming at the end of a decade of fine vintages.

'88

Weather and General Assessment A wet winter and spring were followed by a drier-than-average summer and a warm October. The resulting variations in maturity between the grape varieties were significant, as were those between the same variety at different sites, and this caused noticeable variations in quality. In style, the wines began life as forbiddingly tannic, in the mould of '86, but have become classically elegant and fine.

Médoc and Graves Classically structured wines that seem finer, but have less power, than the '86s. They will be long-lived and harmonious, with fine concentration and breed.

St-Émilion and Pomerol The St-Émilions are exceptionally rich and concentrated, usually superior to the '86s, while the Pomerols are really opulent with great depth of flavour.

Dry Whites The wines have pronounced fruit, with the best Graves having complexity and elegance.

Sweet whites Another classic botrytis year to set beside '83 and '86. The wines have character and great breed, they are well balanced and the top wines are consistent.

'87

Weather and General Assessment After above-average temperatures in July, August and September, heavy rain during the vintage. Wines are soft, fruity and easy to drink young.

Médoc and Graves The Cabernets were caught by the rain, so the Merlots are of more than usual importance. The wines have plenty of fruit and charm, if light in body and rather short. Pleasing, early-drinking wines. Should be drunk up now.

St-Émilion and Pomerol With their high proportion of Merlot, these regions did better than Médoc and Graves. The wines are supple and fruity and have developed quickly. To drink now.

Dry Whites Well balanced with pleasing fruit character.

Sweet Whites Where strict selections were made, good wines have resulted.

'86

Weather and General Assessment Successful flowering and a good summer but heavy rain, especially around Bordeaux, in late September. Exceptionally dry conditions during the harvest. The red wine crop beat the '85 record. The quality of the best wines is excellent, with some classic wines for long keeping. The most tannic year since '75, and a complete contrast to '85.

Médoc and Graves A Cabernet year: many vats of Merlot remained unused. Wines have great power, depth and promise but still need patience.

St-Émilion and Pomerol Here there was less rain and the Merlot did much better. The Pomerols are powerful and tannic, the St-Émilions have more charm but are generally less powerful.

Dry Whites Perfumed and attractive, sometimes better balanced than the '85s.

Sweet Whites Another great Sauternes vintage. The onset of botrytis was more general and rapid than in '85, and the quality more consistent than the '83.

'85

Weather and General Assessment In spite of rain there was an excellent setting of the fruit. The driest September on record, sustained heat, and a warm and dry October. The largest crop of AC reds. Overall quality is high, the wines have charm and breed, classic in the style of '53, but they are more outstanding across the board.

Médoc and Graves Outstanding in Margaux and Graves, more rigorous selection necessary in Pauillac, St-Julien and Médoc: yields were high. Properties that delayed picking their Cabernets until the second week of October did best. Wines are rich in fruit and tannin and harmonious.

St-Émilion and Pomerol Sugar levels in the Merlot were higher than in '82, and the general level amongst the leading growths is more uniform than usual. There were lower yields than in '82 but still excellent considering the exceptionally cold January.

Dry Whites Extremely perfumed fruity wines, but acidity low.

Sweet Whites The few properties that prolonged picking have made excellent wines with great elegance, if less luscious than in '83.

'84

Weather and General Assessment A cold wet May led to the worst *coulure* (failure of flowers to set) in living memory. Late September experienced rain and storms, but a perfect October followed. There are a few successes, but in general the wines appear rather mean.

Médoc and Graves Average yields produced wines that have not lived up to early expectations. A few pleasant surprises.

St-Émilion and Pomerol A small crop of rather average wine which lacks character and can appear mean.

Dry Whites Excellent quality, normal yield. The wines have more delicacy and are lighter than the '83s, with pronounced character, and have aged well.

Sweet Whites Some fine wines were made.

'83

Weather and General Assessment A wet spring, good flowering in June. Early September brought more rain, but the weather was ideal for the vintage. A fine year producing classic wines, mostly now at their best, with style and character.

Médoc and Graves Another large vintage, quality not as regular as in '82 but fine at Cru Classé level with some stylish wines. Most wines are now at their best.

St-Émilion and Pomerol A high yield. Some outstanding wines but more variation than in '82. Most drinking well now.

Dry Whites Good wines with more acidity and style than the '82s.

Sweet Wines A great year, probably the best since '76. Luscious wines, but well balanced and long lived.

'82

Weather and General Assessment A classic hot year, with a large yield and perfect ripeness. Certainly the most outstanding vintage since '61. The wines have a special vintage character.

Médoc and Graves Wines of exceptional concentration and power, with plenty of fruit to cover the high tannin levels. An exceptional year, the most individual since '61.

St-Émilion and Pomerol Wines of exceptional opulence and power, reminiscent of '47. As in '47, some of the top wines have proved remarkable for early drinking, but are still improving.

Dry Whites These wines have charm but are short of acidity. Most should be drunk now.

Sweet Whites The dry hot weather delayed the noble rot; the rain in October started too early, resulting in medium-weight wines that are no more than acceptable for early drinking. Yquem is the exception.

'81

Weather and General Assessment Good weather right through the growing period, but some rain during the vintage. Wines have more breed but less body than in '79.

Médoc and Graves Classic wines with length and finish. Not as powerful as the '79s nor as firm as the '78s but with all the breed of a really fine year.

St-Émilion and Pomerol Elegant stylish wines; the best are full and luscious in flavour, although many are rather light. Some Pomerols have remained lean and dull.

Dry Whites Elegant wines of medium weight. Now mostly drunk.

Sweet Whites The best are luscious, better than the '82s.

'80

Weather and General Assessment The coldest June since '46 caused prolonged flowering and widespread *coulure*. A cold July, a warm August and September. For many this was the latest harvest since '22, with the smallest crop since '69, due to a small harvest of white wines. A useful vintage of stylish wines.

Médoc and Graves Attractive wines for early drinking, now at their best or beginning to show their age.

St-Émilion and Pomerol More variable than Médoc but, since Merlot ripened better than Cabernet Sauvignon, these areas produced many supple, fruity wines.

Dry Whites Light, pleasant wines that should have been drunk.

Sweet Whites The wines are rather light, but the best have a pleasant fruitiness and charm without real lusciousness.

'79

Weather and General Assessment Late flowering and excellent setting; a cold and wet August; but better conditions in September yielded a large crop. Wines have great depth of fruit, vigour and lots of charm, but lack backbone and breed.

Médoc and Graves Wines have a marked vintage character and are rich and dense in texture. They have developed slowly; the best still improving but lacking the finesse of '78.

St-Émilion and Pomerol The Merlot's exceptional ripeness produced more luscious, dense and opulent wines than in '78. This kind of year brings out the best in these districts.

Dry Whites Stylish wines with fruit and breed.

Sweet Whites Vies with '81 as the best vintage between '76 and '83. Luscious, fruity wines.

'78

Weather and General Assessment The wettest March since 1870; exceptionally dry July, August and September. The average-sized vintage was harvested late but in ideal conditions. Classic wines with harmonious balance. They have developed more quickly than expected and are ideal for drinking now.

Médoc and Graves Wines of great character and finesse. Their considerable tannin, well blended with fruit and richness, has given them a long development. They are now at their best.

St-Émilion and Pomerol These wines have developed attractively. Some are rather lean, but most are decidedly stylish. Not such typical wines as the '79s.

Dry Whites A fine year, with the best Graves needing longer to develop than the '79s.

Sweet Whites A freak year, with perfect ripeness but almost no noble rot, leaving the wines lacking in classic character.

'77

Weather and General Assessment Frost at the end of March caused serious damage, especially in Pomerol and St-Émilion. A cold summer, then the driest September, with the most hours of sunshine for 100 years. Some useful commercial wines, but tending to lack appellation character.

Médoc and Graves Many light, pleasing wines, but mostly lacking character of appellation or *cru*. Should have been drunk by now.

St-Émilion and Pomerol Small wines, not without charm, but lacking individuality. Should have been drunk.

Dry Whites A few Graves are stylish and pleasing.

Sweet Whites A year to forget.

'76

Weather and General Assessment Dry, hot weather from April to the end of August. The vintage began September 13 but rain diluted the musts. This mixture of tannin and concentrated fruit, diluted with rainwater, produced diverse wines. Some are deeply coloured, rich and fruity. In others tannin and fruit seem to have separated. It has also affected the development cycle of the wines, which has been relatively rapid.

Médoc and Graves The best wines are supple, powerful and attractive, but there are also disappointments. They have developed well and are by now at their best. To drink rather than to keep.

St-Émilion and Pomerol Overripeness and diluted colours are a feature here. Many wines suffer from low acidity and have aged rapidly. A few have more structure and are delicious now.

Dry Whites Wines low in acidity that needed drinking early. Some top Graves are rich and fine.

Sweet Whites A great vintage, with luscious wines that are more elegant and stylish than the '75s.

'75

Weather and General Assessment Excellent flowering then a dry, hot summer. Some rain in September was just what was needed. A year of moderate yields, good alcoholic degrees and thick skins resulted in tannic wines that are slow to develop. They lack the balance and charm of the '61s which some optimists believed them to resemble at an early stage.

Médoc and Graves At some châteaux this is now looking like the best vintage of the decade, with the tannins peeling away to reveal rich concentrated classic wines with power and fruit. Elsewhere the tannins can seem too dry.

St-Émilion and Pomerol As often happens in a tannic year, the best wines seem better balanced than in the Médoc. The emphasis is on ripeness and opulence: there are many successful wines.

Dry Whites The best Graves are concentrated and powerful but lack the elegance of the '76s.

Sweet Whites Many wines have too much botrytis and are too alcoholic: clumsy, tarry wines that are ageing rapidly (Yquem, Climens, Coutet and Doisy-Daëne are notable exceptions).

'74

Weather and General Assessment Good flowering ensured a large vintage. A fine summer promised good quality but a cold, wet September changed all that. Austere, charmless wines for the most part, which lack any real appellation or *cru* character.

'73

Weather and General Assessment Good flowering conditions ensured a large crop, but the summer alternated between hot and sunny and wet. The vintage was gathered in good conditions in October. Most wines are now past their best.

Médoc and Graves Attractive early-developing wines. Most should have been drunk, but some are holding up surprisingly well.

St-Émilion and Pomerol These are rather overblown wines which had great charm but were short-lived, with a few notable exceptions.

Dry Whites Some stylish Graves have lasted well, but most should have been drunk some time ago.

Sweet Whites Pleasant but moderate wines, on the light side.

'72

Weather and General Assessment A cold spring, a poor summer with rain in August and a late harvest of unripe grapes. A year of high prices and mean, dull wines that are best forgotten.

'71

Weather and General Assessment A cold, wet spring caused a poor flowering and a correspondingly small crop. Then the summer turned warm and sunny with just the right amount of rain. A complete contrast to the previous vintage.

Médoc and Graves Flattering, charming wines that developed quickly and have been at their peak since the late 1970s. With their low acidities, they now need drinking, and many have already turned the corner.

St-Émilion and Pomerol Some great successes here, with rich, luscious but rather overblown wines. They should be drunk up, except for a few Pomerols.

Dry Whites Perfumed, elegant Graves at the top level are lasting well.

Sweet Whites A great classic Sauternes year, combining richness with elegance, usually better than '70.

'70

Weather and General Assessment Ideal growing conditions produced the rare combination of quantity and perfect ripeness. The new plantings of the 1960s yielded quality wines, and 1970 marked the beginning of the great switch from white to red wines and heralded the large yields of the 1970s and 1980s. This was the largest quality year since '34. A fine vintage: slow to develop but generally worth waiting for.

Médoc and Graves These wines have taken much longer to develop than expected, due perhaps to a lack of maturity in parts of the vineyards at this period. Nevertheless, these are classic long-distance wines, well-structured, with breed and fruit to match the tannin. They are now becoming enjoyable to drink, especially the Margaux, St-Juliens and Graves, but there are some disappointments.

St-Émilion and Pomerol These have also been slow to evolve, but they have more charm than many Médocs and are drinking well. The power and the structure of these wines promise a long life.

Dry Whites The best Graves are rich and solid and holding well.

Sweet Whites Big luscious wines, with less style for the most part than in '71. Long-lasting wines.

OLDER VINTAGES STILL DRINKING WELL

'66 – A classic vintage with old-fashioned concentrated wines, the best of the decade after '61.

'64 The Pomerols and St-Emilions are still superb, in many cases the best of the decade. The Médocs are in decline.

'62 Although without the concentration of '66 there are fine classic wines ageing gracefully.

'61 These outstanding wines continue to delight and astonish. They have no rivals today until '82.

'59 – Wines have a roasted character. Some are not far behind '61 but most lack their harmony.

'55 – Some still remarkably fresh, solid and more interesting than they were a few years ago.

What Makes Great Bordeaux

RED

Vineyard

Well-drained, relatively poor soil, high in gravel (Médoc and Graves), limestone (St-Émilion *côtes*), gravel and sand (St-Émilion, Graves) or gravel and clay (Pomerol).

Grape varieties

Cabernet Sauvignon, Cabernet Franc and Merlot.

Mature healthy grapes

The right balance of sugar and acidity; no rot.

Careful vinification

No extraction of acids from the stalks. Fermentation at 28–30°C (82–86°F).

Careful selection

Rejection of any sub-standard *cuves* (grapes from young vines, an inferior part of the vineyard or *cuves* affected by rain or rot).

Addition of vin de presse (*see* page 32).

This adds colour and extracts and so provides additional elements to assist ageing.

Use of new barrels

The percentage of new barrels should be correct for the weight of the wine; it ranges from 30–100 per cent.

Bottling at the right time

After 18–24 months, depending on the wine's tannin and power.

SWEET WHITE

Vineyard

Well-drained, poor soil, characterised by the presence of clay with gravel and limestone.

Grape varieties

Sémillon and Sauvignon.

Overripe grapes affected by noble rot

This must be carefully controlled by selection. Too little botrytis and the wine lacks character; too much, and the wine becomes clumsy.

Selection in the vineyard

The pickers must go through the vineyard from three to six times to select overripe and botrytized grapes.

Slow and long fermentation in cask

The ideal temperature is normally about 20°C (68°F). Because of this and the high concentration of sugar, the fermentation usually lasts two to five weeks.

Cask-ageing

The best *crus* still keep their wines in cask for two to three years. A proportion of the casks is new.

Selection for bottling

Selection is made between pressings (the third is usually the best), and between casks.

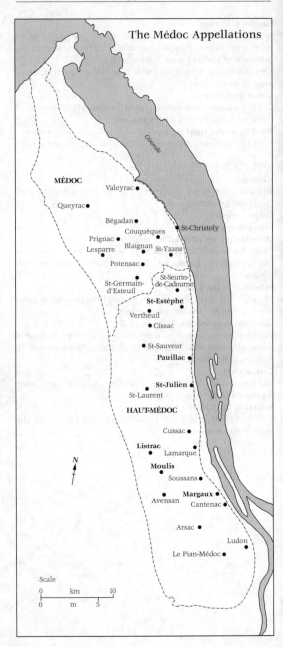

The Médoc Appellations

MÉDOC

Valeyrac

Queyrac

Bégadan

Couquèques

St-Christoly

Prignac

Blaignan

St-Yzans

Lesparre

Potensac

St-Germain-
d'Esteuil

St-Seurin-
de-Cadourne

St-Estèphe

Vertheuil

Cissac

St-Sauveur

Pauillac

St-Julien

St-Laurent

HAUT-MÉDOC

Cussac

Listrac

Lamarque

Moulis

Soussans

Margaux

Avensan

Cantenac

Arsac

Ludon

Le Pian-Médoc

N

Gironde

Scale

0   km   10

0   m   5

Château Profiles by Appellation

This section focuses on properties that merit special consideration. It includes not only the great names of Bordeaux but also many less well-known producers whose wines deserve recognition. The entries are arranged by appellation, and each appellation is introduced with a description of its general character. In the Médoc, which encompasses many important appellations, there is also a general introduction to the region.

After the name of the property, each entry begins with the following details, where obtainable and relevant: classification, owner, administrator, number of hectares planted with vines, number of cases produced annually, grape varieties and respective percentages used in production, and any secondary or other labels. *See* page 5 for a key to the abbreviations.

The Médoc Appellations

Médoc has been the great ambassador for the red wines of Bordeaux the world over. From the early 18th century, when wealthy and discerning Englishmen first paid a premium to obtain better wines, until the second half of the 20th century the fame of the region has centred on the treasure trove of the Médoc.

With its proximity to the city of Bordeaux, the commercial and political centre of the Gironde, it was natural that the Médoc should be developed earlier and more thoroughly than any other piece of land in the region. In the 17th and 18th centuries, the great wine estates there were put together in much the same form as they exist today. Because of the poor, gravelly soil, mixed subsistence farming easily gave way to specialised viticulture. A glance at the map opposite shows the Médoc to be a narrow but lengthy strip of land running along the estuary of the Gironde from just outside the modern suburbs of northern Bordeaux, at Blanquefort and le Taillan, to St-Vivien, 70 kilometres (44 miles) to the north. In few places do the vineyards extend more than ten kilometres (six miles) inland from the river, and most lie to the east of the main Bordeaux-Lesparre-Soulac road. This is where the ridges of gravel are at their deepest and purest. As you go north, the soils get heavier and the gravel more interspersed with clay or sand, while to the west, the land becomes sandy and the pine forests of Les Landes begin.

Viticulturally, the Médoc is divided into two distinct areas: the Haut-Médoc in the south and the Bas-Médoc (called simply Médoc for appellation purposes) in the north. Within the Haut-Médoc, six communal appellations have been carved out. In addition, the name Haut-Médoc itself constitutes a seventh appellation, encompassing wines not covered by the communal appellations. The latter correspond to the area where the great majority of the finest vineyards lie. This is vividly illustrated by the following figures showing the proportion of the area under vine in the five appellations occupied by the Crus Classés (the remaining two contain no Crus Classés). Haut-Médoc 5·5 per cent, Margaux 68 per cent, St-Julien 75 per cent, Pauillac 72·5 per cent, St-Estèphe 19·5 per cent.

Although more and more of the Crus Bourgeois now bottle at least a proportion of their wines at the château, many smaller vineyards find it makes economic sense to join cooperatives where the methods of vinification have been modernised, rather than face the large capital cost of modernising their own *cuviers*. Members of cooperatives account for the following proportions of the areas under vine in these appellations: Médoc 42·5 per cent, Haut-Médoc 17·5 per cent, Pauillac 18 per cent, St-Estèphe 26 per cent, Listrac 24 per cent, Moulis 6·5 per cent. Standards in cooperatives have improved considerably in the past few years and they are now undoubtedly a positive influence on quality.

The predominance of the Cabernet Sauvignon grape in all the vineyards of the Médoc ensures a certain family resemblance, a crispness of definition on nose and palate and a tendency for the tannin to be dominant in the first year or so in bottle. The development of bouquet, combined with bottle-ageing, comes with delicacy and character of flavour, comes with bottle-ageing. Médoc wines all need to be aged, and even quite modest *crus* keep and improve well.

MARGAUX

Margaux is the only one of the six commune appellations that is not restricted to the area bearing its name. Also included under this appellation are most of the commune of Arsac and all of Cantenac, Labarde and Soussans. The area under vine increased by 12 per cent between 1986 and 1996.

The outstanding characteristics of the appellation's wines are finesse and breed, the results of deep, gravelly ridges and a high proportion of Cabernet Sauvignon. But the variations of emphasis are considerable. Labarde wines tend to have more body and richness, the Cantenacs are more elegant and often shorter, as is du Tertre, the sole Cru Classé of Arsac. Many Margaux wines have more tannin and are slower to evolve.

Château d'Angludet
Cru Bourgeois Supérieur Exceptionnel 1932. Owners: Sichel family. 32ha. 14,000 cases. CS 55%, Mer 35%, PV 10%.
Second label: La Ferme d'Angludet.
Angludet was unfortunate not to be classified in 1855. At that time it was divided and had much declined in importance since the 18th century, when it had been ranked with the leading growths. First under Peter Sichel's devoted care then under his son Benjamin's, the wines are becoming steadily better as the vineyard matures. Peter's son Benjamin is now responsible for the winemaking. The excellent vineyard, situated on the plateau of Cantenac, produces wines that are finely perfumed and combine great finesse with elegance and vigour. Since the excellent '78 the wines have been consistently impressive. I would single out the '82, '85, '86, '89, '90, '94, '95, '96 and '98 all of which are fine examples of these vintages.

Château d'Arsac

Cru Bourgeois Supérieur 1932. Owner: Philippe Raoux. 102ha.
26,600 cases. CS 60%, Mer 40%.
Second labels: Ribon Bleu de Château d'Arsac.

From 1995, 40 hectares of this property's vineyards have been classified as AC Margaux, the remainder being AC Haut-Médoc. This *cru* was always something of a curiosity, since it was the only one in Arsac not to benefit from the Margaux AC until recently: when the AC was being established there were no vines planted and the proprietor did not bother to apply for recognition. A start was made in reconstructing the vineyard when it changed hands in 1959, but the real change came when the present dynamic owner arrived in 1986. Since then the massive *chai* has been restored, the *cuvier* modernised and the vineyard increased from only 11·5 hectares to its present 102 hectares. The new vinification facilities were operational for the '88 vintage. The amount of oak ageing has been increased and some new oak is now being used. With the excellent raw materials available, and the dedication and enthusiasm of the owner, the future looks promising.

Château Bel-Air-Marquis-d'Aligre

Cru Bourgeois Supérieur Exceptionnel 1932. Owner: Pierre
Boyer. 17ha. 4,500 cases. Mer 35%, CS 30%, CF 20%, PV 15%.
Second label: Château Bel-Air-Marquis-de-Pomereu.

Confusingly, this is one of the three Margaux properties sporting the name Marquis in its title, and the only one not classified. It lies at the back of Margaux, with part of the vineyard in the adjoining commune Soussans.

Pierre Boyer is a perfectionist who makes his wines with great care from low yields. Only organic fertilizers are used in the vineyards. The wine has real finesse and a certain unctuousness combined with delicacy and freshness.

Château Boyd-Cantenac

3e Cru Classé. Owner: Pierre Guillemet. 18ha. 7,500 cases.
CS 67%, Mer 20%, CF 7%, PV 6%.

This property has a chequered history. It lost many of its vineyards to Cantenac-Brown in 1860, disappeared as a name for 45 years before reappearing again in 1920, then lost its buildings to Château Margaux. Until 1982 the wine was made at Château Pouget, Pierre Guillemet's neighbouring property, but now the wines are separately made.

Although no longer as important as it was in 1855, nor of the standard expected of a Troisième Cru, it still produces well-made wines, rich and supple in style and certainly worthy of a Cru Classé once more; '70, '71, '75, '78 and '79 were all highly successful years. The vintages of the 1980s were bigger and more tannic than their predecessors but seem to have less finesse.

Château Brane-Cantenac

2e Cru Classé. Owner: Henri Lurton. 85ha. 29,000 cases.
CS 70%, Mer 20%, CF 10%. Second label: Le Baron de Brane.

Brane-Cantenac owed its name and pre-eminence in 1855 to Baron de Brane, famed as a viticulturist and responsible for the rise of Mouton. Now it belongs to another family of viticulturalists, the Lurtons. In 1994 Lucien Lurton handed this property to his son Henri, as part of his family plan to pass on specific vineyards to his children.

With vineyards enjoying a prime position on the plateau of Cantenac, this property produces a wine noted for its delicacy, finesse and breed (quintessential Margaux qualities) and this in spite of its high proportion of Cabernet Sauvignon – a sure indication of the influence of soil on grape varieties. Like many Margaux wines it can often be drunk young with enjoyment, but lasts well, as demonstrated by its lovely '66. Good wines were made in '78, '79 and '81; the '82 is outstanding; '83 is rather light; '85 has the breed of the year; '86 is unusually tannic, '88, '89 and '90 combine concentration with great finesse, and '94, '95, '96 and '98 are among the successes of the appellation. A wine on the way up.

Château Cantenac-Brown

3e Cru Classé. Owner: AXA-Millésimes.
Administrator: Jean-Michel Cazes. 32ha. 12,500 cases.
CS 65%, Mer 25%, CF 10%. Second labels: Château Canuet
(Margaux), Lamartine (Bordeaux Supérieur).
The English name Brown is from John Lewis Brown, a Bordeaux merchant of English origin and an artist famous for his animal pictures. He was responsible for this unusual château, described as being in the 'Renaissance Anglaise' style. It now belongs to AXA-Millésimes, which also owns Pichon-Baron and has at its disposal the talents of Jean-Michel Cazes of Lynch-Bages fame.

Cantenac-Brown today does not enjoy the reputation (or sell for the price) it once did. The wine is more tannic with less finesse than the best Cantenacs and has a certain coarseness. Efforts being made by the new owners to improve matters showed some success in '95.

Château Dauzac

5e Cru Classé. Owner: Société Fermière d'Exploitation. 40ha.
29,000 cases. CS 58%, Mer 37%, CF 5%.
Second labels: Châteaux Labarde, La Bastide.
Until recently this property in Labarde had suffered a long period of neglect and obscurity. In 1993 the management of the estate was reorganised as a Société Fermière d'Exploitation, and a substantial shareholding was allotted to the SCEA Les Vignobles André Lurton which took over responsibility for the future management of the property.

The Lurton team is now turning its attention to the vineyard, much of which is planted on unsuitable rootstocks, and this should complete the long process of rehabilitation for this *cru*. The '96 vintage showed a big advance in terms of finesse and breed.

Château Desmirail

3e Cru Classé. Owner: Denis Lurton. 28ha. 5,000 cases.
CS 80%, Mer 15%, CF 5%. Second wine: Château Fontarney.

This famous old growth was resurrected by Lucien Lurton, vineyard owner extraordinary of Margaux (*see* Brane-Cantenac, Durfort-Vivens etc). In 1994 Lucien handed over this *cru* to his son Denis.

The wines are perfumed, soft and elegant in spite of the high proportion of Cabernet Sauvignon. Some outstanding wines were produced from '83 onwards. This is a *cru* rapidly establishing a reputation for itself.

Château Deyrem-Valentin

Cru Bourgeois 1932. Owner: Jean Sorge. 12ha. 6,700 cases.
CS 51%, Mer 45%, PV 2%, Mal 2%.

This small property is situated in the best part of Soussans, and neighbours include Lascombes, Malescot and the two Labégorces. It has belonged to the present family since 1928, and Jean Sorge is very much a working resident proprietor.

The '96 had fine scented fruit, was rich and solid but a shade coarse.

Château Durfort-Vivens

2e Cru Classé. Owner: Gonzague Lurton. 30ha. 5,000 cases.
CS 70%, CF 15%, Mer 15%. Second label: Second de Durfort.

The names come from the Comtes Durfort de Duras, who were the proprietors from the 15th century until the Revolution of 1789; Vivens was added in 1824. As is often the way in Bordeaux, the Vivens and the Durfort families were actually related. From 1937 until 1961 it was under the same ownership as Château Margaux; it was then sold to its present owner. The château itself is still inhabited by Bernard Ginestet, son of the former owner of Château Margaux.

The contrast between Durfort and Brane-Cantenac is always an interesting one. Durfort is always firmer and more tannic but usually has less finesse and charm. In recent vintages, however, the wines have had more richness and fruit to match their tannin.

Gonzague took over from his father in 1994, and the wine of that year was one of the successes of the vintage, with more emphasis on the elegance and breed of the *cru* than was evident in the 1980s. '95, '96, '97 and '98 are all excellent examples of these vintages.

Château Ferrière

3e Cru Classé. Owner: Claire Villars. 8ha. 4,000 cases. CS 75%,
Mer 20%, PV 5%. Second label: Les Remparts de Ferrière.

This small growth was farmed by Château Lascombes on behalf of its owners from 1960. In 1992 the Villars family (*see* Chasse-Spleen, Haut-Bages-Libéral and La Gurgue) bought the vineyard and has already brought its experience to bear. The family's first vintage (of that year) suggests that wines worthy of the property's status will once more be made here.

Château Giscours

3e Cru Classé. Owner: GFA du Château Giscours.
Administrator: Eric Albada-Jelgersma. 82ha. 44,400 cases.
CS 75%, Mer 22%, CF 2%, PV 1%. Second label: Château
Grand-Giscours.

After its acquisition by the Tari family in 1952, much time
and money was invested in this property to restore it to its
former glory. Now it is one of the largest and most important
Margaux properties, as well as one of the most consistent. In
1995 problems in the Tari family led to control passing to
new Dutch owners.

The wines of Giscours are deep-coloured with a pronounced
bouquet combining richness and fruit, while the wine itself
is fruity, vigorous and full-bodied. If not as stylish as the wines
of Cantenac and Margaux, the wine clearly has breed. In the
1980s the wines became more powerful, obscuring the finesse
of previous years, but from 1996 the new owner has produced
some improvements.

Château La Gurgue

Cru Bourgeois Supérieur 1932. Owner: SC du Château La
Gurgue. Administrator: Claire Villars.
10ha. 5,000 cases. CS 70%, Mer 30%.

A well-placed vineyard, together with Desmirail it is the closest
neighbour to Château Margaux on its western boundary. There
was a change of ownership in 1978 and the new investment,
together with the undoubted flair of Bernadette Villars (*see*
Chasse-Spleen and Haut-Bages-Libéral), resulted in a marked
improvement in the wines. The '81, '82, '83, '85, '86, '88, '89 and
'90 were all great successes. Since her mother's tragic death,
Claire Villars has proved herself equally talented.

This is a delicate, perfumed type of Margaux, with style and
breed, nice fruit, not a lot of body but plenty of flavour and refinement. Certainly a wine to follow.

Château d'Issan

3e Cru Classé. Owner: Mme Emmanuel Cruse. 30ha.
12,500 cases. CS 70%, Mer 30%. Second label: Blason d'Issan.

Regum mensis arisque deorum ('for the tables of kings and the high
altar of the gods') says the inscription over the gateway at d'Issan.
This is one of the oldest properties and the most splendid château
in the whole Médoc, with a beautiful early-17th-century château
sitting within the moat of its mediaeval predecessor.

After a long period of neglect, d'Issan was bought by the Cruse
family in 1945 and both château and vineyard have been painstak-
ingly restored to their former glory. Formerly this was a Cruse
(*négociant*) exclusivity; now it is sold on the market, and there
have been marked improvements in the wine in recent years.
This is a wine of great individuality, combining a power and richness rare in Cantenac with great breed and a lovely perfume. Very
good wines were also made in '70, '79, '81, '82, '83, '85, '86, '88, '89
and '90. There is a good '87 to drink now and in '91 it was possi-

ble to make a selection from first-generation grapes, which should provide one of the more successful wines of this frost-affected vintage. In recent years the wines have not been as consistent as might have been expected, but there was a good '95.

Château Kirwan

3e Cru Classé. Owner: Schröder & Schÿler. Administrator: Jean-Henri Schÿler. 34ha. 17,800 cases. CS 40%, Mer 30%, CF 20%, PV 10%. Second label: Les Charmes de Kirwan.

Château Kirwan is named after an Irishman from Galway who lost his head in the French Revolution. It now belongs to the Bordeaux firm of Schröder & Schÿler, which bottled the wines in its Bordeaux cellars until 1966, '67 being the first vintage to be château-bottled.

A great deal of work and investment has gone into improving the quality of Kirwan. New wood was used in the barrel-ageing for the first time in '78. Recent vintages are deep-coloured, powerful, concentrated wines which are beginning to attract favourable comments. The '89 and '90 marked a real step up with more fruit and succulence. The second wine was first produced in '93 as part of the new consultant Michel Rolland's programme for improving quality. The '95 is the best wine yet.

Château Labégorce

Cru Bourgeois Supérieur 1932. Owner: Hubert Perrodo. 31ha. 16,000 cases. CS 55%, Mer 40%, CF 5%.

This is certainly one of the best unclassified wines of Margaux, together with its close neighbour Labégorce Zédé. The vineyards are well placed in Margaux and Soussans and the château has nothing bourgeois about it. The wines have Margaux finesse and delicacy. The property changed hands in 1989 when the Condom family, owners since 1965, sold to an oil tycoon who is also a wine-lover. He has already made a marked improvement.

Château Labégorce Zédé

Cru Bourgeois Supérieur 1932. Owner: Luc Thienpont. Administrator: Luc Thienpont. 27ha. 17,000 cases. CS 50%, Mer 35%, CF 10%, PV 5%. Second Label: Château de l'Amiral.

For some years the wines of Labégorce Zédé took second place to those of its neighbour Labégorce. Luc Thienpont took over in 1979, standards have improved and fine wines are now being made. The emphasis is on finesse and breed with a superbly perfumed bouquet, and this is one of the best unclassified wines of the appellation. Although the château is in Margaux, the greater proportion of the vineyard area lies in Soussans.

Château Lascombes

2e Cru Classé. Owner: Bass Group.
Administrator: Bruno Lemoine. 83ha. 41,500 cases.
CS 55%, Mer 40%, PV 5%. Second label: Château Segonnes.
Second wine: Chevalier de Lascombes.

Lascombes was a small property until its purchase in 1951 by

Alexis Lichine and an American syndicate, who subsequently sold to the giant UK brewery group Bass-Charrington in 1971. Since 1951 its vineyards and production have been greatly increased.

The basic problem at Lascombes has been that the vineyard area was enlarged with scant regard to quality. Under René Vannetelle's stewardship this fact has now been recognised. Only 50 hectares are capable of producing wines of Cru Classé quality: the rest is now sold under the Segonnes label and for making rosé. The result was a marked improvement in the second half of the 1980s. Then a second wine was introduced in '97 to improve the selection for the *grand vin*. René Vannetelle retired at the end of '98 and was succeded by Bruno Lemoine, the talented *régisseur* from Montrose.

Château Malescot-St-Exupéry

3e Cru Classé. Owner: Roger Zuger. 23·5ha. 14,000 cases.
CS 50%, Mer 35%, CF 10%, PV 5%.
Second labels: Château Loyac, La Dame de Malescot.
Since acquiring the property in 1955 from the English firm of WH Chaplin, the Zuger family has done much to rebuild this *cru* which had greatly declined in size and standing. The charming château, now restored and lived in again, stands in the centre of the village of Margaux, while the vineyards are in Margaux (adjoining Château Margaux) and Soussans.

In spite of a fine bouquet, I used to find the wines rather edgy with a certain harshness; there was a marked improvement in the 1980s however, especially from '83 onwards. The '86, '88, '89, '90, '95, '96, '97 and '98 have a degree of breed and finesse allied to concentration that was lacking before.

Château Margaux

1er Cru Classé. Owner: SC du Château Margaux
(Mentzelopoulos family). Administrator: Paul Pontallier. 90ha.
Red: 33,000 cases. CS 75%, Mer 20%, PV and CF 5%.
White: 3,300 cases. Sauv 100%. Second labels: Pavillon Blanc
du Château Margaux, Pavillon Rouge du Château Margaux.
This château has had its ups and down, but new heights of quality and consistency have been achieved since the Mentzelopoulos family acquired the property in 1977. A new underground cellar has been built, the château and gardens restored to their former glory, and much work has been done to improve the vineyard.

At its best Margaux is one of the most sumptuous and sensual of Médoc wines, with all the perfume and finesse of a fine Margaux as found in its neighbours, but allied to more body and remarkable character and individuality. After some great vintages in '45, '47, '49, '50 and '53, its wines became less outstanding and less consistent, although the '66 stands out in this lean period. Then, from '78 to '90 Margaux consistently produced wines that were among the finest examples of their respective vintages. The '93 and '94 are fine wines in the context of the difficult vintages, and magnificent wines were made in '95, '96 and '98. '97 is a fine example of the year.

A second wine, Pavillon Rouge du Château Margaux, is made as a result of the stricter selection now practised. The first vintage was '79. The wines are lighter than the *grand vin*, but have breed and charm and are ready to drink much earlier.

Pavillon Blanc du Château Margaux, an excellent white wine made from only Sauvignon grapes from a vineyard in Soussans, has real distinction. Its bouquet and breed are remarkable – but so, unfortunately, is the price!

Château Marquis-d'Alesme-Becker

3e Cru Classé. Owner: Jean-Claude Zuger. 17ha. 9,600 cases.
CS 30%, Mer 45%, CF 15%, PV 10%.
Second label: Marquise d'Alesme.

This small and little-known Cru Classé was owned by the English firm of WH Chaplin and run partly with Malescot. The present proprietor is the brother of Roger Zuger at Malescot and the château is the original building of Château Desmirail. The vineyards are in Soussans and Margaux.

With its small production and history of obscurity, unfortunately it remains a wine that is hard to find. I have found it possessed of elegant, stylish fruit with a firm backbone. It needs time to develop.

Château Marquis-de-Terme

4e Cru Classé. Owner: Sénéclauze family. 35ha. 14,000 cases.
CS 55%, Mer 35%, CF 3%, PV 7%.
Second label: Terme des Goudats.

A good proportion of this wine is sold direct on the French market, with the result that it is not as widely known on export markets as its size might suggest. Much work has recently been done to make good deficiencies in the *chai*, which is now modern and well equipped. The vineyard is well kept, but yields are high.

I have found this wine to have charm and a certain easy appeal, without being among the best of Margaux in terms of finesse or originality. Since the 1980s there has been a clear advance in quality.

Château Marsac-Séguineau

Cru Bourgeois 1932. Owner: SC du Château Marsac-Séguineau.
Administrator: Jean-Pierre Angliviel de la Beaudelle. 10ha.
4,000 cases. Mer 60%, CS 28%, CF 12%.
Second label: Château Gravières-de-Marsac.

This is a full-flavoured, supple wine which nevertheless lasts well. The vineyard is in Soussans. The wines are exclusively distributed by the *négociants* Mestrezat, who are also in effect the owners, and who have done much to reorganise the vineyards since taking over.

Château Martinens

Cru Bourgeois Supérieur 1932. Owners: Simone Dulos and
Jean-Pierre Seynat-Dulos. 31ha. 11,700 cases. Mer 40%, CS 30%,
CF 20%, PV 10%. Second label: Château Bois du Monteil.

The pleasing château at Martinens was built in 1767 by three sisters from London: Ann, Jane and Mary White. But they sold after only nine years. The present owners have run the property since 1945. It lies in Cantenac and enjoys an excellent reputation for stylish, attractive wines.

Château Monbrison

Cru Bourgeois. Owner: Van der Heyden family. 14ha.
5,500 cases. CS 45%, Mer 35%, CF 15%, PV 5%.
Second label: Château Cordat.

The property was bought in 1921 by Robert Meacham-Davis, an American commissioner in the Red Cross, and the present proprietors are his grandchildren. Jean-Luc Van der Heyden made this one of the most sought-after Cru Bourgeois of the 1980s, and especially from '85 onwards, the price and quality challenged some of the lesser Crus Classés of Margaux. Tragically, Jean-Luc died in 1992 and now his brother, Laurent, is determined to maintain the legacy left to him.

I have found the wine to be most attractive, well structured with plenty of fruit and balancing tannin. This is now one of the most sought-after unclassified wines of the appellation, and although good before, it has been outstanding since '85.

Château Montbrun

Cru Bourgeois 1932. Owner: J Lebègue & Co.
Administrators: Jacques and Alain de Coninck. 8ha.
5,000 cases. Mer 75%, CS and CF 25%.

This small but well-placed vineyard in Cantenac was once part of Château Palmer. With its high proportion of Merlot, it produces rich, full-bodied wines, appropriate for a property run by men from the Libournais. The wine is distributed by *négociants* J Lebègue & Co – now unconnected with the English firm of the same name.

Château Palmer

3e Cru Classé. Owner: SC du Château Palmer.
Administrator: B Bouteiller. 45ha. 12,500 cases.
CS 55%, Mer 40%, PV 5%. Second label: Réserve du Général.

Named after a British general who fought under Wellington, Château Palmer is now owned by French, Dutch and British proprietors (Bouteiller, Mähler-Besse and Sichel). The château lies in the hamlet of Issan, and most of its vineyards were once part of Château d'Issan's domaine. The charming château with its four towers was built in the years 1857–60 when the property was owned by the Péreire family.

The reputation of Palmer has soared in the past 30 years. This was one of the first of the 'Super Seconds', a reputation which effectively dates from the superlative '61. The Chardon family (father Pierre and sons Claude and Yves) have had much to do with the quality and consistency of this splendid wine. Now the Chardon era has finally ended with the retirement of Claude and Yves and the appointment of Philippe Delfon.

The wine is characterised by an opulence and richness that are almost burgundian in the best years, yet this is combined with real finesse and breed. The '70, '71, '75, '76, '78, '79 and '81 were all great successes. The '82 lacks the richness and concentration of the best '82s but is nevertheless a fine and attractive wine. The '83 is reckoned more successful, and is followed by the '85, '86, '88, '89 and '90, all of which are also fine.

In 1995 the wooden vats were replaced by stainless steel. Elegant wines were made in '94, '95 and '96.

Château Paveil-de-Luze

Cru Bourgeois. Owner: GFA du Château Paveil.
Administrator: Baron Geoffroy de Luze. 27ha. 15,000 cases.
CS 65%, CF 5%, Mer 30%.
Second labels: Château de la Coste, Enclos du Banneret.

A fine vineyard on deep, well-drained gravel in Soussans with a charming *chartreuse*-style château, Paveil has belonged to the de Luze family for over a century. The wines were always sound but often rather anonymous, and bottled in de Luze's cellars in Bordeaux. Now the de Luze family has parted from the firm that bears its name and the wine is château-bottled and seems to be improving. At its best this is a wine of some style and distinction: lots of charm and breed rather than body. A wine to watch.

Château Pontac-Lynch

Cru Bourgeois Supérieur 1932. Owner: GFA du Château
Pontac-Lynch. Administrator: Marie-Christine Bondon. 10ha.
6,000 cases. CS and CF 57%, Mer 39%, PV 4%.
Second label: Château Pontac-Phenix.

A little-known *cru* bearing two famous names, Pontac-Lynch apparently sold for higher prices in the mid-18th century than its famous (now classified) neighbours. The wines have been winning medals recently and should be worth looking out for.

Château Pouget

4e Cru Classé. Owner: GFA des Châteaux Boyd-Cantenac et
Pouget. Administrator: Pierre Guillemet.
11ha. 4,700 cases. CS 66%, Mer 30%, CF 4%.

Under the same ownership as Château Boyd-Cantenac. Until the '82 vintage both wines were made here and Pouget was treated as the second wine of Boyd-Cantenac; since '83 however, the wines have had quite separate facilities. Pouget is exclusively distributed by Maison Dubos Frères of Bordeaux.

The wines are well made, rich, supple and worthy of Cru Classé status; '70, '71, '75, '78 and '79 were all successful years. Since the 1980s the wines have become more tannic, but coarser in style.

Château Prieuré-Lichine

4e Cru Classé. Owner: Ballande family. 71ha. 38,000 cases. CS 54%,
Mer 39%, PV 5%, CF 2%. Second label: Château de Clairefort.

The property has been restored and the vineyard enlarged and reconstructed since it was bought by Alexis Lichine in 1952. This charming château in Cantenac, formerly the priory, was Alexis Lichine's European home until his death in 1989. His son Sacha then ran the property until he sold it in 1999.

The quality and reputation of this *cru* have deservedly grown in recent years. The wines are full-bodied and rich, and a consistent standard is maintained.

The firm believes that the fine '82 is surpassed by the '83. Other vintages that have particularly impressed me are '70, '76, '78, '79, '81, '85, '86, '88, '89, '90 and '95.

Château Rauzan-Ségla

2e Cru Classé. Owner: Chanel Inc. Administrator: David Orr. 47ha. 20,000 cases. CS 70%, Mer 28%, CF 2%. Second label: Ségla.

This is one of the oldest and most famous *crus* in Margaux, but unfortunately its wines for some years failed to match their high classification. Having belonged to the Cruse family for several generations, the property was bought by the Liverpool firm of John Holt (now part of Lonrho) in 1960, since when it was managed and marketed by the famous *négociant* Louis Eschenauer.

In 1989 Eschenauer and the château were sold to Brent Walker, who in 1994 resold to Chanel. David Orr, until recently director at Château Latour, was brought in to manage Rauzan on Chanel's behalf. Extensive improvements have been made in both château and *chais*. The new owners have also reverted the original spelling of Rauzan with a 'z'.

In theory this is a long-lasting wine which develops great finesse; in practice too many vintages in the past were austere and charmless. The '82 vintage marked the beginning of a substantial improvement, with the '85 even better. The '86, '88, '89 and '90 vintages have proved to be outstanding, challenging Palmer's reputation as the best wines in the appellation after Margaux.

The new management has made further improvements that have helped to make '94, '95, '96 and '98 all outstanding examples of those vintages.

Château Rauzan-Gassies

2e Cru Classé. Owner: J-M Quié. 28ha. 13,300 cases. CS 65%, Mer 25%, CF 10%. Second label: Enclos de Moncabon.

Until the French Revolution of 1789, this was part of the same property as Rauzan-Ségla. There is no château. Since 1943 it has belonged to the Quié family and in the past some great wines were made. In recent years, however, the wines have been consistent but not top flight.

The style of the wine is more powerful and richer than many Margaux, more in the character of Cantenac, with delicacy and charm developing in bottle. In 1994 Jean-Louis Camp, formerly of Château Loudenne, was brought in here, and at Croizet-Bages and Bel-Orme. He has a clear idea of what needs to be done, and the '96 showed a marked improvement, while '98 is the finest wine for many years.

Château Siran

Cru Bourgeois Supérieur 1932. Owner: William-Alain B Miailhe. Administrator: Brigitte Miailhe. 23ha. 14,000 cases. CS 50%, Mer 30%, PV 12%, CF 8%.
Second labels: Châteaux Bellegarde, St-Jacques.

This is something of a show-place for a Cru Bourgeois, but then the proprietor Alain Miailhe is convinced that it should be a Cru Classé and is eloquent on this topic. There is a heliport here, an anti-nuclear shelter well stocked with the best vintages, and a park famous for the property's cyclamen.

The wines have a charming bouquet and have become noticeably richer and fuller in flavour since around 1970. There is some point of comparison with nearby Giscours, and the wines have more charm and breed than those of their other classified neighbour Dauzac. Michel Rolland has advised since 1995, and it shows.

Château Tayac

Cru Bourgeois. Owner: André Flavin. 34ha. 15,000 cases. CS 65%, Mer 30%, PV 3%, CF 2%.

Lying in Soussans, this is the largest Margaux Cru Bourgeois. Its good reputation is the work of the present proprietor, André Flavin, who inherited the property in 1960. Wines are perfumed and robust with something agreeably rustic in their make-up.

Château du Tertre

5e Cru Classé. Owner: Eric Albada-Jelgersma. 50ha. 14,000 cases. CS 85%, CF 5%, Mer 10%.

The word *tertre* means a knoll, a piece of high ground, and Château du Tertre is a splendidly situated vineyard on the highest ground in the Margaux appellation, Arsac. The soil is classically pebbly. After taking over the property in 1961, Philippe Gasqueton (of Château Calon-Ségur) steadily restored the vineyard, the buildings, then turned to the château itself. In '98 the owner of neighbouring Giscours bought the property.

I believe that this is the most underrated of the Crus Classés. The wines have beautifully vivid fruit and considerable finesse, breed and charm. The record for consistency is also impressive. The '80, for instance, is really fine and has more concentration than many wines of this vintage. The '82, '83, '85, '88, '89, '90, '95 and '96 were also outstanding successes.

Château La Tour-de-Bessan

Owner: Marie-Laure Lurton-Roux. 17ha. 8,300 cases. CS 80%, Mer 20%.

The *tour* is a ruined 15th-century watchtower built during the last years of English rule. The Soussans vineyard, the humblest part of the Lurton's Margaux empire, produces light, supple wines of breed and charm: Lurton Margaux at a more modest price.

Château La Tour-de-Mons

Cru Bourgeois Supérieur 1932. Owner: Clauzel-Crochet. Administrator: Bertrand Clauzel. 35ha. 18,000 cases. CS 45%,

Mer 40%, CF 10%, PV 5%. Second label: Château Rucheterre.
An old property in Soussans with a long-standing reputation. The families that own it also owned Château Cantemerle until 1980. For some time La Tour-de-Mons has been spoken of as a candidate for classification.

Unfortunately the distribution of this excellent wine was for many years a monopoly of the old house of HO Beyermann and, as their fortune declined, the wine was not as widely sold as it deserved to be. Fortunately, with the sale of Cantemerle, there has been some much-needed investment in the property, and a marked improvement in the wines since the 1980s has resulted although there is still a lack of consistency. The wines are wonderfully scented, combining vigour, tannin and breed with plenty of charm. They are long-lived wines of growing distinction.

MOULIS

This is the smallest of the six communal appellations, but there are more outstanding Crus Bourgeois here than in Listrac. The area under vine has increased in the last 20 years but is still under 600 hectares. The vineyards lie northwest of Margaux and directly west of Arcins. The wines are powerful and rich, the best having fruit and finesse as well; they are long-keeping and very attractive.

Château Anthonic
Cru Bourgeois Supérieur. Owner: Jean-Baptiste Cordonnier. 22ha. 12,000 cases. CS 56%, Mer 40%, CF 2%, PV 2%.
This *cru* has carried its present name only since 1922. It appeared in the first edition of Cocks & Féret's *Bordeaux et ses Vins* in 1850 under Puy de Minjon, and changed names once more between then and 1922. The château is on the outskirts of the village of Moulis, and the vineyards are some of the oldest in the commune. After some reconstruction of the vineyards, with an increase in the Merlot at the expense of the Cabernet Sauvignon, the wines are riper and finer. The '90 is a fine example of what this *cru* is now capable of.

Château Bel-Air-Lagrave
Cru Bourgeois 1932. Owner: Mme Jeanne Bacquey. 9ha. 4,500 cases. CS 60%, Mer 35%, PV 5%.
This vineyard is on the gravelly ridges of Grand Poujeaux, certainly the best sector of the Moulis vineyards. It has been in the same family for 150 years. The owners believe in hard pruning and low yields to produce the best quality.

The wines are clearly carefully made. Their charm and fruit is emphasised, and they are softer and more refined than many from this appellation, with individuality and a definite finesse and balance that firmly removes them from any suggestion of the rustic. Wines to watch.

Château Biston-Brillette
Cru Bourgeois 1932. Owner: Michel Barbarin. 21ha. 10,000 cases. CS 55%, Mer 40%, PV 3%, Mal 2%.

An old-fashioned and rather rustic label hardly does justice to the excellent wine now being made here. Typically Moulis with its dense texture, there is also a hint of complexity about its spicy concentrated fruit which lifts it from the general run of wines from this appellation. The emphasis on fruit and balance makes this a wine that can be enjoyed young, but its keeping qualities remain uncompromised.

Château Bouqueyran
Cru Bourgeois. Leased by Philippe Porcheron. 13ha.
3,300 cases. CS 41%, Mer 57%, PV 2%.
With the arrival of a new proprietor, impressively rich, dense-textured wines are now being made here, beginning with '95. 50 per cent new oak is used.

Château Branas-Grand-Poujeaux
Owner: Jacques de Pourquéry. 6ha. 3,300 cases.
CS 50%, Mer 45%, PV 5%.
A small property with a well-placed vineyard and a most enthusiastic owner determined to make fine wines. In a blind tasting of '81 Moulis wines held in 1984 I placed this wine on the same level as some Crus Bourgeois Exceptionnels. At this stage the wine had charm, a fine middle flavour and richness, with real style and breed. All the wine is aged in casks, of which a third are new each year. A wine to watch – if you can find it!

Château Brillette
Cru Grand Bourgeois. Owner: Berthault family.
Administrator: Jean-Louis Flageul. 36ha. 20,000 cases.
CS 50%, Mer 40%, PV 10%.
When Raymond Berthault bought this property in 1976 it had declined badly and there was much work to be done. At the time he was the owner of Viniprix and Euromarché, and Brillette was to be a hobby. One-third new wood is used each year.

Unfortunately Raymond Berthault died in 1981, but his widow and son-in-law continue along the lines already laid down. This was always a good solid Moulis; now it looks like moving into the leading category.

Château Chasse-Spleen
Cru Grand Bourgeois Exceptionnel. Owner: SC du Château
Chasse-Spleen. Administrator: Claire Villars. 73ha.
36,700 cases. CS 60%, Mer 35%, PV 5%. Second labels:
L'Ermitage de Chasse-Spleen, l'Oratoire de Chasse-Spleen.
Chasse-Spleen has long been recognised as not only the leading *cru* of Moulis, but as deserving of Cru Classé status. From the First World War until 1976 it belonged to the Lahary family and was well run. Its present owners include a bank, but the most important partner is the Société Bernard Taillan whose director is the dynamic Jacques Merlaut. Claire Villars has now succeeded her gifted and much-lamented mother, and shows a sure touch. With her marriage now to Gonzague Lurton of Durfort Vivens, two

remarkable Médoc dynasties have been united. The curious name Chasse-Spleen is attributed to a quip of Lord Byron's to the effect that the wine chased away 'spleen' (ill-humour or melancholy).

The wines often have an initial toughness, even coarseness, but this is quickly dispelled and their true character emerges. In mature vintages the wines quickly develop an almost opulent full-ness of fruit on the nose, a lovely flavour with concentration, structure and real breed. It is extremely consistent and makes delicious bottles in lesser years. The '75 is a long-term *vin de garde*; '78 is fine and '79 most attractive. The '82 and '83 are a fine pair, showing the contrasting merits of these vintages; '85 is an approachable wine for its year and '86, '88 and '89 are all powerful tannic wines for long ageing. The '93, '94, '95, '96, '97 and '98 are good examples of their vintages. This wine does not take as long to mature as you might think, it keeps well and seldom disappoints.

Château La Closerie-Grand-Poujeaux

Cru Bourgeois 1932. Owner: GFA Le Grand Poujeaux.
Administrator: Jeanne Bacquey. 7ha. 3,500 cases.
CS 60%, Mer 35%, PV 5%.
This small vineyard was the creation of a former *régisseur* of Chasse-Spleen. Since 1941 it has belonged to the Donat family. For many years the redoubtable Mlle Donat ran the property and was one of the great characters of Moulis. Since 1984 Mme Bacquey has been in charge.

Everything is done in a traditional way and long-lived, solid wines are the result, with the emphasis on body and richness, rather in the same style as Dutruch.

Château Duplessis (Hauchecorne)

Cru Grand Bourgeois. Owner: SC des Grands Crus Réunis.
Administrator: Marie-Laure Lurton. 18ha. 8,900 cases.
Mer 57%, CS 28%, CF 12%, PV 3%.
The wine of this château has for some time been labelled simply as Duplessis. It is now proposed that the word 'Hauchecorne' be added to the label in smaller letters to avoid confusion with the nearby Duplessis-Fabre.

The wines here are rich and supple and are made for reason-ably early drinking. Since Lucien Lurton took over management in 1983, there have been some impressive wines with a more marked character. In 1994 Lucien handed over to his daughter Marie-Laure Lurton.

Château Dutruch-Grand-Poujeaux

Cru Grand Bourgeois Exceptionnel. Owner: François Cordonnier.
23ha. 13,000 cases. CS 45%, Mer 50%, PV 5%.
The wines of Dutruch have long enjoyed a deserved reputation for quality and consistency. The present owner, a relative of the previous owner M Lambert, took over in 1967.

In the 1960s I noted that the wines here were characterised by their body and richness, and this is still the case. These are wines that repay keeping.

Château Gressier-Grand-Poujeaux

Cru Bourgeois Supérieur 1932. Owner: Héritiers de St-Affrique.
Administrator: Bertrand de Marcellus. 20ha. 11,500 cases.
CS 60%, Mer 35%, PV 5%.

This fine old property has been in the hands of the same family
since 1724, and the family arms of the St-Affriques give the label
a distinctive look. Improvements and modernisations have been
made in recent years and new oak is now used in the maturation
process. The wines have always had more fruit and finesse
than those of many neighbouring properties, and have maintained a consistent standard over many years. The '71, '81, '82,
'85, '88, '89 and '90 were all excellent and among the best in
the commune.

Château Lestage-Darquier

Cru Bourgeois Supérieur 1932. Owner: François Pierre Bernard.
8·5ha. 4,400 cases. CS 50%, Mer 40%, CF 10%.

With such a small production it is hardly surprising that this wine
is little known. The vineyard is well placed on the gravelly ridges
of Grand Poujeaux and has belonged to the Bernard family for
several generations. I have found the wines to be deep-coloured,
having a bouquet dense with rich fruit, a distinctive, assertive
flavour, tannic and with the promise of something quite fine
when mature.

Château Maucaillou

Cru Bourgeois. Owner: Dourthe family. 78ha. 44,000 cases.
CS 48%, Mer 35%, CF 10%, PV 7%.
Second labels: Cap de Haut, Franc-Caillou.

Maucaillou is the pride of the Dourthe family. It no longer
controls the *négociant* firm which bears its name, but it has kept
this château, where the business started. Three-quarters of
the vintage is aged in new oak (unusual for a non-classified
growth) and there is a modern stainless steel installation for the
fermentation.

In a blind tasting of '79 Moulis wines held in 1984 I placed
Maucaillou first. The '82, '83, '85, '88, '89, '90, '94, '95 and '96 are
also successful vintages. The wines combine the power of Moulis
with a beautiful flavour, real breed and charm. This *cru* often
competes well with the Crus Classés in blind tastings.

Château Mauvesin

Cru Bourgeois Supérieur. Owners: Vicomte et Vicomtesse de
Baritault de Carpia. 60ha. 30,000 cases. CS 50%, Mer 50%.
(7ha under AC Haut-Médoc producing 3,780 cases.)

Lying in the south of the appellation, this is the largest property in
Moulis. Records show that it belonged to the de Foix family – who
also owned Château d'Issan – until 1647, when it was bought by
Pierre Le Blanc, *conseiller du roi* at the Parlement de Bordeaux. The
Le Blanc family built the large Victorian château that stands on the
property today. The wines of Mauvesin are light, soft and quite
elegant, their easy fruit encouraging early drinking.

Château Moulin-à-Vent
Cru Grand Bourgeois. Owner: Dominique Hessel. 25ha.
12,000 cases. CS 65%, Mer 30%, PV 5%.
Second label: Moulin-de-St-Vincent. 5,000 cases.
Moulin-à-Vent may seem an odd name for a Bordeaux château, but in the Middle Ages mixed agriculture was the norm in the Médoc, and many ruined mills can still be found. Since buying the property in 1977, Dominique Hessel has made a number of improvements including the enlargement of the vineyard, and matures the wine in casks instead of vats.

The wines have a fine flavour and are rich and vigorous, developing a complex bouquet with bottle-age. This property now deserves to be numbered with the leading *crus* of Moulis.

Moulin-de-St-Vincent, the second label, used to be an exclusivity of Ginestet. Under the present management a deliciously fruity, early-maturing wine is being produced.

Château Moulis
Cru Bourgeois Supérieur. Owner: Jacques Darricarrère. 12ha.
4,500 cases. CS 60%, Mer 40%.
In the last century this was a vast estate with around 100 hectares. Now it is a modest one with vineyards grouped around the château just outside the village of Moulis. There is a modern stainless steel installation for vinification, and the wines are matured in wood. All the wine is château-bottled.

Château Pomeys
Cru Bourgeois Supérieur 1932.
Owner: Jean-François Barennes. 8ha. 3,900 cases.
CS 67%, Mer 33%.
This small property has been in the same family for seven generations. It is traditionally run and its wines have a good reputation.

Château Poujeaux
Cru Grand Bourgeois Exceptionnel.
Owners: François and Philippe Theil. 50ha. 30,000 cases.
CS 50%, Mer 40%, CF 5%, PV 5%.
Second label: Château La Salle-de-Poujeaux.
Though Moulis is the name of the appellation, the commune of Poujeaux is where most of the best *crus* are, and there is none better than Château Poujeaux itself.

The wines are deep-coloured with an arresting bouquet – sometimes there are overtones of tobacco and a flavour which is stylish and fine although tannic and powerful. This is a long-lived wine that deserves long maturing in the best vintages (one third is put in new oak) and is certainly always one of the best wines in the appellation. In comparison with its rival Chasse-Spleen, Poujeaux tends to be more fleshy and fruity, but is equally deserving of Cru Classé status. The 1980s have been an impressive period, with '82, '83, '85, '86, '88 and '89 all being outstanding vintages; '87 is also a particularly good example of that year, delicious for drinking now. In the difficult vintages of the 1990s the skills of the winemaking here really came to the fore, producing a highly recommendable '92 and fine examples in '93, '94, '95, '96, '97 and '98.

Château Ruat-Petit-Poujeaux

Cru Bourgeois 1932. Owner: Pierre Goffre-Viaud. 15ha. 7,000 cases. Mer 50%, CS 35%, CF 15%. Second label: Château Ruat.

Petit Poujeaux is a hamlet just outside Moulis and well away from Grand Poujeaux. Ruat was the name of a pre-Revolution property, whose ownership was dispersed during the Revolution but patiently pieced together again after the present proprietor's great-grandfather bought the domaine in 1871. The wines have charm, fruit and typical Moulis richness and solidity, with a tendency to evolve more quickly than many wines of this appellation. This is good middle-of-the-road wine.

LISTRAC

Listrac and its neighbour Moulis differ in important respects from the other four communal appellations. They contain no Crus Classés, and do not border the river where the best *crus* are, but are on a plateau inland. But both produce excellent wines whose distinctive characteristics are increasingly appreciated.

The area under vine here increased by 45 per cent between 1972 and 1986, but has been static since. The wines were often considered to be tough and astringent, but are today markedly less rustic, quite powerful and have finesse and fruit.

Château Cap-Léon-Veyrin

Cru Bourgeois 1932. Owner: Alain Meyre. 22·6ha. 13,900 cases. Mer 62%, CS 35%, PV 3%.

This is an amalgamation dating from 1908 of two vineyards. The wines are matured in cask, including some new oak. They are powerful, long-lived and repay keeping, yet can also be enjoyed young. Also, as the notices on the Bordeaux-Lesparre road point out, the property offers farm holidays, so that visitors can actually stay on the domaine and enjoy traditional Médocain hospitality.

Château Clarke

Cru Bourgeois. Owner: Baron Édmond de Rothschild. 53ha. 31,000 cases. CS 48%, Mer 42%, CF 8%, PV 2%. Second label: Les Granges des Domaines de Rothschild.

One of the most remarkable new developments in the Médoc. Baron Édmond de Rothschild has undertaken a long-term expansion scheme, introducing the most modern installations, and vineyard plantings that will take some years to come to maturity. Prior to the '82 vintage I found the wines rather lean, austere, and marked by new wood. The '82 indicated an improvement, but then rather reverted to type; since then the wines seemed to be ageing rather quickly; the '96 marks a big step forward and is the best yet. An attractive rosé is also made here. There are good facilities for receiving visitors between June and September.

Château Ducluzeau

Cru Bourgeois 1932. Owner: Mme Jean-Eugène Borie. 4·5ha.
2,100 cases. Mer 90%, CS 10%.

In 1850 Charles Cocks listed this château as the second *cru* of Listrac. Since then it has decreased in size and importance, but nevertheless produces some fine wines. They are uncharacteristic of the region in that they come from vineyards planted with 90 per cent Merlot. They are matured in cask for six months and château-bottled. Ideal luncheon wines, they are perfumed and have plenty of fruit.

Château Fonréaud

Cru Bourgeois. Owner: Héritiers Chanfreau.
Administrator: Jean Chanfreau. 34ha. 20,500 cases.
CS 66%, Mer 31%, PV 3%.

The château here is something of a landmark on the main Lesparre road south of Listrac. Part of the crop is aged in vat and part in cask. The wines tend to be elegant, attractive, fruity and easy to drink when young, and are consistent.

Château Fourcas-Dupré

Cru Grand Bourgeois Exceptionnel. Owner: SC du Château
Fourcas-Dupré. Administrator: Patrice Pagès. 44ha.
22,000 cases. CS 50%, Mer 38%, CF 10%, PV 2%.

Guy Pagès lived at and managed this château from 1967 until his untimely death in 1985. During this time he established high standards and made many improvements. He is succeeded by his son Patrice, who is already well-versed in the affairs of the property. There are both stainless steel and concrete vats for fermentation, and casks from leading Crus Classés are used for ageing.

The wines of Fourcas-Dupré are perfumed, quite tannic and powerful in the best years but supple and attractive in lesser ones. Comparison with the neighbouring Fourcas-Hosten is interesting, especially as Patrice Pagès has assisted in the running of the latter for several years. I found them closest in quality in the excellent '78. The Hosten wines tend to have more depth and richness.

Château Fourcas-Hosten

Cru Grand Bourgeois Exceptionnel. Owner: SC du Château
Fourcas-Hosten. Administrators: Bertrand de Rivoyre,
Patrice Pagès, Peter M. Sichel.
44ha. 26,000 cases. CS 48%, Mer 39%, CF 13%.

Until 1972 this château belonged to the St-Affriques of Gressier, and the wines were made and kept there. It now belongs to a French, Danish and American syndicate. The *chai* and *cuvier* have been reconstructed. Some new wood is now used for ageing, and the vineyard has been gradually enlarged. The wines of Fourcas-Hosten have exceptional colour and are notable for their power and richness, with an assertive character but more fruit combined with tannin than the other *crus* of Listrac. This is a consistent wine. The '78 is outstanding; '82 enjoyable; '83 at its best; '85 exceptional; '86 concentrated; '89 and '90 outstanding; '93 above average for the year, and '94, '95, '96 and '98 are fine wines.

Château Fourcas-Loubaney

Cru Bourgeois. Owner: Altus Finances and Château Moulin de Laborde. Administrator: Jean-Claude Maubert. 25ha. 12,500 cases. CS 60%, Mer 30%, PV 10%. Second labels: La Closerie Fourcas-Loubaney, Château La Bécade.

Fourcas-Loubaney's production from low-yielding vines is now of a standard that is creating quite a reputation. Quality has increased recently, with up to 60 per cent new oak casks being used for maturation. The vineyards are on the gravel plateau of Fourcas and date from the beginning of the 19th century, making them some of Listrac's oldest. Recently acquired by a branch of Crédit Lyonnais.

Cave Coopérative Grand Listrac

Owner: Coopérative. 165ha. 77,800 cases.
Mer 60%, CS 35%, PV 5%.

This cooperative has long enjoyed an excellent reputation, especially in France, where Grand Listrac was for many years the best buy on the French Railways. Today there are 70 members. Three Listrac properties are sold under their château names: Capdet, Clos du Fourcas and Vieux Moulis, as are two Moulis wines: Guitignan and Bouqueyran.

Château Lafon

Cru Grand Bourgeois. Owner: Jean-Pierre Théron. 12ha.
6,700 cases. CS 55%, Mer 45%.
Other label: Château les Hauts-Marcieux.

When he bought the estate in the late 1960s, M Thérou found no more than a dilapidated ruin. Everything had to be restored and the vineyard reconstructed and enlarged. The wines are kept only in vat, seeing no wood at all during maturation, and as a result they are ready to drink early. These are pleasant, commercial wines.

Château Lestage

Cru Bourgeois Supérieur. Owner: Héritiers Chanfreau.
Administrator: Jean Chanfreau. 43ha. 24,000 cases.
Mer 52%, CS 46%, PV 2%.

The château, under the same ownership and management as Château Fonréaud, is a large ornate 19th-century mansion. One quarter of the product is aged in new oak, producing supple, early-maturing wine, though I have usually found it quite tannic and sometimes a little dry. It needs bottle-age in the better years.

Château Liouner

Owner: Pierre Bosq. 23ha. CS 50%, Mer 40%, PV 10%.
Second wine: Château Cantegric.

Commendable wines are now being made here. The '96 has enjoyable juicy middle fruit and good structure for drinking in the medium term.

Château Mayne-Lalande
Cru Bourgeois. Owner: Bernard Lartigue. 13.2ha.
One of the up-and-coming smaller vineyards of Listrac. The '96 shows stylish ripe fruit with elegance and medium depth.

Château-Peyre-Labade
Owner: Baron Benjamin de Rothschild. 56ha. 33,300 cases.
Mer 58%, CS 37%, CF 5%.
This vineyard was bought by Baron Édmond de Rothschild in 1979, six years after Clarke, and the vineyard was planted in the 1980s. The first vintage was '88. The management is exactly the same as for Clarke (*see* page 67).

Château Saransot-Dupré
Cru Bourgeois Supérieur 1932. Owner: Yves Raymond.
Red: 12ha. 7,800 cases. Mer 60%, CS 35%, CF 5%.
White: 2·7ha, 1,500 cases. Sém 50%, Musc 40%, Sauv 10%.
Yves Raymond is the third generation of his family to own this *cru* although the family have lived in Listrac for 300 years. Saransot-Dupré is a 225-hectare property which includes woods and pasture. A flock of sheep is kept to provide all the manure necessary for the vineyard.

The '98 has charming fruit, on the light side for early drinking. A small quantity of white AC Bordeaux is also made.

ST-JULIEN
This commune has the highest proportion of Crus Classés. The area under vine increased by under 15 per cent between 1985–95. The soils have more clay than Margaux, and there is quite a difference between the vineyards near the Gironde and those further inland, where more fleshy wines are made. These wines, of great character and originality, with more body and vivid fruit than those of Margaux, match the best Pauillacs for longevity.

Château Beychevelle
4e Cru Classé. Owner: Grands Millésimes de France.
Administrator: Maurice Ruelle. 90ha. 51,000 cases. CS 60%,
Mer 28%, CF 8%, PV 4%. Second label: L'Amiral de Beychevelle.
Other label: Les Brulières de Beychevelle (AC Haut-Médoc).
This is one of the most beautiful châteaux in the Médoc and in the summer months it is set off by a superb bank of flowers at its roadside entrance. When it belonged to the Duc d'Épernon, who was an admiral of France at the end of the 16th century, ships passing by on the Gironde were required to lower their sails as a salute. Thus Beychevelle is a corruption of *baisse voile*, meaning 'lower sail'. In 1984 the Achille Fould family, then the proprietors, sold part of this holding to the GMF, the French Civil Servants' pension fund. The GMF subsequently bought the remainder of the shares, later selling 40 per cent to Suntory (*see* Château Lagrange). All this has resulted in some much-needed investment and a clear raising of standards.

At its best Beychevelle is a glorious example of everything that makes the wines of St-Julien so attractive: a bouquet of great elegance and immediate impact together with a ripe, fresh flavour that asks to be drunk from an early age, although the harmony of the wine also ensures good keeping. The '82, '83, '85, '86, '88, '89 and '90 are all most successful while in the difficult 1990s elegant fruity wines were made in '93 and '94; the '95 and '96 are fine. There has been some inconsistency, and lesser years in particular were unreliable, but recent improvements should lead to greater consistency. A degree of dilution has been noticeable in some excellent years, however – due to high yields one suspects. The '90 is a good example. Les Brulières de Beychevelle comes from a vineyard in Cussac without the St-Julien appellation, and so is sold separately from the Grand Cru and the second wine.

Château Branaire-Ducru

4e Cru Classé. Owner: SA du Château Branaire-Ducru. Administrator: Patrick Maroteaux. 52ha. 25,000 cases. CS 70%, Mer 22%, CF 5%, PV 3%. Second label: Château Duluc.

The simple classical façade of the château here faces Beychevelle but can easily be missed as it stands well back from the road. It would be a pity to miss the wine however. Most of the vineyards lie further inland than those of Beychevelle and Ducru-Beaucaillou, and the wines have less finesse but more body and are not without breed. Jean-Michel Tapie ran the property, which his father bought in 1952, with distinction until he sold his 50 per cent holding to La Sucrière de Toury, a leading French sugar refinery, in 1988. Soon afterwards Patrick Maroteaux gained control when he bought some Tari shares for La Sucrière, and the new owners have been investing heavily: renewing the *cuvier* and *chai*.

The wines have a marked character which often comes through in blind tastings. The bouquet is noticeably powerful with an almost Pauillac assertiveness and a distinct chocolate character in the fat years. The wine has a good deal of body and fruit and is extremely supple: it is often possible to enjoy a Branaire when other wines are still not ready. This is a consistent wine, and excellent examples were made in '75, '76, '78, '79, '81, '82, '83, '85, '86, '88, '89 and '90, while '93, '94 and '95 are charming examples of the vintages. Certainly this is a wine to follow in terms of value for money. It is not yet an 'investment' wine, but is one of exceptional attractiveness. Clear improvements in the wines are now discernable since the change in ownership.

Château La Bridane

Cru Bourgeois. Owner: Pierre Saintout. 15ha. 8,000 cases. CS 55%, Mer 45%.

La Bridane is one of the relatively new Crus Bourgeois in St-Julien, though it has long enjoyed a good reputation. Much of the wine is exported.

Changes occurred during the 1980s when the Cabernet Franc was eliminated in favour of an increased proportion of Merlot. This is good, attractive St-Julien at an accessible price.

Château Ducru-Beaucaillou

2e Cru Classé. Owner: Borie family. 50ha.
19,000 cases. CS 65%, Mer 25%, CF 5%, PV 5%.
Second label: Château La Croix.

This château acquired its name and reputation in the first part of the 19th century when it belonged to the Ducru family. Beaucaillou referred to the name of the vineyard itself. The distinctive château, with its massive Victorian towers and simple, classical façade between them, has been made familiar by the distinctive yellow-brown label. The reputation of the *cru* today is the work of Jean-Eugène Borie, a resident proprietor who was one of the most widely respected winemakers in the Médoc. On Jean-Eugene Borie's death in '98, his son François-Xavier stepped into his shoes. A new *chai* was completed in '99. Ducru-Beaucaillou was the first of the Médoc Crus Classés on the open market to break away from the pack and establish a higher price for itself than the other Second Growths, thus creating the 'Super Seconds' (Palmer had achieved a higher price earlier but was available only though the two *négociant* owners, Mähler-Besse and Sichel).

The wines here have long had elegance, lightness and breed (Jean-Eugène Borie's first great vintage was '53). In recent years they have acquired a little more firmness and richness, especially in the best vintages, although beauty of flavour and finesse are still the hallmarks, rather than the power one finds in Léoville-Las-Cases. The years '78, '81, '82, '83, '85, '88, '89 and '90 all produced classic wines, while '94, '95, '96 and '98 are outstanding examples of those vintages.

Château du Glana

Cru Grand Bourgeois Exceptionnel. Owner: Gabriel Meffre.
42ha. 20,000 cases. CS 65%, Mer 30%, CF 5%.

Château du Glana is not one of the Médoc's more romantic wines. Strictly speaking it has no château, and the ugly little red-brick villa that appears on the label is now not part of the property. More obvious is the massive, functional *chai* sitting amidst the vineyards nearby, close to Gloria and Ducru-Beaucaillou. This and Gloria are the two largest Crus Bourgeois of St-Julien.

The reputation of du Glana has in the past been rather mixed. I can speak only about recent vintages, and have found the wine well made with charm and accessibility. Glana is commercial in the good sense: it provides just the sort of wine, with the character of the appellation, that the wine-lover of today looks for and can enjoy without long keeping.

Château Gloria

Cru Bourgeois. Owner: Héritiers de Henri Martin. 50ha.
20,000 cases. CS 65%, Mer 25%, CF 5%, PV 5%. Second labels:
Châteaux Haut Beychevelle-Gloria and Peymartin.

Gloria is the life's work of Henri Martin, one of the great figures of the Médoc. As *Grand Maître* of the Commanderie du Bontemps he did much to promote the Médoc in general over many years. His son-in-law, Jean-Louis Triaud, who has succeeded him, had already in effect been running the property for some time. The vineyard has been put together in one generation from bits and pieces of Cru Classé vineyards only. For this reason it has not joined the Syndicat des Crus Bourgeois and sells for the same price as some Fifth Growths.

The wine is generous and supple, with breed, fullness and richness of flavour. It is noted for its consistency. The problem is that it is almost certainly not as good as the classified growths of St-Julien, although it is superior to some lesser Margaux and Pauillac classifieds, and it is more expensive than most Crus Bourgeois.

Château Gruaud-Larose

2e Cru Classé. Owner: Group Bernard Taillan.
Administrator: Georges Pauli. 82ha. 44,000 cases.
CS 57%, Mer 30%, CF 7%, Mal 2%, PV 4%.
Second label: Sarget du Gruaud-Larose.

Léoville-Las-Cases and Ducru-Beaucaillou are the archetypical St-Juliens of the riverside vineyards; Gruaud-Larose is the classic example of a St-Julien from the plateau that lies between the riverside properties and St-Laurent. This large estate was created in the 18th century, divided in the 19th then and reunited by the Cordiers in 1934. In 1992 Jean Cordier sold to the Cordier firm which sold on the following year to Alcatel while retaining responsibility for wine-making and sales. In 1997 the Group Bernard Taillan bought the property but Georges Pauli, who supervised the running of the property for many years, remains to provide continuity. In 1995 a new *cuvier* with 14 wooden vats replaced the stainless steel.

As with some other Crus Classés sold as *négoce* exclusivities, Gruaud sold at a more modest price than it would have on the open market. It would be a mistake to allow this to influence assessment of the intrinsic merits of this outstanding *cru*, for Gruaud is certainly worthy of being placed beside Las-Cases and Beaucaillou as a 'Super Second', in quality if not in price. But this may change with the new policy.

The wines here have great concentration and richness and have been decidedly tannic in the past few years, but with maturity they acquire a soft, velvety texture with great breed and charm. Very fine wines were made in '82, '83, '85, '86, '88, '89 and '90. The '80 was slower in developing than most of the wines of its vintage and the '87 looks to be similar, while '93 is one of the best St-Juliens of the vintage, and '94, '95, '96, '97 and '98 are all excellent. The second wine is well worth looking out for. It is packed with fruit and can of course be drunk earlier than the *grand vin*, but still has plenty of structure.

Château Hortevie

Cru Bourgeois. Owner: Henri Pradère. 3·5ha. 2,000 cases.
CS 70%, Mer 25%, PV 5%.

This small vineyard is a good example of the remarkable quality of the *terroir* of St-Julien. In competent hands it cannot avoid producing a wine of charm and breed. It lies behind the village of Beychevelle and its proprietor, who is also the co-owner of Terrey-Gros-Caillou, runs the properties in tandem. A wine of quality.

Château Lagrange

3e Cru Classé. Owner: Château Lagrange SARL.
Administrator: Marcel Ducasse. 113ha. 66,000 cases.
CS 66%, Mer 27%, PV 7%. Second label: Les Fiefs-de-Lagrange.

In 1983 Lagrange was sold to the giant firm of distillers and wine merchants, Suntory, and so became the first Bordeaux Cru Classé to be bought by a Japanese company. The vineyard is well placed on the plateau of St-Julien behind Gruaud-Larose. One of the attractions for its new owners was the considerable potential for increasing the vineyard area. Expansions and improvements complete, this has now increased from 49 to 113 hectares.

The buildings, including the château, have been completely overhauled, the 19th century *chai* restored and two new ones built to cope with the expected increase in production. Marcel Ducasse was brought in by the new owners to manage the property and Michel Delon of Léoville-Las-Cases acts as consultant. There was a time when the wines at Lagrange were tough and coarse in style, but matters have been improving, even in the 1960s, and the '78 had real St-Julien fruit and charm. So all the evidence was there to suggest that something well above the rather modest reputation of recent years was possible.

The '82, made by the previous owners but sold by the new ones, is an excellent example, with a scent of prunes and great depth of flavour and fruit, tannin and complexity; '83 has a good deal of character and finesse with real depth of flavour. It was at this stage that the second wine was first introduced. For the delicious '85, the crop was split 60:40 between the *grand vin* and Les Fiefs. Impressive wines followed in '86, even '87, '88, '89 and '90, Les Fiefs is proving a particularly attractive and stylish second wine. Good wines were made in '93, '94, '95, '96, '97 and '98.

Château Lalande-Borie

Cru Bourgeois Supérieur. Owner: Borie family. 18ha. 8,000
cases. CS 65%, Mer 25%, CF 10%.

This *cru* was created by Jean-Eugène Borie, owner of Ducru-Beaucaillou, from a vineyard that was formerly part of Lagrange. The new vineyard was planted only in 1970 but is now making stylish and elegant medium-weight wines that have charming fruit. The first important vintage was the '79, and the wines have been steadily improving since then. Even the difficult '92 was good here.

This wine offers an excellent opportunity for assessing the Borie family's deft hand with St-Julien at a modest price.

Château Langoa-Barton

3e Cru Classé. Owner: Antony Barton. 17ha. 7,000 cases.
CS 74%, Mer 20%, CF 6%.

This château has belonged to the same family since 1821, longer than any other Cru Classé. When Hugh Barton acquired the property it was known as Pontet-Langlois. It will come as no surprise to anyone familiar with the vagaries of French spelling of proper names to know that Langlois has become Langoa.

The 18th-century château is one of the finest in the Médoc, not as well placed as Beychevelle but not far behind in pure architectural terms. The wines of Langoa and the Barton portion of Léoville were not château-bottled until 1969, but were removed to Barton & Guestier's Bordeaux cellars for bottling.

The wines of Langoa accurately reflect their classification. Usually ready to drink earlier than those of Léoville-Barton, they have a classic St-Julien character but are generally lighter in texture, less tannic but have lots of elegance, fruit and charm – and real breed. Every now and then Langoa produces something surprising, as with the unusually good '74 or the '71 which seems even better than the Léoville. The two seem to have a relationship not dissimilar to that between Gruaud-Larose and Talbot. The vintages here follow those of Léoville-Barton closely: a superb '78; an elegant if lightweight '79; a good '80, and marvellous wines in '81, '82, '83, '85, '86, '88, '89 and '90. Better-than-average wines were made in '92 and '93, while '94, '95, '96, '97 and '98 are excellent.

Château Léoville-Barton

2e Cru Classé. Owner: Antony Barton. 47ha. 20,000 cases. CS 72%, Mer 20%, CF 8%.

Like its neighbour Poyferré, Léoville-Barton was a part of the enormous estate of the Marquis de Las-Cases until the 1820s. In 1826 Hugh Barton, who had bought Langoa only five years before, acquired what was then a quarter share of the original Las-Cases estate and used the cellars of Langoa for making and housing the produce of his new acquisition. One hundred and sixty years later the Barton family still owns the property, with Antony Barton having taken on the burden of management from his uncle Ronald, who lived in the château until his death in 1986.

Léoville-Barton, under Ronald Barton's long stewardship, remained a traditionally made wine: finely perfumed, powerful and rich in tannin at first, then developing that beautiful fruit and richness of flavour that are hallmarks of the best St-Juliens. The style tends towards more richness than Poyferré, but with a shade less elegance. There were some inconsistencies in the 1970s but with stricter selection now evident, good results were obtained in '80, and outstanding wines were made in '81, '82, '83, '85, '86, '88, '89 and '90. The '93, '94, '95, '96, '97 and '98 are fine examples of the vintages.

With the marked improvement that has characterised Léoville-Poyferrés from '80, it is going to be interesting in the future to draw comparisons between the three Léovilles again.

Château Léoville-Las-Cases

2e Cru Classé. Owner: SC du Château Léoville-Las-Cases. Administrator: Michel and Jean-Hubert Delon. 95ha. 44,000 cases. CS 65%, Mer 18%, CF 14%, PV 3%. Second label: Clos-du-Marquis. Third label: Domaine de Bigarnon.

The label of this wine states 'Grand Vin de Léoville du Marquis de Las-Cases' – no mention of château – and serves as a reminder that this is the residue of what was in the 18th century the most important estate not only in St-Julien but also in the Médoc. With its magnificent *clos* adjoining Latour on a gravel ridge within sight of the Gironde, Las-Cases represents half the original estate and runs from the village of St-Julien to Latour. The original château, standing at the southern entrance to the village, is actually divided between Las-Cases and Poyferré, with the Las-Cases portion on the left.

In 1900 the manager – the famous viticulturalist Théophile Skawinski – was given one share in the Société Civile: today his descendants are the majority shareholders! On his retirement in 1930 he was succeeded by his son-in-law André Delon, grandfather of the present administrator Michel Delon. In the 1960s the reputation of Las-Cases recovered from a poor patch, the result of extensive replanting after the Second World War. During the 1970s its reputation soared to fresh heights, so that today Las-Cases is once more regarded as the leading wine in St-Julien.

In style it is firmer and slower to mature than other St-Juliens. Recently the wines seem to have filled out and are now not only elegant but also concentrated and powerful. The bouquet is especially characteristic, reserved at first but slowly evolving to become elegant and firm.

Great wines were made in '82, '83, '85, '86, '88, '89 and '90: all true *vins de garde*. The '80 was slower in developing than most, but the '84 and the '87 especially are much better than most wines from these vintages. In 1991 the Grand Clos was one of the few vineyards to escape the great frost and the resulting wine is outstanding for the vintage, together with that of its neighbour Latour. The '92, '93, '94 and '97 are fine examples of these vintages and '95, '96 and '98 are very good indeed. Las-Cases is certainly now one of the stars of the 'Super Seconds'. The Clos-du-Marquis is one of the best and most consistent of the second wines.

Château Léoville-Poyferré

2e Cru Classé. Owner: Cuvelier family. Administrator: Didier Cuvelier. 80ha. 44,000 cases. CS 65%, Mer 25%, PV 8%, CF 2%. Second label: Château Moulin-Riche.

Like Léoville-Barton, Léoville-Poyferré originally represented a quarter portion of the Las-Cases estate, acquired by the Baron de Poyferré by marriage to a Las-Cases. Unlike the other two Léovilles, Poyferré has not had the same continuity of ownership since that time and its fortunes have been more varied. At its best it has produced wines as fine as Las-Cases, as in '28 and '29. But at that time, although under different ownerships, both were managed by Théophile Skawinski. Now, after a period of inconsistency, a member of the younger generation of the Cuvelier family has assumed responsibility, and the results are beginning to show. First of all the *cuvier* was completely modernised in 1980, then more new wood was introduced and a capable new *maître de chai*, with the reassuringly Médocain name of Dourthe, took over.

The '80 vintage is the watershed here: not obviously a great vintage but elegant and fine – good by the general standard of the year. The '81 has a fine flavour with structure, fruit, elegance and breed; '82 is a glorious example of this exceptional year, a great bottle in the making, while the '83 has length, concentration and harmony. The '85 is a beauty, '86 is more powerful and tannic, while '88, '89 and '90 are outstanding. Good wines were made in '93, '94 and '97; excellent ones in '95, '96 and '98.

Although good wines were made before this (a particular favourite of mine being the delicious '73) the *cru* was certainly not reaching the heights of which it is capable. Now the future looks exciting.

Château St-Pierre

4e Cru Classé. Owner: Héritiers de Henri Martin. 17ha.
8,000 cases. CS 70%, Mer 20%, CF 10%.

This property has certainly had a chequered history. The name derives from a Monsieur St-Pierre who acquired the estate in 1767. Then in 1832 it was divided between different branches of the family, and the suffixes Bontemps-Dubarry and Sevaistre appeared. Although reunited by its Belgian owners after the Second World War, parts of the vineyard had been sold off, notably to Gloria and du Glana. Then in 1982 Henri Martin of Gloria bought the château (now beautifully restored) and most of the vineyard. The original Sevaistre *chai* was bought by Jean-Eugène Borie for his property Lalande-Borie, while St-Pierre is now housed in the same *chai* as Gloria, itself originally the St-Pierre-Bontemps *chai*, which Henri Martin had originally bought without the name.

St-Pierre produced elegant, perfumed, stylish and typically St-Julien wines for some years, but Henri Martin and his son-in-law Jean-Louis Triaud (now in charge since Henri Martin's death in 1991) lifted it to higher plains. From '82 onwards lovely wines of great breed have been made, clearly superior to those of Gloria.

Château Talbot

4e Cru Classé. Owners: Rustmann-Cordier, Bignon-Cordier.
102ha. Red: 54,000 cases. CS 66%, Mer 24%, PV 5%, CF 3%,
Mal 2%. White: Sém 84%, Sauv 16%. 2,500 cases.
Second labels: Connétable Talbot, Caillou Blanc du Château
Talbot (Bordeaux Blanc AC).

It is Talbot's misfortune that it was always obliged to stand in the shadow of Gruaud-Larose. The name commemorates the Earl of Shrewsbury who was killed commanding the English forces at Castillon-la-Bataille in 1453, although it seems doubtful that he ever actually owned the estate. In 1992 Jean Cordier exchanged his holding in Gruaud-Larose for the Company's shares in Talbot, and thus once more became sole proprietor of what had always been his favourite base in the Médoc. On his death in 1994 the estate passed to his daughters.

Talbot has long been noted for its consistency. The wines generally have less tannin and concentration than those of Gruaud-Larose, and are ready to be drunk sooner, but they also keep well. The charm of Talbot is its harmony: no St-Julien is more seductive. The wines are beautifully perfumed and have great St-Julien refinement in their fruit. There is a fine '75 which evolved beautifully and the '81 has developed well and has great finesse. Not surprisingly '82 and '83 are superb. The opulent, rich '85 strongly contrasts with the dense, tannic '86, the '87 was a good follow-up to the '80, and '88, '89 and '90 are a great trio. Good wines were made in '93 and '94; '95 and '96 are excellent.

Since the change of ownership in 1994, Talbot has been sold on the Bordeaux market. Because of Cordier's pricing policy Talbot was always marvellous value for money, especially if bought early.

The second wine, Connetable Talbot, is really delightful, ideal for early drinking, with lots of vivid St-Julien fruit. The white wine is pleasant, fresh and clean and becoming quite impressive.

Château Terrey-Gros-Caillou

Cru Bourgeois. Owners: Annie Fort and Henri Pradère. 15ha. 8,000 cases. CS 70%, Mer 25%, PV 5%.

Ever since I came across this *cru* for the first time – it was the '60 vintage – I have been greatly impressed by the real breed and finesse of the wine. Certainly it is one of the best of the Cru Bourgeois in St-Julien. The vineyard is in several parcels, the most important of which is behind the village of Beychevelle – where the *chai* is – and adjoining Talbot and Léoville-Barton. Another is next to Gruaud-Larose, and yet another adjoins Beychevelle and Ducru-Beaucaillou. A fine '83 here epitomised the virtues of this wine, with its vivid St-Julien fruit on the nose and its lovely flavour combining richness and exceptional breed. This is due not only to good vineyards but also to fine wine-making. Certainly this is a wine to look for if you enjoy St-Julien but do not want to pay Cru Classé prices all the time.

PAUILLAC

The name of Pauillac is assured from the reflected glory of its three First Growths Lafite-Rothschild, Mouton-Rothschild and Latour. The area covered by the Crus Classés here is greater than in any other appellation, even though the village has only 18 compared with 21 in Margaux. The area under vine increased by 18 per cent in the years 1985–95.

It is here that the Cabernet Sauvignon achieves its most characteristic results, producing that marked blackcurrant style for which it is justly famous. The wines are the most powerful, in terms of bouquet, body and flavour, of all Médocs. The best *crus* combine this with a finesse that develops with ageing, although some lesser *crus* have a certain coarseness.

Château d'Armailhac

5e Cru Classé. Owner: GFA Baronne Philippine de Rothschild SA. 50ha. 19,000 cases. CS 50%, Mer 25%, CF 23%, PV 2%.

No leading Bordeaux château has undergone so many changes of name. Acquired by the late Baron in 1933, it retained the original 'Mouton d'Armailhac' until 1956 when it became Mouton Baron Philippe, then in 1975 'Baron' changed to 'Baronne' to commemorate Baron Philippe's second wife. In 1991 his daughter Philippine de Rothschild decided that the names Mouton Rothschild, Mouton Cadet, and the company name Baron Philippe de Rothschild SA were confusing, and that this property deserved a distinctive personality of its own. So we shall now have to get used to Château d'Amailhac, which first appeared with the lovely '89 vintage.

Situated just a few hundred yards from the front gate of Mouton-Rothschild, this château is a curious unfinished building, its classical portico sliced down the middle as if it were a piece of cake. Although only a stone's throw away from the great Mouton, it is run entirely separately but with equal care.

The wines are true Pauillacs, though less rich and opulent than those of their big brother. In the best years they have a good concentration, but in lesser ones they can be slightly mean and dull. As one would expect, they are nearer in style to their other neighbour, Pontet-Canet, than to the great premier Cru, although recent vintages seem more charming and accessible.

Château Batailley

5e Cru Classé. Owner: Castéja family. 60ha. 20,000 cases.
CS 70%, Mer 25%, CF 5%.

The early reputation and classification of Batailley date from the period of Guestier's ownership. Now another *négociant*, Émile Castéja of Borie-Manoux, is in charge.

There is sometimes a tendency to undervalue châteaux that are not sold through the Bordeaux market, especially if, in their pricing policy, they are more concerned with offering continuity to their customers than with what their neighbours are doing. Batailley's real worth should not be underrated on account of its relatively modest price.

All the present vineyard is on land classified in 1855. It lies at the back of Pauillac on the St-Laurent road. Wines are consistent, solid and dependable. In the past Batailley occasionally produced memorable wines (such as the '53, '61, and '64), otherwise they were sound but unexciting. Now they consistently have more fruit and concentration, as well as being more stylish. Years to look out for are '75, '76, '78, '79, '81, '82, '83, '85, '88, '89, '96 and '98.

Château Clerc-Milon

5e Cru Classé. Owner: Baron Philippe de Rothschild SA. 30ha.
13,000 cases. CS 70%, Mer 20%, CF 10%.

This rather neglected property was bought by Baron Philippe de Rothschild in 1970. The vineyard is well placed between the road and the river, north of Pauillac and close to Mouton and Lafite. Milon is the small village where the property lies, and Clerc the name of the proprietor at the time of the 1855 classification.

There was much to be done in the vineyard and for this reason it took time to turn the quality of the wine around. The turning point came with the '81 vintage, when for the first time the wine surpassed Mouton Baronne Philippe (*see* d'Armailhac) in breed and harmonious fruit. After this, the most successful years have been '82, '85, '86, '89, '90, '94, '95 and '96. The higher proportion of Cabernet Sauvignon compared to that of d'Armailhac now sets Clerc-Milon firmly apart.

Château Colombier-Monpelou

Cru Grand Bourgeois. Owner: Bernard Jugla. 25ha.
14,400 cases. CS 65%, Mer 25%, CF 5%, PV 5%.
Second label: Grand Canyon.

For many years this was the best wine to emerge from the Pauillac cooperative. Then in 1970 it was bought by Bernard Jugla, proprietor of the adjoining Château Pédesclaux. Because Colombier parted company with its château and *chai* in 1939 (these now serve as the headquarters of La Baronnie, *négociant* company of Baron Philippe de Rothschild) a completely new installation had to be built. The wines are fermented in metal vats and aged in casks of which a third are new each year. This is good, honest, robust Pauillac that enjoys a growing reputation. The wines have a certain elegance and suppleness and pleasing fruit.

Château Croizet-Bages

5e Cru Classé. Owner: Jean-Michel Quié.
Administrator: Jean-Louis Camp. 26ha. 15,500 cases.
CS 40%, Mer 45%, CF 15%. Second label: Enclos de Moncabon.

This *cru* was created by the brothers Croizet in the 18th century. Its *chai* and *cuvier* are in the hamlet of Bages, close to its more famous neighbour Lynch-Bages, on high ground in the south of Pauillac. It has belonged to the Quié family since 1930. There is no château. The wines are attractively robust, full-flavoured and mellow fairly quickly, yet in my experience they keep well. Following a mediocre period, an improvement was noticeable in '95 and '96 after Jean-Louis Camp assumed responsibility. '98 marked another leap forward.

Château Duhart-Milon-Rothschild

4e Cru Classé. Owner: Domaines Baron de Rothschild. 64ha.
17,000 cases. CS 57%, Mer 21%, CF 20%, PV 2%.
Second label: Moulin-de-Duhart.

When the Rothschilds of Lafite bought the neighbouring vineyard of Duhart-Milon in 1962 it was in a sorry state, with only 16 hectares of vineyards in production and a high proportion of Petit Verdot. The wines were often undistinguished. It takes a long time to see the results when a vineyard has to be almost entirely reconstituted, but good results are now emerging and Duhart is again taking its place as a leading Pauillac.

The vineyard lies mostly on the plateau of the Carruades, and the *chai* and *cuvier* are in Pauillac. There is no château. By the early 1970s a wine of elegance and charm was being produced – not a heavyweight, but rather in the mould of Haut-Batailley. For me the vineyard really came of age with the '78, a wine of immense breed, elegance and outstanding length. The '79 is more powerful and richer, the '80 is a light-weight charmer, the '81, '83 and '85 are all elegant middle-weight wines, while the '82, a true wine of the year, has massive fruit but is complex and fine. The '86 has extra concentration and opulence; '88, '89 and '90 also have promise. But there was still a degree of coarseness until Charles Chevalier, who had taken over in 1994, moved the wine into a new mode in '96. This wine deserves to be placed among the leading Pauillacs and has truly realised its potential again.

Château La Fleur-Milon

Cru Grand Bourgeois. Owner: Héritiers Gimenez.
Administrator: Claude Mirande. 11·7ha. 7,400 cases.
CS 65%, Mer 25%, PV 10%.

The vineyards of this *cru* are indeed well placed. Its *chai* is in the village of Le Pouyalet (there is no château), and the various small plots of vineyard adjoin Mouton-Rothschild, Lafite-Rothschild, Duhart-Milon and Pontet-Canet. Until recently the wines were decidedly rustic, but now the judicious use of new oak and better winemaking is resulting in polished tannins and mellow fruit.

Château Fonbadet

Cru Bourgeois Supérieur 1932. Owner: Pierre Peyronie. 17ha.
7,500 cases. CS 60%, Mer 20%, CF 15%, PV 5%.
Second labels: Châteaux Haut-Pauillac, Padarnac,
Tour-du-Roc-Milon, Montgrand-Milon.

This charming 18th-century château lies south of the village of St-Lambert, just past the two Pichons as you drive from Bordeaux. The trees in its park stand oasis-like in a sea of vines. The present owner is very much the working, resident proprietor. Twenty-five per cent new casks are used.

This is a sound, classic Pauillac from old vines, made with meticulous care. It often does well in blind tastings and fully deserves its excellent reputation.

Château Grand-Puy-Ducasse

5e Cru Classé. Owner: SC du Château.
Administrator: Jean-Pierre Angliviel de la Beaumelle.
39·8ha. 14,200 cases. CS 62%, Mer 37%, PV 1%.
Second label: Château Artigues Arnaud.

Until the present proprietors bought it in 1971, Grand-Puy-Ducasse was a small vineyard of only ten hectares, adjoining Mouton and Pontet-Canet. The new owners bought two additional vineyards, one adjoining Batailley and Grand-Puy-Lacoste on the plateau behind Pauillac, the other adjoining the two Pichons, so that it now has vineyards in all three main sectors of Pauillac.

The château is a pleasing neo-classical building on the quayside near the centre of the village of Pauillac. For many years it also served as the Maison du Vin.

The new regime has produced mixed results. The wines at their best are classic Cabernet Sauvignon blackcurrant Pauillacs, and the structure supple, rich and harmonious. The '75, for instance, was splendid. Since then the best years have been '79,

'81, '82, '85, '88, and '89. However, too many wines in the 1990s have been marred by tough, astringent tannins: it seems that the potential is only fitfully being realised here.

Château Grand-Puy-Lacoste

5e Cru Classé. Owner: Borie family.
Administrator: Xavier Borie. 50ha. 16,700 cases.
CS 75%, Mer 25%. Second label: Lacoste-Borie.

This *cru* has long had an excellent reputation for producing typically robust and fine Pauillacs. Raymond Dupin was owner from 1932 until extreme old age caused him to sell to the Borie family in 1978. If some things had begun to slip in his last few years this should not detract from his achievements. The Bories decided to replace the old *cuvier* with stainless steel after the '80 vintage, and the previously dilapidated château has been tastefully renovated.

Most of the vineyard is in one piece in front of the château on the Bages plateau, and is of the highest quality. The consistency and excellence of the wines reflect this. These wines are powerful and often rather tannic and tough at first. The Bories are still making concentrated wines, but are trying to emphasise the fruit a little more. With the '81 the wines seemed to acquire an extra dimension; '82, '83, '85 (exceptional), '86, '88, '89 and '90 all produced fine wines and in the difficult vintages of '92, '93, '94 and '97, excellent wines were made. The '95, '96 and '98 are outstanding. This is now among the finest wines in Paulliac, after the Pichons.

Château Haut-Bages-Libéral

5e Cru Classé. Owner: SC du Château.
Administrator: Claire Villars. 27ha. 13,300 cases.
CS 80%, Mer 20%. Second label: Chapelle de Bages

This *cru* has had a chequered history. When it was bought by the Cruses in 1960 it lost part of its vineyard to Pontet-Canet and its wines were Bordeaux-bottled in the Cruse's cellars. With the introduction of compulsory château-bottling for the Crus Classés in 1972 and the sale of Pontet-Canet, the Cruses were obliged to build a new installation for handling the wines. In 1983 they sold to a company that also runs Chasse-Spleen and La Gurgue, and that company has made important investments to bring the property and vineyards up to standard.

The vineyard is on the plateau of Bages and adjoins Latour, Lynch-Bages and Pichon-Longueville Baron. The 'Libéral' has no political connotations but was the name of the property's 19th-century owner at the time of the classification.

In the last years of the Cruse management there were improvements: the wine was rich and fruity – the '76 and '82 were particularly attractive. But Mme Villars soon made her mark. The '85, was good; '86 even better; '88 and '89 equally impressive; '94, '95, '96, '97 and '98 were all good wines. The future seems assured.

Château Haut-Bages-Monpelou

Cru Bourgeois. Owner: Héritiers Castéja. 15ha. 8,100 cases.
CS 70%, Mer 25%, CF 5%.

One of the lesser lights of the Borie-Manoux stable. The vineyard was once part of Duhart-Milon. The wines are full-bodied but elegant and drinkable relatively young. This is pleasant, dependable, easy-to-drink wine at a modest price.

Château Haut Batailley

5e Cru Classé. Owner: Mme de Brest-Borie. Administrator: François-Xavier Borie. 22ha. 10,000 cases.CS 65%, Mer 25%, CF 10%. Second label: Château La Tour-d'Aspic.

When the Borie family bought Batailley in 1942 it was divided between the two brothers: *négociant* Marcel and François, who bought Ducru-Beaucaillou. Haut-Batailley is much the smaller part. Its vineyard had to be replanted and took time to mature. There is no château, as the house stayed with the main part of the property, and the wine is vinified at La Couronne.

There is a marked contrast in style between Haut-Batailley and Batailley, the former producing wines of less weight but real elegance. Comparing Haut-Batailley with Grand-Puy-Lacoste shows the same sort of contrast. Grand-Puy and Batailley are more assertively – even aggressively – Pauillac. Haut-Batailley is consistent, the beautifully balanced fruit and mature tannins making it drinkable relatively young but still able to age attractively.

Château Lafite-Rothschild

1er Cru Classé. Owner: Domaine Rothschild. 100ha. 21,000 cases. CS 70%, Mer 15%, CF 13%, PV 2%. Second label: Carruades de Lafite-Rothschild.

Lafite has experienced something of a renaissance in recent years. In the 1960s and early 1970s there were far too many disappointments for a wine of Lafite's standing. In 1974 a new era began with the appointment of a younger generation of the family, Baron Eric de Rothschild, as the member responsible for Lafite. In 1975 Professor Peynaud was called in to advise and Jean Crété was subsequently appointed *régisseur*, with his invaluable experience under Paul Delon at Léoville-Las-Cases behind him. The combination of these changes was most beneficial for Lafite and showed up vividly in the glass. Jean Crété retired in 1983 and was followed by Gilbert Rokvam. Since '85 there has been much stricter selection with more wine being set aside for the Carruades label, which, as a result, is much improved. Further changes occurred and the practice of keeping the wine in cask for three years, irrespective of the character of the vintage, was abandoned. In 1987 a new second-year cask cellar in an innovative circular design was finished, and in the following year a new *cuvier* of stainless steel vats was introduced to supplement the traditional oak ones. On Gilbert Rokvam's retirement in 1994, he was succeeded by Charles Chevalier, who has made such a success of Rieussec. His first vintages – '94, '95 and '96 – have confirmed that he is a winemaker with green fingers and a touch of magic. Expect even greater things in the future.

The features that one notices about recent Lafite vintages compared with those of previous years are their depth of colour, richness and concentration of flavour. The most outstanding recent vintages here are '76, '79, '82, '85, '86, '88, '89 and '90. In the more challenging early vintages of the 1990s, after a fine '91 and honourable '92 came a successful '93 and a '94 which is almost entirely Cabernet Sauvignon yet is still, above all, Lafite, and magnificent '95, '96, '97 and '98. To drink a bottle of Lafite should be one of the ultimate experiences for any wine-lover, and it is good to know that in future there should be no disappointments.

Château Latour

1er Cru Classé. Owner: François Pinault. Administrator: Frédéric Engerer. 65ha. 31,700 cases. CS 78%, Mer 17%, CF 4%, PV 1%. Second label: Les Forts de Latour. 10,000 cases.

In 1963 the Pearson group bought a majority shareholding in Latour, with Harveys of Bristol taking a 25 per cent holding. Harveys later became part of Allied-Lyons, which in 1989 also acquired Pearson's share of the property. Jean-Paul Gardère as administrator was the dominant influence on the wines of Latour from his appointment in 1963 until his retirement in 1987. In 1993 Allied-Lyons, having bought at the top of the market in 1989, sold out at the bottom to François Pinault who, like André Mentzelopoulos before him, has made his money through retailing in France. In 1999 Christian Le Sommer left after ten years of excellent winemaking. The energetic Frédéric Engerer is the President, not the winemaker.

Latour has produced monumental wines for generations. The modernisation of the *cuvier* and improvements in the vineyard have simply tended to make the wines more accessible. But retrospective tastings show that Latour has lost none of its legendary characteristics: its great depth of colour, classic Cabernet nose and remarkable concentration of fruit and tannin. Admirers of Latour often used to bemoan the fact that they doubted they would live long enough to enjoy the most recent vintages. After the legendary '61, the great vintages were '62 and '66, with '64 and '67 above average for these years. In the 1970s the outstanding wine is '75, followed in quality by '70 and '78, with an exceptional '73 and a good '76. Of the 1980s, the '81 is probably one of the best wines of its year, the '82 is a great classic, '86, '88, '89 and '90 are outstanding and long-maturing, while '85 is lovely and more quickly maturing. In '91 the vineyard escaped the worst of the frost and one of the best wines of the vintage resulted. After one of the best '92s, '93 and '94 showed the advantages of a *terroir* which allows the Cabernet Sauvignon to ripen earlier than it does in neighbouring properties and produced outstanding wines in each vintage. The '95, '96 and '98 are great years here.

Les Forts de Latour is produced partly from vineyards whose produce does not go into the *grand vin* and partly from the younger vines of Latour. There is a shorter fermentation, and the wine has the characteristics of Latour but with less concentration, so it develops more quickly. The wine used not to be placed on the market until it was ready to drink but in 1991 a break with this tradition was made when the '90 was offered *en primeur*.

Château Lynch-Bages

5e Cru Classé. Owner: Cazes family.
Administrator: Jean-Michel Cazes. 85ha. 35,000 cases.
CS 75%, Mer 15%, CF 10%. Second label: Château Haut-Bages-
Averous (7,000 cases).

Lynch-Bages arouses markedly varying opinions among claret-lovers. Some admire it unreservedly; others call it the poor man's Mouton or claim that it lacks finesse and breed.

From an objective point of view, this is a marvellously attractive, almost plummy, Pauillac with a really concentrated blackcurrant bouquet and flavour. At the same time it is less tannic and aggressive than many Pauillacs, with an emphasis on fruit and suppleness. This *cru* also has a fine record for making good wines in lesser vintages.

The château, which is the home of Jean-Michel Cazes who now runs Lynch-Bages, stands on the edge of the plateau of Bages, commanding views across the Gironde with the vineyards behind it. In recent years there has been an impressive programme of enlarging and modernising both *cuvier* and *chai*. Certainly standards have never been higher than they are today. Recent outstanding years have been '82, '83, '85, '86, '88, '89 and '90. Honourable wines were made in the difficult vintages of '92, '93 and '94 and very good wines were made in '96 and '98.

Haut-Bages-Averous is something of a cross-breed. There are five hectares of good Cru Bourgeois, the produce of which is assembled with those vats of Lynch-Bages that have been eliminated from the *grand vin*. The result is a light, deliciously fruity and easy-to-drink wine.

Château Lynch-Moussas

5e Cru Classé. Owner: Castéja family. 30ha. 11,000 cases.
CS 75%, Mer 25%.

This *cru* has belonged to the Castéja family for many years and there were many members of the family involved until Émile Castéja was able to buy out the others in 1969. At that time the production had fallen to less than 2,000 cases and the property was in a run-down condition. Émile Castéja, who is also responsible for all Borie-Manoux's properties, has had to rebuild and re-equip the *cuvier* and *chai* and replant the vineyard, which adjoins Batailley and is the most westerly of all Pauillac *crus*. Part of it lies near the hamlet of Moussas, the rest near Duhart-Milon and Lafite to the north and near Pichon and Latour to the south.

Before the restoration this was a pleasant but rather light wine, without much distinction. The wines are now more stylish without being big and have charm and breed. After good wines in '94 and '95, Lynch-Moussas excelled in '96 with probably the best wine produced here.

Château Mouton-Baronne-Philippe

See Château d'Armailhac.

Château Mouton-Rothschild

1er Cru Classé 1973.
Owner: GFA Baronne Philippine de Rothschild. 75ha.
27,000 cases. CS 80%, CF 10%, Mer 8%, PV 2%. White: Aile d'Argent (Bordeaux Blanc Sec) 4ha. 100% Sauv. 1200 cases.
Second labels: Le Second Vin ('93 only), Le Petit Mouton.

The Mouton-Rothschild we know today is the life's work of one man – Baron Philippe, who, from the day he took charge in 1923 until his death in 1988, set about making something special. He was the first to introduce compulsory château-bottling, along with the other First Growths, though at this time Mouton itself was not a First. He hit upon the idea of having an artist design an original work for each year's label, something that has happened every year since 1945. Finally he cut through the petty jealousies of Bordeaux to see Mouton proclaimed an official Premier Cru Classé in 1973. In his last years he persuaded his only child, Philippine, to become involved, and she now ably fills her father's place.

Mouton wines are quintessential Pauillacs, curiously closer in style to Latour, on the other side of the commune, than to its near neighbour and long-time rival, Lafite. There is a similar concentrated blackcurrant bouquet, and flavour combined with a richness and opulence that disguise the tannin more than at Latour. Recent great vintages have been '82, '83, '85, '86, '88, '89, '90, '95 and '96. In 1985 Patrick Léon took over as technical director with a sure touch. The second wine was introduced in '93. Aile d'Argent's first vintage was '91. Like Pavillon Blanc at Margaux, it is a 100 per cent Sauvignon, fermented in new oak, and needs two to three years in bottle to show its class.

Château Pédesclaux

5e Cru Classé. Owner: Jugla family. Administrator: Bernard Jugla. 20ha. 12,200 cases. CS 65%, Mer 25%, CF 5%, PV 5%.

This is one of the more obscure Crus Classés. Its vineyards and *chai* are just to the north of the village of Pauillac, near to Pontet-Canet. The name comes from a *courtier* (wine broker) who was proprietor at the time of the 1855 classification. It was bought by the Jugla family in 1950, and the facilities have been improved and the production increased under their management. Belgium is the principal export market.

The reputation of Pédesclaux is for making solid, honourable Pauillacs rather than exciting ones – but following a new collaboration with Dourthe, there has been a marked improvement in quality beginning with the '85 vintage.

Château Pibran

Cru Bourgeois. Owner: AXA-Millésimes. Administrator: J-M Cazes. 9·5ha. 4,000 cases CS and CF 60%, Mer 24%, CF 11%, PV 5%.

This *cru* lies just outside Pauillac to the northwest of and adjoining Pontet-Canet. It belonged to the Billa family from 1941 to 1987 and the wine established a good reputation. Now under Jean-Michel Cazes' supervision and part of the new AXA empire, attractively fruity, assertive wines are being made.

Château Pichon-Longueville Baron

2e Cru Classé. Owner: AXA-Millésimes.
Administrator: J-M Cazes. 50ha. 14,000 cases.
CS 75%, Mer 25%. Second label: Les Tourelles de Pichon.

The château here is a notable landmark on the *route des châteaux*, its slender turrets and high-pitched roof giving it a fairy-tale look. In 1855 the property was undivided and, apart from Mouton (now elevated to Premier Cru status), was the only Pauillac in the Deuxième Cru category. The vineyard is superbly situated, adjoining Latour. The new owners have restored the château, which has been little more than a shell since the war, and have also built a new *chai* and *cuvier*, whose size and extent are rather too dominating for their surroundings.

There was a time when Pichon-Baron (as it is usually called to distinguish it from the neighbouring Comtesse) was normally the better of the two wines but the 1960s and especially the 1970s were disappointing times under the previous management. Since AXA-Millésimes bought the property in 1987, Jean-Michel Cazes has quickly turned things round again and produced classic wines in '88, '89 and '90. In the early 1990s the wines seemed over-oaked for these rain-troubled vintages, but returned to form with the '94, '95 and '96 vintages. This is quintessential Pauillac, compared to the more feminine character of Comtesse across the road.

Château Pichon-Longueville Comtesse-de-Lalande

2e Cru Classé. Owner: May Elaine de Lencquesaing. 75ha.
40,000 cases. CS 46%, Mer 34%, CF 12%, PV 8%.
Second label: Réserve de la Comtesse.

Unlike its neighbour, the Baron, Pichon-Comtesse has a charming château which is now lived in for much of the time by the present owner and administrator, Mme de Lencquesaing. It was her father, Edouard Miailhe, who originally acquired the property in 1926. But it is really since Mme de Lencquesaing took over in 1978 that the reputation of Pichon-Comtesse soared into the top category of Second Growths. A new *cuvier* was ready for the reception of the '80 vintage, further extensions have been made to the *chai*, and the facilities for receiving guests and providing tastings have been much improved.

The wines here have always had great finesse and breed. The fact that part of the vineyard lies in St-Julien helps to give the wine a special character, more opulent and feminine than a Pauillac, yet richer than a St-Julien. The introduction of the Réserve de la Comtesse has led to a more rigorous selection and a corresponding rise in quality. Outstanding wines have been made in '78, '79, '81, '82, '83, '85, '86, '88, '89, '90, '94, '95, '96 and '98 while '80, '84, '87, '92, '93 and '97 have produced wines above the years' general levels. This is now one of the most prized wines in the Médoc after the Firsts.

Château Plantey

Cru Bourgeois. Owner: Gabriel Meffre. 26ha. 15,000 cases.
CS 50%, Mer 45%, CF 5%.

This good Cru Bourgeois is well placed between Ch d'Armailhac and Ch Pontet-Canet. Gabriel Meffre, who owns extensive vineyards in the Rhône, also owns du Glana in neighbouring St-Julien. Good, rich, robust traditional wines are made here, and the quality is very consistent in the '90s.

Château Pontet-Canet
5e Cru Classé. Owner: Guy Tesseron. 78ha. 38,000 cases.
CS 62%, Mer 32%, CF 6%. Second label: Les Hauts de Pontet.
This large property lies north of Pauillac and adjoins Mouton-Rothschild. For many years it was the pride of the Cruse family, who sold it in 1975 to Guy Tesseron, member of a well-known Cognac family who married a Cruse.

The château, fine *chai* and underground cellar (a feature in few Médoc properties) are impressive. Unfortunately, during the latter years of the Cruse regime the reputation of Pontet-Canet declined. The wine was bottled in their Bordeaux cellars and not at the château. Now all the wine is château-bottled.

Under the new ownership the fortunes of Pontet-Carnet might have been expected to improve but so far progress has been less than rapid. Often these powerful tannic wines seem to lack breed, and sometimes they seem dry and austere. Alfred Tesseron has made a determined effort to improve matters though and has had the benefit of Émile Peynaud's advice. The introduction of the new second label in 1982 has resulted in a stricter selection. The best vintages have been '75, '81, '82, '85, '86, '88, '89 and '90. The wines made a real breakthrough in '94 and '95, replacing dry tannins with ripe fruit and much better balance. '98 was outstanding.

Cave Coopérative La Rose Pauillac
Owner: Groupement des Propriétaires-Viticulteurs de Pauillac.
80ha. 46,000 cases. CS and CF 45%, Mer 40%, PV 15%.
This cooperative, founded during the crisis year of 1933, marked the beginning of the cooperative movement in the Médoc. There were 52 members initially, rising to 125 in the mid-1980s, but today membership is in decline, with individuals leaving to make their own wines. Most of the wine is sold under the label of La Rose Pauillac, but Château Haut-Milon and Château Haut-St-Lambert make their own declaration. Château le Fournas Bernadotte is also vinified at the cooperative, the *élevage* being carried out by the proprietor.

This cooperative enjoys a reputation for producing good, solid Pauillacs which are fruity and not too tannic or austere.

ST-ESTÈPHE
In many ways this is a transitional area between the two parts of Médoc. The wines exhibit a wide range of qualities from the breed and power of the leading *cru*, Cos-d'Estournel, to some rather lean, austere wines with a distinct *goût de terroir*. But improved methods of vinification have rendered many wines less rustic than they were. There has been little change in the area under vine, which has increased only slightly in the past 15 years.

Château Andron-Blanquet

Cru Grand Bourgeois Exceptionnel. Owner: Domaine Audoy.
Administrator: Bernard Audoy. 16ha. 11,000 cases.
CS 40%, Mer 30%, CF 30%. Second label: Château St-Roch.

Since 1971 Andron-Blanquet has been under the same ownership
and direction as Cos-Labory, whose vineyards it adjoins at some
points. This wine has that strong *goût de terroir* found in some St-
Estèphes, especially when young, but it is matched by sufficient
fruit and richness to become a pleasing wine with quite a strong
flavour. A wine of character – if you like the character!

Château Beau-Site

Cru Grand Bourgeois Exceptionnel. Owner: Héritiers Castéja.
32ha. 20,000 cases. CS 70%, Mer 30%.

The name means 'beautiful spot', and the view from the small
courtyard in front of the château and *chai* explains why it was
chosen. The village of St-Corbian, where it is situated, is on high
ground and there is a splendid prospect across the vineyards of
Calon-Ségur and towards the Gironde. The property is owned by
the Castéja family and the wines are distributed exclusively by
the Bordeaux *négociants* Borie-Manoux.

The wines, like many St-Estèphes, have quite a strong flavour
at first but soon develop the richness to produce harmonious and
pleasing wines. There can be a touch of austerity about the finish,
but this usually rounds off with ageing. A good Cru Bourgeois.

Château Beau-Site-Haut-Vignoble

Cru Bourgeois 1932. Owner: Jean-Louis Braquessac. 15ha.
8,000 cases. CS 69%, Mer 22%, PV 5%, CF 4%.

Beau-Site-Haut-Vignoble is in St-Corbian, the same village as Beau-
Site. This wine is distinctly more artisanal and although carefully
made it is not in the same class as its neighbour. There is a lack of
richness combined with toughness, giving a certain leanness and
other features characteristic of many lesser St-Estèphes. This is
nevertheless an honourable wine, typical of its region.

Château Le Boscq

Owner: Dourthe-Kressman. 17ha. 10,000 cases. Mer 51%, CS
38%, PV 7%, CF 4%.

This property is in the north of St-Estèphe on gravelly ridges overlooking the Gironde. I remember an excellent '53 bottled by
Calvet, but in recent years the wine was little heard of until the
present owners took over at harvest time in 1995. This is a very
new oak-influenced style of wine, but the '96 shows delicious fruit
and remains sweet at the finish.

Château Calon-Ségur

3e Cru Classé. Owners: Capbern-Gasqueton and Peyrelongue
families. Administrator: Mme Gasqueton. 58ha. 20,000 cases.
CS 65%, Mer 20%, CF 15%. Second label: Marquis de Ségur.

This is the oldest of the leading St-Estèphe *crus*. In the 12th century it was given to a bishop of Portiers, Monseigneur de Calon,

while in the 18th century it belonged to the famous Marquis de Ségur, who was proprietor of Lafite and Latour. He is supposed to have said that, although he made his wine at Lafite, his heart was at Calon – hence the heart-shaped device seen on the label and in many places at the property.

After the death of his uncle in 1962, Philippe Gasqueton ran the property and maintained the wine's reputation for consistency. In 1984 a large new underground cellar was completed. It is L-shaped and runs along two sides of the *chai*, 60 metres long on one side and 50 metres on the other. The beautiful old wooden *cuvier* is still preserved but has not been used since 1973. The new stainless steel *cuvées* are of 100 hectolitres each – this size representing half a day's picking – enabling control and selection. Since Philippe Gasqueton's death in 1995, Mme Gasqueton has been in charge.

This is a wine that seldom comes top in comparative tastings of cask samples of Cru Classé St-Estèphes, but then often does better in bottle. The wines are noticeably softer and fruitier, and more generous than Cos or Montrose, but less fine perhaps. In a blind tasting in Paris in 1976 for *La Nouvelle Guide de Gault-Millau*, Calon received the highest average mark of a group of leading Crus Classés. The vintages tasted were '66, '70, '71 and '83. Of the recent vintages the '78, '79 and '81 are all good and there is a delicious early-drinking '80. The '82 is among the leading wines of the vintage and '83 is soft and forward though rather overproduced. The '85 is a little atypical but impressive and '88, '89 and '90 are classic Calons. Excellent wines were made in '95 and '96.

Calon was always a great favourite in England, but in recent years its reputation has been rather eclipsed. Perhaps it has just not made the headlines, but all the evidence points to this being just the sort of wine one wants – easy to drink yet lasting well, with plenty of character, and not over-expensive.

Château Capbern-Gasqueton

Cru Grand Bourgeois Exceptionnel. Owner: Capbern-Gasqueton family. Administrator: Mme Gasqueton. 35ha. 10,000 cases. CS 65%, Mer 20%, CF 15%. Second label: Le Grand Village Capbern (exclusively distributed by Dourthe).

The château, a solid mansion in the centre of St-Estèphe, is the home of the Gasqueton family and has been for many generations. The vineyard is in two parts, one adjoining Calon-Ségur, the other near Meyney. All the wine is matured in casks but ten per cent new wood is used.

As at Calon-Ségur, the fruit is emphasised to avoid the harshness often associated with St-Estèphe.

Château Chambert-Marbuzet

Cru Bourgeois 1932. Owner: SC du Château (H Duboscq & Fils). 7ha. 4,700 cases. CS 70%, Mer 30%.
Second label: MacCarthy.

Another outpost of the Duboscq empire around Marbuzet (*see*

Haut-Marbuzet). The wine is well made and most attractive, even when young, yet clearly has the ability to age well. I have found it scented and packed with fruit, well supported by ripe tannin, with an attractive flavour.

Château la Commanderie

Cru Bourgeois 1932. Owner: Gabriel Meffre. 8·5ha.
5,000 cases. CS 55%, Mer 40%, CF 5%.

This is a northerly outpost of Gabriel Meffre's empire. At one time all the wines were made at du Glana; now they have their own *chai*. The name goes back to the Middle Ages when this was a *commanderie* of the Knights Templar.

Château la Commanderie is situated in the southern part of the commune, between Marbuzet and Leyssac. The wine is exclusively distributed by Dourthe and Kressmann.

Château Cos-d'Estournel

2e Cru Classé. Owner: Group Bernard Taillan. Administrator:
Jean-Guillaume Prats. 64ha. 25,000 cases. CS 60%, Mer 38%,
CF 2%. Second label: Les Pagodes de Cos.

Cos is a landmark familiar to all who travel the *route des châteaux* on account of its pagoda-like façade; it is strikingly placed on a hill overlooking Lafite. This building is in fact the *chai*, for there is no château. The present ownership dates back to 1919 when it was bought by Fernand Ginestet, the grandfather of Bruno Prats. The latter was in charge from 1971 until the sale to the Taillan Group in 1998, when his son took over. Cos has usually been considered as the leading *cru* of St-Estèphe and certainly develops more finesse and breed in bottle than any other, as well as being long-lived. There was a period in the 1960s when it was less convincing, but after Bruno Prats assumed the direction, Cos has become established as one of the leading Deuxièmes Crus Classés once more.

When this wine is in cask it is always most impressive, concentrated and tannic but finely balanced with great breed. There is often a dull patch in the early years in bottle, but then the fruit, balance and breed come into their own. This is a most rewarding wine to keep. Fine and often exceptional wines were made in '78, '79, '81, '82, '83, '85, '86, '88, '89 and '90, while in the challenging 1990s '91, '92 and '93 are all exceptional for the vintages. The '94 is fine, while '95 and '96 are again outstanding.

Château Cos-Labory

5e Cru Classé. Owner: Domaine Audoy.
Administrator: Bernard Audoy. 18ha. 10,000 cases.
CS 50%, Mer 35%, CF 10%, PV 5%.

The style of the wines here is light and elegant, and they mature rather quickly. There is certainly more refinement here than is usual in St-Estèphe, but not the weight and character of the leading growths. The '86, however, marked the beginning of more concentrated and impressive wines and, in spite of this, there is still not the consistency one would hope for.

Château Coutelin-Merville

Cru Grand Bourgeois. Owner: Guy Estager et Fils.
Administrator: Bernard Estager. 19ha. 12,000 cases.
CS and CF 43%, Mer 40%, PV 17%.

Until 1972 this property was run with adjoining Château Hanteillan in Cissac, but inheritance problems forced the sale of the latter, so this *cru* now stands on its own.

Wines are matured in cask and no new oak is used. They have power and good structure and require bottle-age to round off and give of their best.

Château Le Crock

Cru Grand Bourgeois Exceptionnel. Owner: Cuvelier family.
Administrator: Didier Cuvelier. 32ha. 17,500 cases.
CS 58%, Mer 24%, CF 12%, PV 6%.

Since 1903 Le Crock has belonged to the Cuvelier family, which also now owns Léoville-Poyferré. This property is managed by the enthusiastic Didier Cuvelier, assisted by Francis Dourthe, the Poyferré *maître de chai*.

I do not know what the wines were like in the past, but recently they have been most impressive. They are scented, powerful and complex on the nose, with a marked and agreeable personality; rich, with structure and depth on the palate. A wine to look out for, especially since its revitalised management took charge.

Château Haut-Beauséjour

Cru Grand Bourgeois Exceptionnel. Owner: Champagne Louis Roederer. 19ha. 9,000 cases. Mer 54%, CS 39%, PV 4%, Mal 3%.
Since its purchase by Roederer in 1992, steady progress has been made here. Very elegant, fruity wines are produced which drink well young.

Château Haut-Marbuzet

Cru Grand Bourgeois Exceptionnel. Owner: SCV Duboscq.
Administrator: Henri Duboscq. 50ha. 25,000 cases.
CS 50%, Mer 40%, CF 10%.
Second label: Tour de Marbuzet.

In the last 25 years or so, Henri Duboscq has built up a formidable reputation for his wines. Haut-Marbuzet, situated around the village of Marbuzet just to the south of Montrose, was his starting point. Now he has added MacCarthy, Chambert-Marbuzet and Tour-de-Marbuzet to his empire.

One remarkable feature of this Cru Bourgeois is that all the wine is matured in new oak, something even most Cru Classés do not attempt. One might expect this to result in austere, tannic wines, especially in St-Estèphe, yet in my experience the wines are outstandingly attractive. The colours are deep and dense, the nose rich and concentrated with fruit and well-married oak. The wine is well balanced and stylish with an outstanding flavour. It can be drunk when relatively young yet is a good keeper. The consistency is also unusually good.

Château Houissant

Cru Bourgeois Supérieur 1932. Owner: Jean Ardouin. 26ha.
16,000 cases. CS 70%, Mer 30%.

This *cru* is well situated on high ground inland from Montrose, in the southern sector of the appellation. The wines have long enjoyed a solid and consistent reputation.

Château Houissant is not currently rated because it is not a member of the Syndicat des Crus Bourgeois, it is nevertheless a commendable Cru Bourgeois.

Château Laffitte-Carcasset

Cru Bourgeois 1932. Owner: Vicomte Philippe de Padirac.
33ha. 19,000 cases. CS 65%, Mer 35%.
Second label: Château La Vicomtesse.

The name is not an attempt to ape the Premier Cru Classé but the name of an 18th-century owner. The property is well placed, lying just past the Cave Coopérative as one travels north. The wines are carefully made, the emphasis being on finesse, although they also have plenty of body. This property is not a member of the Syndicat des Crus Bourgeois.

Château Lafon-Rochet

4e Cru Classé. Owner: Tesseron family.
30ha. 22,000 cases. CS 55%, Mer 40%, CF 5%.
Second label: Le Numero 2 de Lafon-Rochet.

Since Guy Tesseron (a Cognac *négociant* who married into the Cruse family) bought this *cru* in 1960, great efforts have been made to rebuild its reputation. There was much to be done in the vineyard as well as the *chai*, and an entirely new château was built, designed in a suitably traditional mould. It is clearly visible from the road just past Cos-d'Estournel on the *route des châteaux*.

For many years I have criticised this *cru* for mean, dry tannins, especially at the finish. This was mainly a problem of too much Cabernet Sauvignon for the soil. The wine first came into balance in my judgement with the '90 – but that was an exceptional year. More impressive were the ripe fruit and fine harmony achieved in more demanding vintages such as '93, '94 and '95. On such form Lafon-Rochet is one of the best buys in St-Estèphe.

Château Lavillotte

Cru Bourgeois. Owner: Jacques Pedro. 12ha. 4,200 cases.
CS 72%, Mer 25%, PV 3%.

This offers a good example of the vagaries of French spelling. When this *cru* hit the headlines by coming out above some Crus Classés in a Gault-Millau blind tasting, I rushed off to my *Bordeaux et ses Vins* (Édition Féret) to look it up, but there was no entry under this name. Later it transpired that it was entered as La Villotte! The château label spells the name as one word.

Jacques Pedro is a perfectionist, and this is reflected in his wines. They are matured in cask and not filtered so decanting is essential. It is not hard to see why this wine did so well in a blind tasting. It tends to be heavily perfumed and rich with distinctly minty overtones and real intensity. The flavour is fine and speaks of breed and complexity. I particularly like its attack and fruit up-front, yet there is also finesse, with slightly less body than expected.

Château Lilian Ladouys
Cru Bourgeois. Owner: SA Château Lilian Ladouys. 50ha. 20,000 cases. CS 70%, Mer 30%.
When Christian and Lilian Thieblot bought this property in 1989, they transformed a rather run-down member of the cooperative into a Cru Bourgeois worthy of the name.

The vineyard was increased from 20 hectares to 50 by some judicious purchases from neighbours, and a new *cuvier* and *chai* were constructed around the charming 'Directoire' *chartreuse* château, close to Cos.The first vintage to be bottled, '89, is impressively rich and spicy in character, with plenty of fruit and the character of the year. That and an equally delicious '90 suggest that this is a property of real potential. Unfortunately, the recession and the run of poor vintages in the early 1990s were too much for the new owners, who were obliged to sell in 1995. But with Georges Pauli (*see* Gruaud-Larose) now consulting here, good wines are still made.

Château MacCarthy
Cru Grand Bourgeois. Owner: Henri Doboscq. 7ha. 4,700 cases. CS 65%, Mer 35%. Second label: Château Chambert-Marbuzet
As we know from the history of Lynch, Dillon and Kirwan, exiled Irishmen did well in Bordeaux in the 18th century, not to mention those like the Bartons who came of their own volition. The MacCarthys are not so famous, but they were people of consequence two centuries ago, and have left behind this small property and a street in Bordeaux to keep their name alive.

In 1988 Henri Duboscq (*see* Haut-Marbuzet) bought this property, so further increasing his holding around the village of Marbuzet. The vineyard has been joined to Chambert-Marbuzet and the name retained for the second label.

Château de Marbuzet
Cru Grand Bourgeois Exceptionnel. Owner: Domaines Prats. 7ha. 3,900 cases. Mer 60%, CS 40%.
The handsome château here is the home of the Prats family of Cos-d'Estournel, which has no château of its own. The wine was treated as the second wine of Cos until the '94 vintage when it became a wine in its own right again. The first vintages have been stylish and fine.

Cave Coopérative Marquis de St-Estèphe
Owner: Société de Vinification de St-Estèphe. 170ha. 102,000 cases. CS 65%, Mer 25%, PV 4%, CF 3%, Mal 3%.
The *Cave* here was founded in 1934 by just 42 *viticulteurs*. Now there are over 200 members, and this is one of the most up-to-date and best-run cooperatives in the Médoc, or indeed the Gironde.

Only grapes from the St-Estèphe appellation are received here. Apart from the wine sold under its own *marque* of Marquis de St-Estèphe, the wines of a number of other important properties are kept separately and bottled *à la propriété* to be sold under their own names. They are: Chateaux de Mignot, Lille-Coutelin, Giraud, L'Hôpital, La Croix des Trois Soeurs, Palmier, Les Pradines, La Croix de Pez, Balangé, Graves de Blanquet, Haut-Verdon, Les Combes, and Violet. Of course the quality of these wines varies according to the soil and the *cépages* planted, but all are carefully made. No wood is employed, and the wines normally show well after four to six years.

Château Meyney
Cru Grand Bourgeois Exceptionnel. Owner: Domaines Cordier.
52ha. 29,000 cases. CS 67%, Mer 25%, CF 5%, PV 3%.
Second label: Prieur du Château Meyney.

St-Émilion abounds with old ecclesiastical buildings or their remains, but they are rare in Médoc, and Meyney certainly has the best-preserved example. The present buildings, finely situated on a ridge with views across the Gironde, date from 1662–66. The courtyard still has a rather monastic atmosphere. Until recently the old name Prieuré des Couleys appeard on the label.

The wines balance fruit and tannin judiciously; they are quite dense in texture and strong but always juicy in flavour. I find that they are normally at their best when on the young side, and that although they seem to have the structure for ageing, if kept too long they dry up and acquire a bitter finish. Of recent vintages '82, '83, '85, '86, '88, '89, '90, '95 and '96 were all, in their different ways, great successes here. This is clearly one of the leading non-classified wines of St-Estèphe, in my judgement just behind de Pez and Phélan-Ségur as it lacks a little in breed.

Château Montrose
2e Cru Classé. Owner: Jean-Louis Charmolüe. 68ha.
30,000 cases. CS 65%, Mer 25%, CF 10%.
Second label: La Dame de Montrose.

Disappointingly for the Scots, the name has no Scottish affiliation but refers to the old name for this vineyard, the 'rose-coloured hill'. This is the most recently planted of all the great Crus Classés, developed from completely uncultivated land, formerly part of Calon-Ségur, at the beginning of the 19th century. Like the neighbouring Meyney, it commands fine views of the Gironde from its ridge nearby. Montrose has belonged to the Charmolüe family since 1896 and is meticulously run. The present owner, Jean-Louis Charmolüe, is a resident working proprietor, like his much-respected mother before him. The *cuvier* is still completely traditional, with beautifully kept wooden vats, and this is traditional wine. The only modern note is struck by a new *chai*.

I have always admired Montrose in cask. Although it is less marked by Cabernet Sauvignon than it used to be in the past, it has a lovely clean, crisp, tannin flavour with new oak, tannin and fruit well matched. But this is not a wine to hurry over, and plenty of patience is required.

As for vintages, the '76 is outstanding for the year, concentrated and rich; '78 elegant and mature, with '79 more powerful but less fine. The '81 is especially impressive with its nice touch of sweetness over powerful tannins; '82 is fine but in no way outstanding, and '83 needs drinking. The benefits of a more severe selection after the high yields of '82 and '83 are evident, beginning with '84 which was exceptional for this vintage with its scented fruit and rich supple flavour. The '85 is a beauty; '86 has a glorious cedar-like scent and beautiful flavour and balance; '88 is still closed; '89 less dense with unctuous fruit and '90 even richer and finer with its lovely sweetness – one of the great wines of this great vintage. The '91 is one of the few outstanding wines of its year, thanks to a largely frost-free vineyard; '92, '93, '94, '95, '96 and '98 are all among the leading wines of these vintages.

Montrose has clearly moved up a notch in the last decade, and should now be regarded as one of the 'Super Seconds'.

Château Morin

*Cru Grand Bourgeois. Owners: Marguerite and Maxime
Sidaine. 10ha. 6,000 cases. CS 48%, Mer 50%, PV 2%.*
This *cru*, just outside St-Corbian in the appellation's northern sector, has been in the same family for several generations. It still uses a delightful old label, distinctly 19th century in appearance, and the property is run on traditional lines. The strongly flavoured wines are reasonably supple and of good repute.

Château Les Ormes-de-Pez

*Cru Grand Bourgeois. Owner: Cazes family.
Administrator: Jean Michel Cazes. 32ha. 15,000 cases.
CS 55%, Mer 35%, CF 10%.*
The great gift for winemaking that the Cazes family has brought to Lynch-Bages is also evident here. I have been agreeably surprised over the years by the consistently attractive wines. Even in difficult years they are usually supple and fruity, quite without the leanness or austerity of many St-Estèphes. In 1981 new stainless steel fermentation vats were installed and a new ageing *chai* constructed. Previously the wines had been kept at Lynch-Bages.

The wines have plenty of concentration but are well balanced with suppleness, fruit and plenty of character. Very good wines were made in '82 (especially rich), '83, '85, '86, '88, '89, '90 and '96. While Ormes-de-Pez sometimes lacks the breed of neighbouring de Pez, it seldom disappoints, which makes it one of the best and most reliable of St-Estèphe's Crus Bourgeois.

Château de Pez

*Cru Bourgeois Supérieur 1932. Owner: Champagne Louis
Roederer. 23·2ha. 15,600 cases. CS 70%, CF 15%, Mer 15%.*
The grand twin-turreted château of this old property is clearly visible from the *route des châteaux* as it winds its way throught the hamlet, just to the west of St-Estèphe. When Robert Dousson took

over the management here for his aunt in 1955 the reputation of this *cru* grew, and it was regarded as the best non-classified *cru* in the commune. But then in the late 1980s things seemed to slip, and Phélan-Ségur overtook de Pez in reputation and consistency of quality. Then in 1995 Louis Roederer bought the property, so developments will be watched with keen interest.

The quality that de Pez has, and which is missing in most other Crus Bourgeois of the commune, is breed. This comes out clearly in blind tastings. There is an attractive spiciness on the nose, together with elegance, charm, and a lot of fruit, while the flavour has good concentration and richness, with breed and balance. Some years can be a little lean, but the balance is preserved. Very fine wines were made in '75, '76, '78, '79, '82, '83, '85 and '86. After a good '95, '96 is exceptional.

Château Phélan-Ségur
Cru Grand Bourgeois Exceptionnel.
Owner: Château Phélan-Ségur SA (President: Xavier Gardinier).
66ha. 40,000 cases. CS 56%, Mer 34%, CF 10%.
Second label: Franck Phélan. 8,330 cases.
As with neighbours Meyney and Montrose, this is a château you will not see from the *route des châteaux*. The handsome building is on the southern edge of St-Estèphe village on high ground with a fine view across the river. There is a massive *chai*. In 1985 the Delon family, who had owned the property since 1924, agreed to sell to Xavier Gardinier, the former President Director-General of Champagne Pommery.

At its best this *cru* can make fine long-lasting wines which are rich and supple, with complexity and breed. In the latter days of the Delon ownership there was a lack of consistency and some poor wines were produced. In 1987, Xavier Gardinier impressed Bordeaux by announcing that he would take back all the '83 vintage and was not going to sell the '84 or '85 under the château label. Then, starting work with a clean slate, the château proceeded to make an excellent '87 (in the context of that year), followed by impressive wines in '88, '89 and '90, while '92 and '93 are well above average for these vintages. The '94 and '95 are good, the '96 excellent. Phélan is once again challenging as one of the best unclassified wines of St-Estèphe.

Château Pomys
Cru Bourgeois Supérieur 1932. Owner: SARL Arnaud. 21ha.
14,000 cases. CS 50%, Mer 30%, CF 20%.
The picturesque château is now under separate ownership. The wines, however, often seen in England, are reliable, attractive and well balanced.

Château Segur de Cabanac
Owner: Guy Delon. 6ha. 3,000 cases. CS 50%, Mer 30%, CF 20%.
Guy Delon, whose family were the former owners of Phélan-Ségur, bought this property in 1985. It is made up of as many as nine small parcels of vines with neighbours such as Calon-Ségur

and Meyney. The new *chai* and *cuvier* are down at the port of St-Estèphe. The '96 is a high-class wine with lovely rich fruit and quality tannins in good harmony. Unfortunately their prices are rising as fast as the quality!

Château Tour de Pez

Owner: S.A. Tour de Pez. 23ha. 13,500 cases. CS 45%, Mer 40%, CF 10%, PV5%.

It seems likely that some parts of the vineyard were once part of Ch de Pez. There are parcels in Leyssac and Aillan, as well as on gravelly slopes adjoining Calon-Ségur and Montrose. Since the present owners bought the property in 1989, there have been heavy investments. I found the '96 had lovely sweet fruit, length and elegance, a wine of real quality. Definitely a name to look out for.

Château Tour-des-Termes

Cru Bourgeois 1932. Owner: Jean Anney. 21ha. 14,500 cases. CS 55%, Mer 35%, PV 10%.

A good-sized property situated near the village of St-Corbian in the north of the appellation. The wines I have come across are robust with plenty of character but also supple and quite fine. They are aged in cask. Tour-des-Termes is not a member of the Syndicat des Crus Bourgeois.

Château Tronquoy-Lalande

Cru Grand Bourgeois. Owner: Arlette Castéja-Texier. 15 ha. 9,000 cases. Mer 45%, CS 45%, PV 10%.

I have always been attracted by the charming château with its two distinctive towers at each end of a *chartreuse*-style building. Lalande is the place, Tronquoy the name of an early-19th-century owner. At that time this *cru* was included in several unofficial classifications, but did not make the all-important one in 1855.

This is now a carefully managed property, for which Dourthe has exclusive distribution rights and provides technical assistance. The wines are matured partly in *cuve* and partly in wood and are inclined to be tough and rustic when young, improving with time. The '96 was much more balanced and attractive than usual.

HAUT-MÉDOC

The decline that this area suffered in the years of depression has been triumphantly reversed. The area under vine nearly doubled between 1973 and 1988, which is remarkable enough; between 1988 and 1995 there has been a further 20 per cent increase. This is *par excellence* the area of the Crus Bourgeois, which here account for 62 per cent of the area in production and cover a greater area than in any other part of Médoc. Wines are produced in 15 diverse communes but in only ten of these are more than 100 hectares planted. The most important are St-Seurin, St-Laurent, Cussac, St-Sauveur, Cissac and Vertheuil.

The styles of wine vary considerably, with the largest-producing northern communes making robust, full-flavoured wines, and softer, lighter ones being made in the south.

Château d'Agassac

Cru Grand Bourgeois Exceptionnel. Owner: Groupama. 35ha.
10,000 cases. CS 54%, Mer 40%, CF 6%.

This is one of the few remaining examples of a genuine mediaeval fortress to survive in the Médoc. It is also the most important
cru in Ludon, after La Lagune. After Philippe Gasqueton (*see*
Calon-Ségur, Capbern and du Tertre) took over 30 years ago,
marked improvements were made and the reputation of the wine
was much enhanced. After his death it was sold to the present
owners in 1996.

The wine has marked and attractive individuality; it is vividly
perfumed, with a special fruitiness and pronounced flavour. Much
of the crop is traditionally exported to Holland. It is a pity that
this wine is not better known in Britain.

Château Aney

Owner: Raimond family. 30ha. 16,000 cases. CS 65%, Mer 25%,
CF 7%, PV 3%.

If you are driving through Cussac-Fort-Médoc you cannot miss
this *cru*, it is right on the road. The '96 has very solid supple tannins and pleasing fruit.

Château d'Arcins

Cru Bourgeois 1932. Owner: SC du Château d'Arcins. 97ha.
39,000 cases. CS 51%, Mer 49%. Second label: Tour de Mayne.

Castel Frères are the largest shareholders in the company
running Château d'Arcins. They have in recent years invested
much in the development of this property, which is the best in its
commune. The wines have many of the qualities evident in the
neighbouring growths of Margaux and Moulis, and are sold mostly
in the north of France.

Château Arnauld

Owners: M et Mme Maurice Roggy. 27ha. 11,000 cases.
CS 60%, Mer 40%. Second label: Château Chambore.

Originally a priory, this property took its name from a *procureur*
at the court of the Parlement de Bordeaux – Pierre-Jacques
Arnauld. It was bought by the Roggy family in 1956. The vineyards were replanted and improvements in vinification followed
the marriage of one of the Roggy daughters to François Theil of
Château Poujeaux. The '85 is an early developer, with fruit and
charm; '88 is much more powerful. A wine to look out for.

Château d'Arsac *See* page 51.

Château d'Aurilhac

Owner: Erik Nieuwaal. 16ha. 9,500 cases. CS 67%, Mer 27%,
CF 3%, PV 3%.

This is very much a newcomer. The vineyard, the most westerly
of St-Seurin de Cadourne was only planted in the late '80s. The '96
is very new oak-influenced, the 50 per cent is probably too high
for young vines, but with massively rich, ripe tannins, and more

like Châteauneuf-du-Pape than Médoc. The amazing 13.5 degrees alcohol confirmed this impression. It is nevertheless very attractive in its new-wave way. Obviously a wine to watch.

Château Barreyres
Cru Bourgeois 1932. Owner: SC du Château Barreyres. 109ha. 38,000 cases. CS 50%, Mer 50%. Second label: Tour Bellevue.
Castel Frères have, as at Château d'Arcins, invested much in this property, completing a new *cuvier* and *chai* in 1981 to enable improved vinification of this château's large output. The wines are attractive with pleasant fruit character but can be slightly coarse.

Château Beaumont
Cru Grand Bourgeois. Owner: Grands Millésimes de France. Administrator: Jacques de Chancel. 105ha. 66,700 cases. CS 60%, Mer 35%, CF 2%, PV 3%. Second labels: Châteaux Moulin d'Arvigny and Les Tours-de-Beaumont.
In marked contrast to those of their neighbour, Tour-du-Haut-Moulin, the wines of Beaumont tend to be light, fruity and ready to drink early. They are perfumed, with well-integrated new oak, tannin and fruit, combining to make a harmonious whole, most attractively flavoured. The '85 is typically fruity and succulent; '86 has more depth and firmness; '88 is forward, with attractive spicy fruit for drinking now; '89 is exceptional in terms of depth and structure while the '90, '95 and '96 are more flattering and forward. The ownership here is the same as at Beychevelle (*see* page 70).

The second wines, designed for early drinking, are a selection of about 25 per cent of the production, mostly from young vines.

Château Bel-Air
Owner: Héritiers d'Henri Martin. 37ha. 20,000 cases. CS 65%, Mer 35%.
Henri Martin – owner of Château Gloria and one of the Médoc's greatest personalities until his death in 1991 – bought this property in 1980. It is now managed by the highly capable Jean-Louis Triaud, Martin's son-in-law, who coordinates Bel-Air's three separate vineyards. These are dense-textured wines, with fruit and a good perfume. They are certainly wines to watch for.

Château Belgrave
5e Cru Classé. Owner: GFA. Administrator: Jacques Begarie. 53ha. 30,000 cases. CS 40%, Mer 35%, CF 20%, PV 5%.
Until the CVBG group (Dourthe-Kressman) bought this property in 1979 it had suffered from under-investment and neglect for decades. Consequently the wine was little known and its reputation negligible. The vineyard, however, was well situated on gravelly ridges behind Lagrange, and has good potential. The new owners have carried out improvements to the *chai* and new casks are being used for maturation. After extensive investment in the *chai* and *cuvier* a new phase began in '86 with Professor Alain Reynier in the vineyard and Michel Rolland as winemaker. The improvement in the wine is considerable, but they still lack Cru-Classé class.

Château Bel-Orme-Tronquoy-de-Lalande

Cru Grand Bourgeois. Owner: Jean-Michel Quié.
Administrator: Jean-Louis Camp. 26ha. 13,000 cases.
Mer 45%, CS 40%, CF 10%, PV 5%.
Not to be confused with Tronquoy-Lalande in nearby St-Estèphe,
this property once belonged to the Tronquoy family. The words
bel orme mean 'beautiful elm'.

The wines are powerful, solid and traditional, and they last
marvellously, as was proven by some bottles from the 1920s that
I sampled. The wines have benefited from Jean-Louis Camp's
improvements and the '96 is a big mouthful of wine with ripe tannins promising a long evolution.

Château Bernadotte

Owner: Mme May-Eliane de Lencquesaing. 26ha. 16,000 cases.
CS 62%, Mer 36%, CF/PV 2%.
This property straddles the boundary between Pauillac and St-
Sauveur. When the new owner, who also owns Ch Pichon-
Longueville Comtesse de Lalande bought it in 1996 it was decided
that only the Haut-Médoc portion of the vineyard should carry
the name of Bernadotte. The vineyard adjoins that of Liversan.
The wines have real quality with rich tannins and expansive fruit.
'96 was already impressive, while '97 was above average for the
year, and '98 has delicious fruit and harmony. This is a wine to
watch and follow.

Château Le Bourdieu

Cru Bourgeois. Owner: Richard family. 40ha. 24,000 cases.
CS 60%, Mer 25%, CF 10%, PV 5%.
Second labels: Châteaux Victoria and Picourneau.
This is probably the best-reputed *cru* in Vertheuil today,
the vineyards run from the village of that name to the boundary
with St-Estèphe. The wine is matured in cask and well reflects
the careful winemaking, the results of which combine
robustness with finesse. The style is typical of a good, lush
St-Estèphe.

Château du Breuil

Cru Bourgeois Supérieur. Owner: Vialard family. 25ha.
13,300 cases. Mer 34%, CS 28%, CF 23%, PV 11%, Mal 4%.
This is the oldest recorded property in the Médoc, records being
traceable through the barony of Breuil back to the sixth century.
The château is a mediaeval fortress, inhabited until 1861 but now
sadly deteriorated, though still majestic and imposing.

The current owners are the Vialard family (*see* Château
Cissac) who acquired the property in 1987; the *chai* and *cuvier*
were in a run-down state at this stage and needed much care and
attention. Although some respectable wines were made before
this, under the Vialard ownership the situation has been transformed. Since '88 (the second vintage under the new
management) the wines provide an interesting contrast to Cissac
with its more flattering Merlot style.

Château Cambon-la-Pelouse
Cru Bourgeois Supérieur 1932. Owner: Indivision Carrère Fils Frère & Gendre. 60ha. 33,000 cases. Mer 50%, CS 30%, CF 20%.
The *cru* has been resurrected by an energetic family of growers from St-Émilion, which also owns Château Grand Barrail-Lamarzelle-Figeac.

The wines have real breed, with emphasis on elegant fruitiness. They are soft and develop quickly for early drinking – no casks are used for the maturation but this is a good example of how clean, fresh and attractive such wines can be. This approach clearly makes good commercial sense. I noted a lovely scent of cherries and liquorice, a delicious flavour, rich if simple fruit. This certainly seems to be a *cru* with an interesting future.

Château de Camensac
5e Cru Classé. Owner: Forner family. 65ha. 29,000 cases.
CS 60%, CF 20%, Mer 20%.
Like the other Crus Classés of St-Laurent, Camensac had sunk into a state of complete obscurity and neglect when it was rescued by the Forner brothers in 1965. Of Spanish origins (they produce a fine Rioja) and new to Bordeaux, they sought the help of Professor Émile Peynaud in rebuilding this *cru*. Much of the vineyard had to be replanted, and the *chai* and *cuvier* completely modernised and re-equipped.

In the '80s the wines seem to have a strong, coarse flavour, even when, as with the '82, there is a lot of richness and ripeness. Wines seem too extracted and heavily oaked for their weight. But '95 was an improvement, good wine made within its limitations.

Château Cantemerle
5e Cru Classé. Owner: Société Assurance Mutuelles du Bâtiment et Travaux Publics. Administrator: Philippe Dambrine. 67ha. 40,000 cases. Mer 40%, CS 35%, CF 23%, PV 2%. Second label: Villeneuve de Cantemerle.
This famous old property, after a period of decline, has now been rapidly restored to its former glory. It achieved a great and deserved reputation when Pierre Dubos was proprietor, a regime which lasted over 50 years and corresponded roughly with the first half of this century. Then came the division among a number of heirs – a constant problem in France – and the result was a lack of money and direction, so decline and decay set in.

The turning point for Cantemerle came in 1980 with the sale to a syndicate of which Domaines Cordier is part. Cordier is responsible for the management and marketing, its partners have provided the finance. The *cuvier* and *chai* have been modernised, with stainless steel fermentation vats taking the place of the old wooden ones.

The style of Cantemerle leans towards lightness and elegance combined with good richness in the middle flavour. With the *cuvier* being rebuilt at the time, I found the first vintage of the new regime disappointing and dull. The '81 was better but not special, but then in '82, '83 and '85 superb wines were made, with an opulence and richness encountered only in exceptional years. Unfortunately the '86 crop suffered from the effects of hail. Then, after a great and flattering '88, '89 and '90 are rich opulent wines. Good wines were also made in '94, '95, '96 and '98.

Canterayne

Owner: Cave Coopérative de St-Sauveur. 72ha. 42,000 cases. CS 60%, Mer 35%, CF, Mal and PV 5%.

There are 69 members of this cooperative, which was founded in 1934. It produces some 3,800 hectolitres of wine annually, which is well made and expresses the firmness and solidity characteristic of the region's wines.

Château Caronne-Ste-Gemme

Cru Grand Bourgeois Exceptionnel. Owners: Jean and François Nony-Borie. 45ha. 20,000 cases. CS 65%, Mer 33%, PV 2%. Second label: Château Labat.

This good *cru* is deservedly becoming much better known since François Nony-Borie became involved in the early 1980s. The family has owned the property since 1900. The vineyards are separated from Camensac and the rest of St-Laurent by the Jalle du Nord, which divides St-Julien from Cussac, and the nearest vineyard is Lanessan in Cussac, so their situation is rather special.

My overall impression of the wines here is that they are well-made, have more style and breed than most St-Laurent wines, with nothing rustic about them. But there is a strong assertive character which comes through clearly, nicely balanced with fruit, and resulting in some complexity. The '82 is excellent, with the concentration typical of the year. The '83 is tannic but has plenty of fat, bigger than the '81 and finer perhaps than '79; '85 and '86 are both concentrated and attractive, with the latter being slightly more powerful. '96 again has all these qualities. This is really a top Cru Bourgeois, with excellent keeping qualities.

Château Charmail

Owner: Roger Sèze. 22ha. 14,000 cases. Mer 48%, CS 30%, CF 20%, PV 2%.

This property is excellently situated on the gravelly ridges of St-Seurin-de-Cadourne, near to the river. It was bought and restored in the 1970s by a Burgundian, Monsieur Laly, who came to the Médoc as he was unable to afford a vineyard in his home region. Roger Sèze, owner of Château Mayne-Vieil, took over in the early 1980s and is now producing rich, supple and charming wines, likely to improve as the vineyards mature. The '96 was more concentrated.

Châtelleine

Owner: Cave Coopérative de Vertheuil. 66·7ha. 40,000 cases. CS 50%, Mer 50%.

The total annual output of the 70 members of this cooperative is 7,000 hectolitres. They are solid wines of good quality, some of which are marketed under their own château labels: Châteaux Ferré Portal and Julian.

Château Cissac
Cru Grand Bourgeois Exceptionnel. Owner: Vialard family.
50ha. 25,000 cases. CS 75%, Mer 20%, PV 5%.
Second label: Reflets du Château Cissac.

Cissac has been inseparably linked for over a generation with Louis Vialard, who comes from an old Médocain family. The family has owned Cissac since 1885, and Louis Vialard has lived here since 1940. Extensive modernisation has been carried out and traditional methods – old vines, wooden fermenting vats and oak ageing casks (of which 50 per cent are normally new) – have been supplemented with new vats of stainless steel. In 1971 Louis Vialard made some important changes in his methods. He stopped adding *vin de presse*, using only the free-run juice; he began harvesting later and he increased the proportion of Cabernet Franc at the expense of the Cabernet Sauvignon.

In 1983 he gave a tasting of the vintages of the 1960s and 1970s to assess the results. For me the most noticeable difference was made by the *vin de presse*, it gave the older vintages a background of flavour and complexity lacking in most of the younger wines – the exception being the '75, itself a year unusually rich in tannin and extract. In otherwise excellent years such as '76, '78 and '79, a certain leanness was perceptible. Of the more recent vintages '86 is a real *vin de garde*; '88 fine and classic and '89 and '90 big raw-boned wines for keeping, '96 is still very austere. The Cabernet Franc at Cissac tended to lack body and colour, somewhat diluting the final blend, and this grape is no longer used. This is a fine *cru* whose wines have real breed and elegance and reward keeping.

Château Citran
Cru Grand Bourgeois Exceptionnel.
Owner: Groupe Bernard Taillan. 90ha. 47,000 cases.
CS 58%, Mer 42%. Second label: Moulins de Citran

This is the most important *cru* in Avensan. Part of the vineyard lies close to the village, but the oldest part is between the château and Paveil-de-Luze. When the Miailhe family bought the property in 1945 there was hardly any vineyard left. Jean Miailhe of Château Coufran ran the property until 1980. He expanded the vineyards and established a fine reputation for the wine. He then handed over to his sister and brother-in-law, who sold to the Japanese company Fujimoto in 1986. In 1997 Fujimoto sold to the present owners (*see* Chasse-Spleen, page 63–4).

The wines now have a good reputation and I have found them to have an excellent bouquet with pronounced fruit. They have a good flavour and balance with a certain earthiness. From 1979 until the sale in 1996 they were less consistent: dilute and dry in large vintages, especially the '79 and '83. But the first efforts under the new regime, '88, '89 and '90, together with an attractive new label, were most rewarding. Good wines were made in '94, '95, '96, '97 and '98.

Château Clément-Pichon

Owner: Clément Fayat. 25ha. 13,000 cases.
CS 50%, CF 10%, Mer 40%.

Originally called Château Parempuyre, this property was owned by the Pichons until 1880. The subsequent owners built the flamboyant château that stands there today – of a similar romantic-Gothic style to Châteaux Lanessan and Fonréaud and by the same architect. Clément Fayat – it was he who changed the name – made his fortune building *autoroutes* and has invested in replanting and creating a new drainage system in the vineyards. The *chai* has been similarly modernised and new vats installed enabling computer-controlled fermentation. The vineyards need more time to mature but the wines are already pleasant, if light.

Château Coufran

Cru Grand Bourgeois. Owner: SC du Château.
Administrator: Jean Miailhe. 75ha. 45,000 acres. Mer 85%, CS 10%, PV 5%. Second label: Château La Rose Maréchale.

The high proportion of Merlot here is unusual for the Médoc, even on these heavier soils. The result is an easy, supple, fruity wine for early drinking that does especially well in good years, but can be light in lesser ones. This is good commercial claret however and fulfils its declared purpose of producing easy-to-enjoy Médoc available a reasonable price.

Château Dillon

Cru Bourgeois 1932. Owner: Lycée Agricole de Bordeaux-Blanquefort. 35ha. 20,000 cases. Red: CS 50%, Mer 39%, CF 5%, PV 5%, Carmenère 1%. White: Sauv and Sém.
Second label: Château Linas (Bordeaux Blanc) 5ha.

This *cru* takes its name from an emigré Irishman who acquired the property in 1754. It has belonged to the Lycée Agricole since 1956, which has made improvements in the *cuvier* in order to carry out temperature-controlled fermentation.

At their best, the wines produced here are light and elegantly flavoured, but there have been lapses in consistency. Some good wines were made in the 1970s, especially the '70, '75 and '79. Since then an extension of the vineyard was added and little or no selection practised: the wines have therefore taken a step backwards in quality.

Château Fontesteau

Cru Grand Bourgeois. Owners: Christophe Barron and Dominique Fouin. 20ha. 11,000 cases.
CS 45%, Mer 25%, CF 30%.

From 1939 until 1984 the owner of Fontesteau was René Église. Since 1984 it has been owned by Jean Renaud. The name comes from *fontaines d'eau*, because there are a number of old wells on the property. The wines are made quite traditionally, with fermentation in concrete vats and ageing in casks. The wines tend to be quite tough and tannic.

Château Grandis

Cru Bourgeois 1932. Owner: GHF du Château Grandis.
9·2ha. 3,800 cases. CS 50%, Mer 40%, CF 10%.
Second label: Murac-Major.

Grandis was bought in 1857 by Armand Figerou and it has remained in the family ever since; today it is run by his ancestor François Vergez. The wines have the solidity typical of St-Seurin-de-Cadourne and are traditionally made. Certainly a ripe, powerful wine that repays keeping.

Château Hanteillan

Cru Grand Bourgeois. Owner: SARL du Château Hanteillan.
Administrator: Catherine Blasco. 83ha. 50,000 cases.
CS 52%, Mer 40%, CF 5%, PV 3%.
Second label: Château Laborde.

In 1972 this property was bought by a group of partners connected to France's largest construction company. It used to share the same owners as Château Coutelin-Merville in St-Estèphe, and the vineyards adjoin one another. Despite Coutelin-Merville's superior appellation, I have found that Hanteillan today makes a more impressive wine. The high proportion of Merlot grown reflects the clay present in parts of the vineyard.

This is a serious wine with some real breed and should be followed with interest as the vineyard matures.

Château Haut-Logat

Owner: Marcel and Christian Quancard. 20ha. 10,000 cases.
CS 60%, Mer 30%, CF 10%.
Second wine: Ch La Croix Margautot.

This good *cru* in Cissac owned by the members of the family négociants Cheval Quancard, and is close to their neighbouring property at Ch Tour-St-Joseph, which, however, has more Cabernet Sauvignon. I found the '96 to have fruit and charm with distinct style and moderate body.

Château Haut-Madrac

Owner: Castéja family. 20ha. 12,000 cases. CS 75%, Mer 25%.

Bought by Émile Castéja's father in 1919, this property adjoins the family's other property in Pauillac (Lynch-Moussas). It produces wines that are well made, charming and good for early drinking. Typically these wines have light, fresh and fruity characteristics.

Château La Lagune

3e Cru Classé. Owner: SC Agricole. Administrator: Jean-Michel Ducellier. 70ha. 38,900 cases. CS 60%, Mer 20%, CF 10%
PV 10%. Second label: Château Ludon-Pomiès-Agassac (changing to Moulin de La Lagune for the '98).

The restoration of La Lagune began when it was bought by Georges Brunet in 1957. This dynamic man replanted the vineyard and reconstructed the *chai*, where he installed a marvellous system of stainless steel pipes to bring the new wine straight from the vats to the barrels and also to carry out racking entirely mechanically and without contact with the air. It was a revolutionary system when installed over 30 years ago, but no one else has yet copied it, which seems surprising.

Burnet undertook many costly improvements within a short time and as a result ran short of money so had to sell in 1961, having made the mistake of selling that great year *sur souche* (on the vine, before the harvest). La Lagune was bought by Champagne Ayala for whom Jean-Michel Ducellier is the administrator. The *régisseuse* is Caroline du Vivier the daughter of the redoubtable Mme Boyrie; she succeeded her mother who died unexpectedly in 1986, and her meticulous hand creates some fine wines.

Now the vineyard has come of age a series of splendid wines has given La Lagune an enviable reputation. It is extremely reliable and excellent value. This is a wine of great elegance; perfumed, usually rather marked by new wood at the start (100 per cent new wood was usual here but has now has been reduced 80 per cent) but this is soon absorbed to give a rich, supple flavour with great finesse. The '82, '83, '85, '86, '88, '89, '90, '93, '94, '95, '96 and '97 are all great successes. Since '93 there has been more serious selection with 25 per cent set aside for the second wine in '95 and '96 and 30 per cent in '97.

Château de Lamarque
Cru Grand Bourgeois. Owner: SC Gromand d'Évry.
Administrator: Roger Gromand. 48ha. 25,000 cases. CS 46%,
Mer 25%, CF 24%, PV 5%. Second label: Donjon de Lamarque.
The château here is the best-preserved and most impressive fortress in the Médoc of those that survive from the English period in Aquitaine. Although parts of it date from the 11th and 12th centuries, the main structure is 14th century with some 17th-century alterations. It lies between the *route des châteaux* and the ferry to Blaye, but is well concealed amid the trees of its park. Until recently the wine of Lamarque was unknown, but reconstruction of vineyards and *chai* was undertaken in the 1960s and is now bearing fruit.

Ownership of the château has passed through inheritance since 1841 when it was acquired by the Comte de Fumel, passing via a daughter to the present owner Marie-Louise Burnet d'Évry, who married Roger Gromand. He is the driving force behind the renaissance of Lamarque, and with Professor Émile Peynaud's constant advice and supervision he has again established a reputation for the wines. The wine is matured in casks, 30 per cent of which are new each year.

In the 1970s I found the wines light and agreeable in good vintages but without much personality. Then in the 1980s they filled out and became more powerful and much richer. Clearly the vineyard has come of age, and this is a wine to watch.

Château Lamothe-Bergeron
Cru Bourgeois. Owner: SC Grand-Puy-Ducasse. 66ha.
19,000 cases. CS 52%, Mer 34%, CF 14%.

The name Lamothe-Bergeron comes from the word *motte* (a piece of high ground) and from the name of a previous owner of the château. This *cru* has a reputation for producing well-made, reliable and reasonably priced wines. Particularly attractive vintages were the '82, '85, '86 and '87; the '88 and '89 were even better.

Château Lamothe-Cissac

Owner: SC du Château Lamothe. Administrator: Vincent Fabre. 33ha. 18,000 cases. CS 70%, Mer 26%, PV 4%.

This is an old property: it was a *maison noble* in the 17th century and evidence of Roman occupation has also been found here. The château itself does not share this history and was built comparatively recently in 1912. Lamothe-Cissac was bought by the Fabre family in 1964 in an extremely run-down state. Since then a new *cuvier*, *chai* and underground cellar have been built. 20 per cent new oak is used each year for maturation, and as the vineyards develop some impressive wines are emerging. The wines are stylish, with solidity and fruit. They are mostly sold direct, not via Bordeaux *négociants*.

Château Lanessan

Cru Bourgeois Supérieur 1932. Owner: Bouteiller family. Administrator: Hubert Bouteiller. 40ha. 17,700 cases. CS 75%, Mer 20%, PV 4%, CF 1%. Second label: Domaine de Ste-Gemme.

Since 1790 this property has effectively been in the same family, the Delbos, whose name still appears on the label alongside that of Bouteiller. It was handed from father to son until 1909, when the daughter of the last male Delbos inherited. She married Étienne Bouteiller. Hubert Bouteiller, the present member of the family in charge, has his home here. A feature of Lanessan unrelated to wine is the carriage museum, where the stables and harness room are displayed with a fine assortment of carriages.

The wines of Lanessan have a marked personality. There is a tendency to firmness at first, but in good years the wines have marvellous fruit and richness and considerable breed. They are also consistent. There is a great capacity for ageing. I have tasted a number of old vintages going back to 1916, all of them well preserved and many outstanding. Even the '77 was good from this property and a useful and elegant '80 was also made. Recently '81, '82, '85, '86, '87, '88, '89, '90, '95 and '96 were all excellent examples. This is a wine for those who love fine Médocs for their own sake and are not slaves to labels.

Château Larose-Trintaudon

Cru Grand Bourgeois. Owner: Assurances Générales de France. Administrator: Jacques Papon. 172ha. 83,300 cases. CS 60%, Mer 25%, CF 15%. Second label: (since '90) Larose St-Laurent. Ch Larose Perganson (for hand harvested old vines).

Bought and developed by the Forner family in the 1960s this is now the largest vineyard in the Médoc. Élisée Forner continued as administrator until the autumn of 1988, when the new owner's management team took over. Under Jacques Papon's leadership,

Franck Bijon came from Latour in April 1989 to become technical manager, with Mattheas von Campe joining as marketing manager in September. Mechanical harvesting is used, but all the wines are matured in casks of which 30 per cent are new each year.

The new director is making clear improvements in the wines with more selection. The '86 is a big, rich wine, but with rather dry tannins; '88 is more classic with riper tannins; '89 still rather awkward, needing time; '90 the best wine yet: its lovely velvety texture fills the mouth and shows the potential of this *cru*. After a supple, attractive '92 made for early drinking, the '93 is a little dry, and '94 has more fruit structure and character. The Médoc's largest vineyard seems to have found its way. In '96 between 12 and 15 per cent of the older vines were hand harvested and sold as Larose-Perganson. The contrast in quality is marked.

Château Lestage-Simon
Cru Bourgeois. Owner: Charles Simon. 40ha. 20,000 cases.
Mer 60%, CS 35%, CF 5%.
The wines here are typical of St-Seurin: fine, robust and solid, with the Merlot giving fruit and suppleness. I was once given a bottle of the '29 by a former proprietor, and I found it had kept splendidly. In the '80s wines were made for earlier drinking but were none the worse for that. They are widely distributed in good restaurants in France. The '81, '82, '83 and '85 are good examples. But I found the very concentrated '96 too oaky.

Château Liversan
Cru Grand Bourgeois. Owner: Boncampe family.
Administrator: Jean-Michel Laplu. 48ha. 22,000 cases. CS 49%,
Mer 38%, CF 10%, PV 3%.
In 1983 Liversan was bought by the Polignacs, formerly the principal shareholders of Champagne Pommery, but following the death of Prince Guy de Polignac in 1996 the family sold to the owners of Patache d'Aux. The Polignacs' first move upon purchase was to install a new *cuvier* with stainless steel fermentation vats.

The wines are now to be aged in oak with a good proportion of new wood. The scented, opulent yet elegant '85 and the '86, for which only 65 per cent of the crop was included in the final *assemblage* and only 25 per cent of that was Merlot, show the potential of this *cru*. Excellent wines were made by the Polignacs following considerable investment. This has continued under the new owners. The sumptuous '96 is unfiltered.

Château Magnol
Cru Bourgeois. Owner: Barton & Guestier.
16·2ha. 7,200 cases. Mer 50%, CS 40%, CF 10%.
Most of the vineyards at this château were planted within the last 40 years. The current owner is a subsidiary of the Seagram group. Vinification is carried out with much care, using modern temperature-controlled stainless steel vats and producing wines that are full-flavoured, rich and supple. Wines to be drunk young.

Château Malescasse

Cru Bourgeois. Owner: La Société Alcatel Alsthom.
Administrator: Jean-Pierre Petroffe. 32ha. 16,000 cases. CS 70%,
Mer 20%, CF 10%.
Second wine: La Closerie de Malescasse.

A charming high-roofed château, dating from 1824, overlooks this property which is on the gravelly ridges of the commune of Lamarque. Its vineyards are some of the best in the area between Margaux and St-Julien. During the inter-war recession the area under vine had dwindled to only four hectares. A programme of replanting started in 1970 was completed in 1992. In 1992 Alcatel bought the property from the Tesserons of Pontet-Canet.

The style and solidity of these wines is particularly impressive for a vineyard that is not yet fully mature, the '85, '86, '88, '89, '90, '94, '95 and '96 are all of a high standard, and sold at modest prices. A *cru* proving to be one of the appellation's best buys.

Château de Malleret

Cru Grand Bourgeois. Owner: SC du Château (Marquis du Vivier). 66ha. 38,900 cases. CS 55%, Mer 35%, CF 5%, PV 5%.
Second label: Châteaux Barthez and de Nexon,
Domaine de l'Ermitage Lamouroux.

These wines are extremely scented and elegant, fruity with real length of flavour and a quite seductive charm. In recent years the proportion of Merlot has been increased at the expense of Cabernet Sauvignon. Consistently attractive wines are made here.

Château Le Meynieu

Cru Grand Bourgeois. Owner: Jacques Pédro. 15ha.
6,700 cases. CS 62%, Mer 30%, CF 8%.

The energetic, meticulous Jacques Pédro is mayor of Vertheuil as well as proprietor of this *cru* and those of Lavillotte and Domaine de la Ronceray. His aim is to make typical Médocs with supple fruit, delicious for early drinking.

Château Muret

Owner: Philippe Boufflerd. 22ha. 14,000 cases. Mer 55%, CS 45%. Second wine: Château Tour du Mont.

The present owner acquired this old *cru* in the western part of St-Seurin de Cadourne in 1985 and has since completely renovated it. To help control yields grass is grown between the rows of vines. I found the '96 to have a marked spicy scented character with rich, rather extracted tannins but undeniably attractive. As the vineyard matures the wines can only improve.

Cave Coopérative La Paroisse

Owner: Union de Producteurs. 90ha. 36,700 cases.

The cooperative was founded in 1935 and is considered to be the best in the Haut-Médoc appellation. Most of the wine is sold in bulk to *négociants* or under the La Paroisse brand, but a few property wines are kept separate: Château Quimper, Domaine du Villa and Château La Chicane. In recent years the cooperative has lost a number of members as new owners decide to make their own wines. These are solid, well-balanced wines which resemble the lesser St-Estèphes but usually have more flesh.

Château Paloumey

Owner: Martine Cazeneuve. 18.5ha. 11,000 cases. CS 55%, Mer 40%, CF 5%. Second wine: Les Ailes de Paloumey.

This *cru* had an excellent reputation in the 19th century but the vineyard was finally up rooted in 1954. The present owner replanted the vineyard in 1990. In spite of the youth of the vines I found the '96 attractively fruity and ripe for early drinking. Watch this space!

Château Peyrabon

Cru Grand Bourgeois. Owner: Jacques Babeau. 48ha. 20,000 cases. CS 50%, Mer 27%, CF 23%.

This distinctive twin-towered château has been owned by the Babeau family since 1958 and they are proud to be able to say that Queen Victoria once attended a concert here.

Prior to 1958 Peyrabon wines were relatively unknown as they were mostly sold privately; they now have a good reputation and are classics of the northern Médoc, with a note of *terroir* on the finish. The vineyards are extensive and were supplemented by land bought from Château Liversan in 1978. They are fermented in concrete vats and matured in wood, 33 per cent new. The '96, despite strong tannins, is attractively robust and fruity.

Château Pontoise-Cabarrus

Cru Bourgeois. Owner: SICA de Haut-Médoc. Administrator: François Tereygeol. 29ha. 16,700 cases. CS 60%, Mer 30%, CF 6%, PV 4%.

A modest Cru Bourgeois with an interesting history. Owned by the Cabarrus family during 'The Terror' in Bordeaux, the daughter of the house, Thereza Cabarrus, saved many lives in her role as mistress of the notorious Tallien. A colourful character, she was later a witness at the wedding of Napoleon and Josephine.

The Tereygeols bought the château in 1960 and built up the seven-hectare property to its current size. They produce carefully made, solid wines with flavour, needing plenty of time to reveal their best characteristics.

Château Puy-Castéra

Cru Bourgeois. Owner: Marès family. 25ha. 15,600 cases. CS 57%, Mer 30%, CF 9%, Mal 3%, PV 1%. Second label: Château Holden.

Puy-Castéra was given a new lease of life in 1973 when it was bought by Henri Marès. At this stage the buildings were dilapidated and the vineyards had been returned to pasture. Replanting was gradual: 25 hectares were in production by 1980. Winemaking was put into the hands of Bertrand de Rozières from Château Sestignan. The vineyards are well sited and as they mature yield wines of increasing quality. Attractive, early-drinking wines.

Château Ramage-la-Bâtisse

Cru Bourgeois. Owner: MACIF. 40ha. 24,400 cases.
CS 45%, Mer 45%, CF 5%, PV 5%.
Second label: Château Dutellier.

This is a combination of several properties which have been put together since 1961. The wines are scented (I detected a smell of violets) and extremely fruity and easy to drink. It is easy to see why these wines rapidly gained a good reputation.

Château du Retout

Cru Bourgeois 1932. Owner: Gérard Kopp. 30ha. 18,900 cases.
CS 70%, Mer 23%, CF 5%, PV 2%.

An old mill tower (dating from 1395) stands on this property: it was used in the Seven Years' War (1756–63) to look out for British ships advancing up the Gironde estuary.

This is yet another example of a property where extensive restoration has been needed. Its wines are now well made and sold at reasonable prices.

Château Reysson

Cru Bourgeois. Owner: Mercian Corporation. Administrator: Jean-Pierre Angliviel de la Beaumelle. 67ha. 15,800 cases. CS 56%, Mer 44%. Second label: Château de l'Abbaye.

Château Reysson was restored by the Mestrezat Group who bought it in 1972, subsequently selling to the Mercian Corporation (part of the Japanese Ajimoto group). Pleasant wines, suitable for drinking young, are produced at reasonable prices.

Chevaliers du Roi Soleil

Owner: SICA des Viticulteurs de Fort-Médoc.
56ha. 33,000 cases. CS 50%, Mer 40%, CF 10%.
Other labels: Fort-Médoc, Châteaux Les Capérans, Église Vieille, les Jacquets, Le Neurin, Le Moreau and Grand-Merrain.

Initially a small group of growers who pooled their efforts in 1966 to improve their output and to market it more efficiently. Today a *négcciant*, Ginestet, is also involved with this group of producers which is based in a modern site complex, somewhat startling for the traveller in the Médoc countryside as it intrudes on the flat landscape en-route from Lamarque to Cussac.

Some 22 members now produce wines under the label 'Chevaliers du Roi Soleil'. They are unlike cooperative wines in that they reflect the character and personality of their château origins.

Château St-Paul

Owner: Boucher family. 20ha. 12,400 cases. CS 60%, Mer 35%, CF 5%.

This vineyard was created in 1979 from parcels of vineyard in St-Seurin de Cadourne belonging to two St-Estèphe properties just across the communal boundary, Le Boscq and Morin. Lovely, rich ample wines with good structure and fruit are now being made. This is yet another excellent St-Suerin de Cadourne wine.

Château Sénéjac

Cru Bourgeois Supérieur 1932. Owner: Charles de Guigné.
26ha. 14,400 cases. CS 60%, Mer 25%, CF 14%, PV 1%.

There is an international air about Sénéjac. The proprietor is an American citizen of French origin, and during the 1980s when he was assisted by New Zealand oenologist Jenny Bailey, considerable progress was made. Unfortunately she left in 1994. The wines are good and have made progress recently. They are completely different from those of de Malleret, the other important *cru* of Pian. They are deep-coloured and perfumed, but classically austere and tannic. These wines are made to last and do last, as the older vintages show. They have a good following among many traditional English wine merchants and it is easy to see why.

Château Sociando-Mallet

Cru Grand Bourgeois. Owner: Jean Gautreau. 50ha.
25,000 cases. CS 60%, Mer 25%, CF 10%, PV 5%.
Second label: La Demoiselle de Sociando-Mallet.

The aim here is to produce traditional Médocs. There is long vatting, for maximum extraction of colour and tannins, and maturing in casks, of which between 80 and 100 per cent are new – a high proportion for a Cru Bourgeois. When young the wines are taut and marked by new wood – at a stage when other wines are beginning to be drinkable. The '79 was like this in 1984. With patience the wines develop a fine flavour and character and during the 1980s they seem to have filled out and become much richer – '82, '83, '85, '88, '89 and '90 are especially impressive, then after a fine '93 '94, '95 and '96 are all great successes. These are certainly the most impressive Haut-Médocs in the north of the appellation.

Château Soudars

Cru Bourgeois. Owner: Eric Miailhe. 22ha.
13,900 cases. CS 44%, Mer 55%, CF 1%.

Eric Miailhe cleared 2,500 tons of stones before planting his new vineyards here in 1973. The property is near to those owned by his father and grandfather – Verdignan and Coufran – but they were discouraged from using this land by the quantity of stones and boulders covering it.

Miailhe's care and attention has produced some fine wines: the '82, '83, '85, '86, '89, '90, '95 and '96 are evidence enough that this *cru* has a good future.

Château du Taillan

Cru Grand Bourgeois. Owner: Mme Henri-François Cruse.
22ha. 11,000 cases. Red: CS 48%, Mer 30%, CF 22%.
White: Château La Dame-Blanche. 4ha. 2,200 cases.
Sauv 56%, Col 30%, Sém 14%.

This property has belonged to the Cruses since 1896. The château and the even older cellars are classified as historic monuments. The wine is kept mostly in large wooden *foudres* of 80–170 hectolitres, but 20 per cent passes through new casks of the conventional size.

The aim here is to produce supple, easy-to-drink wines without much tannin. The white wine, La Dame-Blanche, with its heavy dose of Colombard, is rather different in character from the usual Bordeaux Blanc, having much more obvious flowery fruit.

Château La Tour-Carnet

4e Cru Classé. Owner: Mme Marie-Claire Pelegrin. 40ha.
20,000 cases. CS 53%, Mer 33%, CF 10%, PV 4%.
Like so much else in St-Laurent, La Tour-Carnet was on its last legs when Louis Lipschitz bought it in 1962. In the early days the Ginestets gave technical assistance and sold the wine on an exclusive basis. After Louis Lipschitz died his daughter and her husband continued the work. The wines are conscientiously made, and a third of the wood used in making them is new. At their best they are vivid in colour, fruity and intense in flavour, but light.

In the late 1980s, many changes were made and great efforts went into improving the wine; '90 seemed a big step forward but since then the wines have been irregular. Let us hope that this *cru* can again deserve its place in the classification.

Château Tour-du-Haut-Moulin

Cru Grand Bourgeois. Owner: Laurent Poitou. 31ha.
17,800 cases. CS 50%, Mer 45%, PV 5%.
The vineyards of this *cru* lie beside those of Beaumont around the village of Cussac, but the wines are different.

Laurent Poitou is the fourth generation of his family to own this property, and he makes fine traditional wines. They are aged in wood, of which 25 per cent is new. The result is a wine of exceptional colour that is also rich in extract. Tannic and powerful but well balanced, these wines have great character, and with ageing their real breed emerges. This is consistently one of the best Crus Bourgeois.

Château Tour-du-Mirail

Cru Bourgeois 1932. Owners: Hélène and Danielle Vialard.
18ha. 10,800 cases. CS 75%, Mer 20%, PV 5%.
This property has belonged to the daughters of Louis Vialard of neighbouring Château Cissac since 1970. Everything is quite separate from Cissac.

Vinification is in stainless steel vats and the wines are matured in cask. They have a lot of flavour and a well-projected and quite perfumed bouquet. At the same time they are fairly light in body and have a certain Cabernet Sauvignon 'edge'. Despite their firmness, I find these wines are at present more enjoyable when fairly young (five to seven years), before the fruit begins to fade. This is an honourable Cru Bourgeois, but at present lacks the style and character of Cissac.

Château Tour St-Joseph

Owner: Marcel and Christian Quancard. 10ha. 5,000 cases.
CS 70%, Mer 25%, CF 5%.
The owners head the family *négociant* business of Cheval

Quancard, and also the neighbouring Cissac property of Haut-Logat. The vineyard is situated on the highest point of the commune, and the old vines produce wines with good fruit and elegance and some style.

Château Tourteran
Cru Grand Bourgeois.
Owner: SC du Château Ramage-la-Bâtisse. 20ha. 12,000 cases.
CS 50%, Mer 50%. Second label: Château Terrey.
The same management as and an adjoining vineyard to Ramage-la-Bâtisse; younger vines, a different name but the same objectives.

Château Verdignan
Cru Grand Bourgeois. Owner: SC du Château.
Administrator: Eric Miailhe. 60ha. 36,000 cases. CS 55%,
Mer 40%, CF 5%. Second label: Château Plantey-de-la-Croix.
Coufran is the most northerly château in the Haut-Médoc and this is the second most northerly – both are administered or owned by Jean Miailhe. Verdignan has an attractive château with a tall turret, easily visible from the road.

When Jean Miailhe bought the property in 1972 the reputation of Verdignan was not good. I remember wines of a rather tough character during the 1960s. Now Jean's son Eric is in charge of the winemaking, as he is at Coufran. The wine is fermented in stainless steel and matured in cask and, as one would expect of a wine from St-Seurin, it is solid and well-structured with a strong flavour. It also has lots of fruit, something that was lacking in the past.

Château de Villegeorge
Cru Bourgeois Supérieur Exceptionnel 1932.
Owner: Marie-Louise Lurton. 15ha. 2,200 cases.
Mer 60%, CS 30%, CF 10%.
Villegeorge has long enjoyed a good reputation. It was one of only six Crus Bourgeois classified as Exceptionnel in 1932, and was again classified as Exceptionnel in 1966. The soil here is extremely gravelly, resembling that of Margaux, and has been largely abandoned by *vignerons* in recent years, becoming prey to gravel merchants, so the countryside is now scarred with water-filled pits. Lucien Lurton campaigned to prevent further spoiling of his land. In 1994 he handed over the property to his daughter Marie-Louise.

The fermentation is in stainless steel, and the wine is matured in cask with 25 per cent new wood used. The vineyard here is particularly prone to frost damage which often causes low and irregular yields. The high proportion of Merlot is most unusual in the Médoc. The wines of Villegeorge have always been deep-coloured, with a strong character, and they remained so under Lucien Lurton with the difference being that they are now rather more polished and less rustic than they sometimes were. Excellent wines were made in '79, '81, '82, '83, '85, '88, '89, '90, '95 and '96.

MÉDOC AC

The fortunes of this area have revived considerably in recent years. Between 1985 and 1996 the area under vine increased by over 50 per cent to 4,741 hectares. Wine is now produced in 16 communes, of which the most important are Bégadan (by far the largest), St-Yzans, Prignac, Ordonnac, St-Christoly, Blaignan and St-Germain-d'Esteuil. Because of the heavier soils, even where there are outcrops of gravel, more Merlot is found here than in the Haut-Médoc and there is therefore a lower proportion of Cabernet Sauvignon. The wines are pleasantly perfumed, especially when young, and develop some finesse in bottle. They are mostly light in body but well flavoured. There are plenty of good Crus Bourgeois – nine were designated as Grands Bourgeois in 1978.

Cave Coopérative Bellevue
Owner: Société Coopérative de Vinification d'Ordonnac.
260ha. 153,000 cases. Mer 50%, CS 45%, CF 5%.
The cooperative at Ordonnac was founded in 1936 and has members drawn from this commune and the neighbouring one of St-Germain d'Esteuil. The following individual *crus* are vinified here: Châteaux de Brie, Belfort, Mareil, Moulin-de-la-Rivière, l'Oume-de-Pey, La Rose-Picot, and Les Graves. The cooperative is also a member of Uni-Médoc, the association of *caves coopératives* of Médoc, and supplies much wine in bulk for *négociants'* own brands as well as under its own *marque* of Pavillon de Bellevue. This is good, dependable Médoc.

Château Blaignan
Cru Bourgeois. Owner: SC du Château Taffard.
Administrator: Mestrezat Domaines SA. 75ha. 37,500 cases.
CS 60%, Mer 40%. Second label: Château La Garenne.
A consistent, well distributed wine run by *négociants* Mestrezat. It is the largest vineyard in the commune of the same name.

Château de By
Cru Bourgeois. Owner: J-C Baudon. 11·4ha. 6,100 cases.
Mer 40%, CS 30%, PV 20%, CF 10%.
Located on the ridge of By, between Bégadan and the Gironde, this *cru* is unusual in that a high percentage of Petit Verdot is grown, giving de By's wines a distinctive vivid colour. The proprietor, Monsieur Baudon, also believes in chaptalizing as little as possible – another unusual factor – which lends the wines a refreshingly natural, crisp character.

These are wines which develop quickly and are full of Médoc style, with finesse and plenty of individuality.

Château La Cardonne
Cru Grand Bourgeois. Owner: Domaines C.G.R. 70ha.
30,000 cases. Mer 50%, CS 45%, CF 5%.
This large property, the most important in Blaignan, was acquired by Domaines Rothschild in 1973, since when the vineyard has been considerably expanded, the existing buildings restored and

the equipment replaced. The vineyard is well placed on the highest plateau of the region. The wines saw no wood at all prior to 1990 when the Rothschilds sold to the present owner.

These wines are deep-coloured, perfumed, fruity, frank and fresh: archetypical Médoc, straightforward and easy to enjoy young. It has moved up a gear in recent years and now has more fruit and succulence – this is especially noticeable from the '88 vintage onwards. In 1996 Eric Fabre, formerly at Lafite, took over management. One third new oak is now usual in the maturation.

Château Castéra
Cru Bourgeois. Owner: D G Tondera. 50ha. 22,000 cases.
CS 45%, Mer 45%, CF 7%, PV 3%. Second label: Château
Bourbon La Chapelle.
This is one of the principal *crus* of St-Germain-d'Esteuil. It is an old property which has links with the Black Prince, who besieged the original château. It belonged to Alexis Lichine & Co, the *négociants*, from 1973 to 1986, when they sold to the present owners. This is a good, solid, enjoyable Médoc, developing a mellow, fruity character, full and soft when quite young. Can be enjoyed from three years onwards.

Château La Clare
Cru Bourgeois. Owner: Paul de Rozières. 21·8ha. 13,700 cases.
CS 57%, Mer 36%, CF 7%.
Second labels: Châteaux Laveline and du Gentilhomme.
Situated on the ridge of By, 50 per cent of La Clare's vineyards have been replanted by the present owners over the last 20 years. These are mostly mechanically harvested, but grapes for the older vines – some over 60 years old – are hand-picked.

The Rozières, owners since 1969, originally came from Tunisia and used their experience as vineyard owners there to advantage, producing excellent wines which are attractive and well-made with spiciness, opulence and plummy fruit.

Château de la Croix
Owner: Francesco family. 20ha. 11,000 cases. CS 50%, Mer
45%, CF 4%, PV 1%. Brands: Château Roc-Taillade, Château
Terre-Rouge, Château Côtes de Blaignan.
This *cru* was created in 1870, and has been in the hands of the same family ever since. The domaine has gradually been increased in size, so comprises numerous parcels in Ordonnac. I found the '96 had rich tannins and good fruit balance with an attractive and distinctive character.

Château Les Grands Chênes
Owner: Jacqueline Gauzy-Darracade. 7ha. 4,400 cases.
CS 65%, Mer 30%, CF 5%. Second label: Le Chêne Noir.
This small St-Christoly property has carved out quite a reputation for itself in recent years for its well-made concentrated wines of character that repay ageing. One-third new oak is used. The wines are sold direct from the château.

Château Greysac

Cru Grand Bourgeois. Owner: Domaines Codem.
Administrator: Philippe Dambrine. 60ha. 27,800 cases.
CS 45%, Mer 45%, CF 5%, PV 5%.

Since the late Baron François de Gunzburg bought this château in 1973 its importance has increased. Fermentation is in stainless steel *cuves* and the wine is aged in cask with 20 per cent new wood. I have found the wines to have an expansive, almost opulent fruit flavour, with a rather overripe style in the best vintages. They can be drunk with pleasure when three to four years old.

Château Haut-Canteloup

Owner: S.C.I. du Château Haut-Canteloup. 38ha. 23,500 cases.
Mer 60%, CS 30%, CF 10%. Second wine: Château les Mourlanes.

This good property in St-Christoly is now making very good wines. The '96 had lovely rich, unctuous, expressive fruit and harmony, with elegance and persistence of flavour; a very stylish wine.

Château Lacombe-Noillac

Owner: Jean-Michel Lapalu. 28ha. 12,500 cases.
CS 58%, Mer 32%, CF 6%, PV 4%.

The vineyard was reconstructed only in 1980, but is now regarded as the leading *cru* in Jau-Dignac-et-Loirac, the most northerly of the Médoc vineyards. The well-made, attractive wines are made with 15 per cent new oak in their maturation.

Château Laujac

Cru Grand Bourgeois. Owner: Bernard Cruse. 27ha. 14,000 cases.
CS 60%, Mer 30%, CF 5%, PV 5%.

A widely-known château belonging to the Cruse family, Laujac is situated on the Médoc's central plateau. This large property used to produce much more wine, of higher repute than it does now. The wines lack much of the character evident in neighbouring *crus*.

Château Les Moines

Cru Bourgeois. Owner: Claude Pourreau.
24ha. 13,200 cases. CS 70%, Mer 30%.
Other label: Château Tour St-Martin (aged in vat only).

A good *cru* in Couquèques, adjoining Les Ormes-Sorbet. The grapes are mechanically harvested and matured in cask, of which 25 per cent are renewed annually. This is solid and well-made serious wine, fruity and consistent.

Château Livran

Cru Bourgeois. Owner: Robert-Yves Godfrin. 48ha. 27,800
cases. Mer 55%, CS 35%, CF 10%. Second label: Château La
Rose-Goromey.

Once owned by the de Goth family – one of whom became Pope Clement V in 1305 – this château's history is as impressive as its appearance. It was also owned by a London wine merchant – James Denman – until the Second World War. The present proprietor is its former manager. Pleasant, well-made wines.

Château Loudenne

Cru Grand Bourgeois. Owner: W & A Gilbey Ltd. 50ha.
Red: 27,000 cases. CS 50%, Mer 43%, CF 6%, Mal 1%.
White: 5,000 cases. Sauv 62%, Sém 38%.

The wines tend to be lighter in colour but have more perfume and finesse than most wines of the Médoc AC. There is a real elegance about them which becomes more noticeable as the wines mature in bottle. The '90 and especially '96 are good here.

The excellent white wine is fermented in stainless steel at between 17° and 20°C (62° and 68°F). It is delicious, perfumed and elegant soon after bottling in the spring, but the Sémillon lends the potential for ageing as well.

Château de Monthil

Cru Bourgeois. Owner: Les Domaines Codem. 30ha.
27,800 cases. CS 30%, CF 30%, Mer 30%, Mal 5%, PV 5%.

Les Domaines Codem also owns Châteaux Greysac, Bégadan and Les Bertins in the same commune. Before they bought the property in 1986, the traditionally made wines were mostly sold to restaurants within France. Now they are exported too, and with their fine reputation – they have established a loyal following – they ought to do well. A wine to look out for.

Château Noaillac

Cru Grand Bourgeois. Owners: Xavier and Marc Pagès. 41ha.
22,500 cases. CS 55%, Mer 40%, PV 5%. Second labels: Moulin de Noaillac, La Rose Noaillac, Les Palombes de Noaillac.

Another example of *pieds noirs* enterprise (*see* La Tour de By, page 123). The Pagès family bought the property in northern Jau-Dignac-et-Loirac in 1983 and replanted the vineyard. The wines are deep-coloured with pronounced fruitiness and depth of flavour. Fifteen per cent new oak is used as well as *cuves* for the maturation, but the wines spend only ten months in cask, which adds dimension to the wines without drying them.

Château Les Ormes-Sorbet

Cru Grand Bourgeois. Owner: Jean Boivert. 21ha.
12,000 cases. CS 65%, Mer 30%, CF 2%, PV 2%, Carmenère 1%.

The wines here are nicely perfumed and elegant, with a strong, assertive Cabernet flavour and plenty of structure. Like many wines in the Bas-Médoc, they have lots of flavour but not much body. Note the replanting of Carmenère, an important variety in the pre-phylloxera days, which virtually disappeared due to its flowering problems when grafted. In the '80s robust, solid wines with a distinct *goût de terroir* were made, but the excellent '96 shows more suave style.

This is an excellent example of what the Bas-Médoc can do with care and dedication.

Château Patache-d'Aux

Cru Grand Bourgeois. Owner: SC du Château. Administrator: Patrice Ricard. 43ha. 25,600 cases. CS 70%, Mer 20%, CF 7%,

PV 3%. Second label: Le Relais de Patache-d'Aux.

This *cru* has had a good reputation for many years and belonged to the Delon family (*see* Léoville-Las-Cases and Potensac) until a syndicate of *pieds noirs* headed by Claude Lapalu bought it in 1964. The actual château now belongs to the municipality. The fermentation is still partly in wooden *cuves* and partly in concrete and stainless steel vats, but all the wine is matured in cask with 20 per cent new oak.

The wines are finely perfumed, with clear overtones of violets and Cabernet; finely flavoured, fruity and supple, quite light in body but with a good backbone.

Château Plagnac

Cru Bourgeois. Owner: Domaines Cordier. 33ha. 19,000 cases. CS 70%, Mer 30%.

The present owners acquired this property in Bégadan in 1972 and have brought about many changes and improvements since then: the vineyards have been adapted for mechanical harvesting, stainless steel vats bought in for fermentation, and wooden casks for maturation. This progress has produced consistently attractive wines throughout the '80s and '90s.

Château Pontey

Owner: Quancard family. 11ha. 5,000 cases. CS 60%, Mer 40%.
Second label: Château Vieux Prezat.

Situated partly on the higher plateau of Blaignan, this good *cru* belongs to the family *négociants* Cheval Quancard. They certainly seem to know what the wine-lover looks for. New oak (one third) is cleverly used to show off not smother the sweet fruit, resulting in rich, charming wines that are a joy to drink young, yet can also keep.

Château Potensac

Cru Grand Bourgeois. Owner: Delon family. Administrator: Michel and Jean-Hubert Delon. 52ha. 26,000 cases. CS 60%, Mer 25%, CF 15%. Second labels: Châteaux Gallais-Bellevue and Lassalle, Goudy la Cardonne.

There is a good gravelly outcrop at Potensac lying between St-Yzans and St-Germain-d'Esteuil, where the Delon family (*see* Léoville-Las-Cases) owns four vineyards. Good wines have been made here for years, but in the last two decades, under Michel Delon's management, they seem to have gone from strength to strength. The biggest vineyard is Potensac itself, then come Lassalle, Gallais-Bellevue and Goudy la Cardonne, and the four are effectively run together. The *cuvier* has been re-equipped with stainless steel *cuves*, and the wines enjoy a long, slow fermentation, followed by ageing in casks of which 20 per cent are new each year – with a further proportion from Léoville-Las-Cases. The wines are characterised by their depth of colour and a nose full of vigour, typical of the Médoc, which often has spicy or floral overtones. They have a concentrated, complex and powerful flavour, and a rather angular structure. Usually five or six years are needed before these wines are at their best for drinking, and they last well. The '81, '82, '83, '85, '86, '88, '89, '90, '92, '93, '94 and '95 are all good. This is certainly one of the best wines being made today in the Médoc AC.

Château Preuillac
Cru Bourgeois. Owner: Raymond Bonet. 30ha. 17,000 cases.
Mer 50%, CS 45%, CF 5%.

Lesparre's most important *cru*, Preuillac is one of the best-kept properties in its commune. Vinification is by traditional methods, and due to the high proportion of Merlot the wines tend to be quite full-bodied.

Château Ramafort
Owner: Domaines C.G.R. 15.7ha. 10,000 cases. CS 50%, Mer 50%.

Of the three properties in Blaignan now being run by Eric Fabre for Domaines C.G.R., this now seems to be yielding the best results. Probably the absense of Cabernet Franc gives it the edge over La Cardonne. It recently won the Coupe de Médoc in face of competition from many leading *Crus Bourgeois* from Haut-Médoc. I noted lovely smoky, rich, ripe fruit and more personality than Le Cardonne in the '95, very harmonious, promising '97 and a '98 of real ripeness and excellent potential.

Château Rollan de By
Owner: Jean Guyon. 15ha. 6,500 cases. Mer 70%, CS 25%, PV 5%. Cuvée Special : Château Haut-Condessas.

This property in Bégadan really hit the headlines when its special *cuvée* performed spectacularly on the tasting circuit. The normal wine has length of flavour, supple fruit and an attractive personality. The Condessas really pulls out all the stops including malolactic fermentation in 100 per cent new oak. This is top new-wave wine manipulation, but very well done.

Château Roquegrave
Owner: M M Joannon et Lleu. 30ha. 20,000 cases.
CS 70%, Mer 25%, PV 5%.

A well-known and well distributed property at Valeyrac, the most northerly of the riverside communes of the Médoc. A mixture of *cuves* and casks is used. Decent, straightforward, robust wines.

Château St-Bonnet
Cru Bourgeois 1978. Owner: Michel Solivères. 51ha.
32,000 cases. CS 50%, Mer 50%.

Some excellent wines are made in St-Christoly, and this is one of the most important *crus* there. It is a traditional Médoc with a marked character. The wines are deep in colour with a distinctively spicy bouquet and a robust, powerful flavour where tannin and fruit are well balanced. There is a distinct *goût de terroir* which is arresting but attractive.

Cave Coopérative St-Jean

President: René Chaumont. 455ha. 268,600 cases.
Mer 50%, CS 24%, CF 24%, PV 2%.

The Cave St-Jean, also referred to as the Cave Coopérative de Bégadan, is by far the largest cooperative in the Médoc AC. Its 170 members come not only from this commune but also from the neighbouring ones of Valeyrac and Civrac. The Cave is also a member of Uni-Médoc, a group of four cooperatives which store and mature the wines of the region. The external buildings have a capacity of more than 60,000 hectolitres.

The following châteaux vinify their wines separately at the cave: La Caussade, Le Bernet, Le Monge, Bégadanet, Logis Sipian, Moulin du Bourdieu, Pey-de-Pont, Haut-Condisas and du Verdasse.

The produce of this cooperative has a good reputation. Much of it is supplied to *négociants* for their own generic blends. These wines are characteristic and attractive Médocs.

Cave Coopérative St-Roch

Owner: Société Coopérative de Vinification de Queyrac.
190ha. 113,000 cases.

This cooperative was founded in 1939 and now has 165 members, drawn from the communes of Queyrac, Gaillan, Jau-Dignac-et-Loirac, Vensac, Valeyrac and Vendays. A number of individual *crus* are vinified here: Châteaux du Berton, les Gabriaux, Laubespin, Les Trois-Tétons and Pessange.

The cooperative is a member of the Uni-Médoc and, apart from its own *marque* of St-Roch, a large proportion of the wine made here is sold in bulk to *négociants* for their own blends and contributes to the good overall standard of generic Médoc.

Cave Coopérative de St-Yzans-de-Médoc

Owner: Société Coopérative. 200ha. 111,000 cases.
Mer 55%, CS 40%, CF 2%, PV 2%, Mal 1%.

The cooperative of St-Yzans has 120 members and was established in 1934. The wines are sold under the name of St-Brice or in bulk to *négociants* for their own *marques*. The *cave* has a good reputation for making fine typical Médocs. Apart from those in St-Yzans itself, St-Brice also has members in Blaignan, Couquèques and St-Christoly. Two châteaux, Martignan and La Flanquette, vinify their grapes here. There is some ageing in cask.

Château Sestignan

Cru Bourgeois. Owner: Bertrand de Rozières. 19·5ha.
12,200 cases. CS 60%, Mer 25%, CF 13%, Mal 1%, PV 1%.

On the edge of the Bas-Médoc region, this château is surrounded by alluvial *palus* and drainage ditches. This is a wine that has performed consistently well in a number of comparative tastings. The wines spend 16 months in *cuves* and four months in cask.

When Bertrand de Rozières began with just a few wines in '73, he was one of the first to begin the reconstruction of the vineyards of Jau-Dignac-et-Loirac which had been completely abandoned after the war. It is therefore a *cru* to look out for. There is a charming '96.

Château Sigognac

Cru Grand Bourgeois. Owner: SC Fermière.
Administrator: Colette Bonny-Grasset. 45ha. 25,000 cases.
CS 33·3%, CF 33·3%, Mer 33·3%.

A Roman villa once stood on this site, and some of the pottery found here may be seen at the *mairie* (town hall) at St-Yzans. This vineyard had been reduced to only four hectares of vines when Paul Grasset bought it in 1964. It was then transformed, first by him and then, after his death in 1968, by his wife, now married to M Bonny. The fermentation is in concrete vats and the wine is matured partly in vat and partly in cask, with 20 per cent new oak. The wine has a good colour and is full and soft on the nose, with pleasant fruit and tannin on the palate: elegant rather than powerful. If it lacks the finesse of its more illustrious neighbour, Château Loudenne, it is nevertheless a pleasant, honourable Médoc of a good general standard.

Château La Tour-de-By

Cru Grand Bourgeois. Owner: SC (Cailloux, Lapalu, Pagès).
Administrator: Marc Pagès. 73ha. 46,000 cases. CS 58%,
Mer 36%, CF 4%, PV 2%. Second labels: Châteaux La Roque-de-
By and Moulin-de-la-Roque, Cailloux de By.

This fine *cru*, on one of the highest and best gravelly ridges in the whole of the Bas-Médoc, has an attractive château and parts of the other old buildings are also pleasing. The tower, an old lighthouse, stands on high ground nearby. Since buying the property in 1965, Marc Pagès and his partners have made many improvements. They have expanded the *chai* and installed some stainless steel (retaining the old wooden *cuves*). The wine, matured in cask with 20 per cent new oak, is deeply coloured and finely scented, and the lively, sappy fruit is often reminiscent of violets. The flavour is harmonious and attractive; it is also powerful, with real depth, and quite tannic. Other marked characteristics are elegance and length of flavour. This château certainly has a good claim to be considered as the finest wine of the Médoc appellation.

The special position of the vineyard paid off in '91 when it was much less frosted than most in the northern Médoc, and an excellent wine was made from first-generation grapes. The consistent quality can be judged by the wines made in '92 and '93.

Château La Tour-Haut-Caussan

Cru Bourgeois. Owner: Philippe Courrian. 16ha. 10,000 cases.
CS 50%, Mer 50%. Second label: La Landotte.

A windmill dating from 1734 stands on this property in Blaignan and is evidence of the polyculture that held sway in this part of the Médoc before the 19th century. The current owner comes from a family of true Médocains, whose history here is traceable to 1615. He believes in traditional methods of viticulture, and vinification is carried out with the utmost care, using high temperatures for the fermentation of his Merlots and lower temperatures for the Cabernets. The wines are then blended and matured in oak, 33 per cent of which is new. The results have been successful and won many awards, the wines are in high demand from good French restaurants but are also widely distributed in France and on the export markets.

Château La Tour-St-Bonnet

Cru Bourgeois. Owner: Pierre Jacques Merlet-Lafon. 40ha. 17,000 cases. Mer 50%, CS 28%, CF 22%. Second label: Château La-Fuie-St-Bonnet.

This is the largest and probably the best known *cru* in St-Christoly. The vineyard is splendidly placed on the best gravelly ridges of the commune, with its distinctive tower among the vines. The wines, typical of the Médoc, are highly coloured, vigorous and powerful. They require some ageing to show of their best.

Château La Valière

Cru Bourgeois. Owner: Cailloux family. 15ha. 7,500 cases. CS 74%, Mer 25%, PV 1%.

Situated on the gravelly ridges of St-Christoly, this château is one of the best in its commune, producing charmingly fruity wines with good solidity. Consistent wines are made here.

Château Vernous

Cru Bourgeois. Owner: Champagne Deutz. Administrator: André Lallier. 21ha. 11,000 cases. CS 70%, Mer 23%, PV 7%. Second label: La Marche de Vermous.

Deutz invested a great deal in this good Lesparre *cru* in the 1980s. The vineyard has one of the few gravelly *croupes* (ridges) in this part of the Médoc. One-third new wood is used in the maturation. This is stylish, well-made wine.

Vieux Château Landon

Cru Bourgeois. Owner: Philippe Gillet. 40ha. 17,800 cases. CS 70%, Mer 25%, Mal 5%.

This property has been in the same family for several generations. The present owner married his predecessor's daughter. It is one of a number of excellent *crus* in the commune of Bégadan and produces attractive wines with lots of fruit and plenty of Médocain character.

Caves Les Vieux Colombiers

Owner: Uni-Médoc. 310ha. 165,000 cases. CS 50%, Mer 40%, CF 10%

This large cooperative, located in Prignac, collects the produce of 200 members in this commune and also those of Lesparre and St-Germain-d'Esteuil. It also produces two independent *crus* which are vinified separately: Château de Beusse and Château Lafon.

Château Le Vivier
Owner: Domaines C.G.R. 8ha. 5,000 cases.
CS 50%, Mer 50%.
This is still a very young vineyard, and because of this Eric Fabre (*see* La Cardonne and Ramafort) keeps the wine entirely in stainless steel and bottles early. This preserves the fruit. Despite the wines still being fairly simple and on the light side, there is definitely good potential here.

Graves

It is not easy to get to grips with this disparate region. Geographically, it is a continuation of the Médoc, but in the north many vineyards have disappeared beneath Bordeaux's urban sprawl, and further south one can travel for miles, see nothing but trees and believe one is already in Les Landes. This used to be a region of many mediocre whites and a few aristocratic reds, but this picture has changed significantly in the past 30 years. The changes can be gauged to an extent from the following tables comparing production figures for 1976 and 1996. Since the region is now divided into two appellations, Pessac-Léognan and Graves, I have shown these figures separately for 1996:

	1976 (hl)	1998 (hl)	Increase (hl)
Graves Rouge	} 57,760	124,692 }	118,102 (+204%)
Pessac-Léognan		51,170	
Graves Blanc		50,590	
Pessac-Léognan	} 48,243	14,192 }	22,195 (+36%)
Graves Supérieur	13,708	19,356	
	119,711	260,008	140,297 (+117%)

This demonstrates the two important trends: from white to red, and from alcoholic whites (12 per cent minimum alcohol by volume, plus some residual sugar) to drier, lighter (11 per cent) ones. The term Graves Supérieur refers to the higher alcohol level: such wines usually also have some residual sugar. Until 1975, more Graves Supérieur than Graves Sec was made: in '95 and '96 there was a large increase. The table also shows the revival in the district as a whole, with total production up 117 per cent. Over a similar period, the areas under vine have developed as follows:

	1976 (ha)	1996 (ha)	Increase (ha)
Graves Rouge	} 1,230	2,128 }	1,889 (+154%)
Pessac-Léognan		991	
Graves Blanc		809	
Pessac-Léognan	} 1,393	282 }	397 (+28%)
Graves Supérieur		699	
	2,623	4,909	2,286 (+87%)

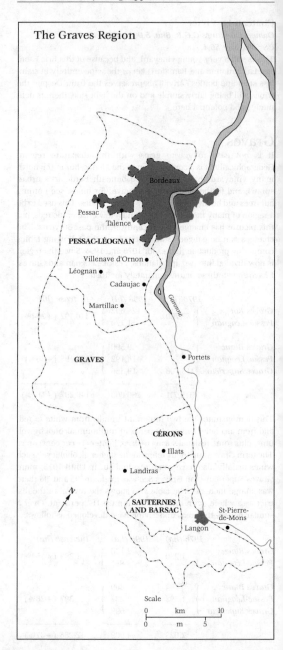

The Graves Region

Bordeaux

Pessac
Talence

PESSAC-LÉOGNAN

Villenave d'Ornon ●
Léognan ●
Cadaujac ●
Martillac ●

Garonne

GRAVES

● Portets

CÉRONS

● Illats

● Landiras

**SAUTERNES
AND BARSAC**

St-Pierre-
de-Mons
Langon ●

N

Scale

0   km   10
0   m   5

While the major expansion has been in the red wine vineyards, there has been some increase in the white wine vineyards, following a lengthy decline. New vineyards and better husbandry have brought much higher yields. The 1982 edition of Cocks & Féret's *Bordeaux et ses Vins* monitors the decline of the vineyards which have been caught up in the expansion of the town of Bordeaux. In the four communes most affected, Gradignan, Mérignac, Pessac and Talence, there were 119 winemaking properties in 1908; by 1981 there were only nine. In the whole of Graves in 1981 there were 33 communes where some declarations under the Graves AC were being made (in several others entitled to the appellation, only Bordeaux or Bordeaux Supérieur was declared). Most of the wines are made in eight communes: Léognan and Martillac in the north; Portets, Illats, Cérons, St-Pierre-de-Mons, and Langon and Landiras in the south. Of these, Illats and Cérons produce both Cérons and Graves, though 80 per cent of the whites made in these communes seem to be declared as Graves, as are the reds, and the proportion is rising.

There are plenty of hopeful signs that the region is coming out of its long decline. There is the general improvement in the quality of dry white Graves through the use of cold-fermentation methods; the gospel preached by Professor Peynaud in the 1960s has been put into practice by men like André Lurton and Pierre Coste. André Lurton, for example, has reclaimed large tracts of abandoned vineyards in the best parts of the northern Graves; Pierre Coste has made delicious and inexpensive white and red wines in the southern Graves, and Denis Dubourdieu and Peter Vinding-Diers have shown how the whole gamut of modern technology, including yeast selection, can transform the quality of wines coming from even modest sites in the southern Graves. Recently there has been a strong movement back to cask fermentation, with excellent results.

There are differing views as to the best *encépagement* for white wines. Traditionally the Sauvignon and Sémillon are blended. The Sauvignon gives the initial fruit, on the nose especially, and acidity while Sémillon provides the possibility of bottle-ageing, its bouquet gradually taking over as the Sauvignon begins to fade after one to two years in bottle. Sémillon also gives the wine body. However, in the search for freshness and fruit for early drinking, some properties have abandoned Sémillon entirely. Such wines tend to lose their charm rather quickly and my impression is that many growers are now realising that this grape has a role to play in giving balance.

The list of red wines available ranges from some of the greatest wines in Gironde (Haut-Brion, La Mission-Haut-Brion, Domaine de Chevalier, Haut-Bailly and Pape-Clément) to a host of modestly priced and deliciously vivid wines of individuality. All have Cabernet Sauvignon as their major grape variety, assisted by Merlot and Cabernet Franc.

It is taking time to bring the wine-drinker back to an appreciation of white Graves, so poor has its image been. But as more and more fine wines come onto the market at reasonable prices, their following is bound to grow. As far as the red wines are concerned, the special charm of those whose blend is based on Cabernet, which are quite distinct in character from their Médocain cousins, will surely win them more friends as they become more widely available.

On the quality front, the growers in the north have now won the right to the appellation Pessac-Léognan, which came into force in 1987, with the '86 vintage the first to bear the new title. It covers the communes of Cadaujac, Canéjean, Gradignan, Léognan, Martillac, Mérignac, Pessac, St-Médard-d'Eyrans, Talence and Villenave-d'Ornon. André Lurton, who has done so much to revive the vineyards of this area, was the driving force behind this new appellation.

So the prospect of Graves taking a larger share of Bordeaux's prosperity in the future looks bright. The worldwide demand for good dry white wines and the continuously growing market for middle-price red wines of quality must make Graves a happy hunting ground for wine-lovers.

PESSAC-LÉOGNAN

Château Baret

Owner: Héritiers A Ballande.
Red: 13ha. 6,500 cases. CS 60%, Mer 35%, CF 5%.
White: 5ha. 2,500 cases. Sém 65%, Sauv 32%, Musc 3%.
Philippe Castéja has run this property since 1981, when he took over after the death of his father-in-law André Ballande. He commercialises the wines through the family's *négociant* house of Borie-Manoux.

Although Château Baret's wines have always had a good reputation, there has been a marked improvement in vintages of recent years. The red wines are light but have depth and plenty of spicy fruit. The whites are stylish, classic wines.

Château Bouscaut

Cru Classé. Owner: SA du Château Bouscaut (Sophie and Louis Lurton). Red: 37ha. 22,000 cases. Mer 55%, CS 35%, CF 5%, Mal 5%. White: 8ha. 3,300 cases. Sém 70%, Sauv 30%.
Second label: Valoux.
The only important *cru* in Cadaujac, and the Graves Cru Classé closest to the Garonne. Between 1968 and 1980 an American syndicate led by Charles Wohlstetter rescued the property from neglect by installing up-to-date equipment and restoring the 18th-century château. During this period, Jean Delmas, *régisseur* of Haut-Brion, acted as *régisseur* here. In 1980 the Americans sold to Lucien Lurton, proprietor of Brane-Cantenac and Durfort-Vivens in Margaux as well as Climens in Barsac.

The vineyards, which adjoin the Bordeaux-Toulouse road, are on gravelly ridges over limestone: perfect for natural drainage. Stainless steel vats are used for red and white wines and the whites are fermented at 18–20°C (64–68°F). The reds are matured in casks of which a quarter are new, and the whites are also cask-aged, spending six months in wood.

I must confess to disappointment at the Bouscaut wines of recent vintages. The reds are relatively light in colour and body, supple and pleasant but lacking in personality or any real distinction, although there has been some improvement, notably with the '85. To put it in context, there are a number of Crus Bourgeois in the Médoc that make better wine.

The white wines often seem to lack breed and 'lift' or projection of flavour, though the '83 was an improvement, and '85 and '88 were even better. In 1994 Lucien Lurton handed the property to his daughter Sophie. His son Louis oversees the winemaking. The new generation is already making a perceptible difference.

Château Brown

Owner: Bernard Barthe.
Red: 21ha. 10,000 cases. CS 70%, Mer 25%, PV 5%.
White: 4ha. 2,100 cases. Sauv 70%, Sém 25%, Musc 5%.
Second label: Le Colombier (red and white).

This property takes its name from the family that owned Cantenac-Brown until the middle of the last century. Its vineyards are well situated on two gravel ridges in the commune of Léognan. The present owner acquired the property in 1994, and has re-equipped the cellars and carried out drainage work in the vineyards. The previous owners had already worked on the vineyards and were producing attractive wines, but '94 and '95 show a big improvement. A delicious cask-fermented white is also made.

Château Carbonnieux

Cru Classé. Owner: Société des Grandes Graves. Administrator: Antony Perrin. Red: 41ha. 13,000 cases. CS 60%, Mer 30%, CF 7%, Mal 2%, PV 1%. White: 37ha. 12,000 cases. Sauv 65%, Sém 34%, Musc 1%. Second label: La Tour Léognan.

This famous old property first had vineyards in the 12th century, and winemaking was revived by the Benedictine monks who took over in 1741. Marc Perrin bought and restored the property in 1956, and his son now administers the estate. The white wine is fermented in stainless steel and used to see no wood at all, but recently has been put in new oak for about three months. The reds are matured in cask, of which a third are new oak.

The more famous white Carbonnieux comes from the largest vineyard of the Graves Crus Classés. The high proportion of Sauvignon and early bottling mean that it is delicious when young (nine to 18 months), then often goes through a dull stage as the primary Sauvignon fruit fades, only to emerge again as the Sémillon begins to mature and flower (after about two and a half years). In recent years this has been a most consistent wine, the best of the Crus Classés available in commercial quantities.

The red has been rather rustic, and is not among the top classified Graves, but determined efforts have been made in recent vintages to improve the quality. The '85, '86, '88, '89 and '90 have all shown more structure and breed than was evident in the past.

Château Les Carmes-Haut-Brion

Owner: Chantecaille family. Administrator: Didier Furt.
3·9ha. 2,000 cases. Mer 50%, CF 40%, CS 10%.

The unusual combination of grape varieties yields wines that are concentrated, have deep colour and tannin, but which are rather coarse. This may be due to the low percentage of Cabernet Sauvignon. The wine has been château-bottled only since 1985.

Domaine de Chevalier

Cru Classé. Owner: SC du Château. Administrator: Olivier
Bernard. Red: 31ha. 16,700 cases. CS 65%, Mer 30%, CF 5%.
White: 4ha. 2,000 cases. Sauv 70%, Sém 30%.

From 1865 to 1983 Chevalier was the property of the Ricard family, and Claude Ricard owned it from 1948. He was obliged to sell but the new owners, the Bernard family, contracted him to manage the *cru* for a further five years and pass on his vast experience to Olivier Bernard, who was deputed to look after the property. The red wine is fermented at a slightly higher temperature than is fashionable, 32°C (90°F), to facilitate the maximum tannin extraction from the grape skins. For the maturation in cask 50 per cent new oak is used. The white wine fermentation takes place entirely in cask at a low temperature, the wine is then matured in oak (a small proportion of which is new) for 18 months – a traditional practice that was for a time abandoned elsewhere in Graves, but has now been revived. The results of this meticulous winemaking are exceptional wines. The reds are deep in colour, the bouquet takes time to open out and is then complex, with overtones of tobacco, while the flavour is compact and well structured with great breed, power and length of flavour. This wine in some years can approach the quality of Haut-Brion and La Mission. It is also a slow developer. The '76 and '80 were charming examples of their years while outstanding wines were made in '78, '79, '81, '82, '83, '85, '86, '88, '89, '90, '95 and '98.

The white wine has a different style from that of Laville or Haut-Brion, perhaps because of its cask-ageing. It is perfumed, firm and compact of flavour and slowly opens out only after six to eight years. It has extraordinary delicacy and finesse, and can improve and last for 15 to 20 years.

Château Couhins

Cru Classé. Owner: Institut National de la Recherche
Agronomique. Red: 10·8ha. 5,600 cases. CS 48%, Mer 40%,
CF 11%, PV 1%.
White: 4ha. 1,700 cases. Sauv 80%, Sém 20%.

A curious situation exists at Couhins, which is now divided between the National Agricultural Research Institute (INRA), which owns the main part, and André Lurton, who has a smaller section (*see* Couhins-Lurton). For many years the Gasqueton and Hanappier families were owners and produced only white wines (this is the sole property in Graves where only the white wine is classified). Then the INRA bought the property in 1968.

The estate lies on an elevated site in Villenave-d'Ornon, with vineyards near the Garonne. The modern, low-temperature-fermented wine, is fresh and elegant. Unfortunately, with the division of the property and the production of unclassified red wine, the small quantities available mean that it is hard to find.

Château Couhins-Lurton

Cru Classé. Owner: André Lurton. White: 6ha. 3,000 cases.
Sauv 100%. Second label: Château Cantebau.

André Lurton began as *fermier* here in 1967, just before the INRA bought out Gasqueton-Hanappier, and made the wine for the whole of Couhins during most of the 1970s. The INRA then took a major part of the property into their own control and André Lurton was able to buy this part. The gravelly soil has traces of clay in the subsoil and this gives body to the wine. Unlike the INRA part, which is classically planted with both Sémillon and Sauvignon, this vineyard is 100 per cent Sauvignon. Fermentation takes place in new casks (since 1982) at 16–18°C (61–64°F), followed by ten months' ageing before bottling. Generally these wines are at their most attractive at between two and four years due to the Sauvignon. There are plans to plant Cabernet Sauvignon and Merlot to produce red wines, and the white vineyard, already extended from 1·5 to six hectares, will be further enlarged. In 1992 André Lurton bought the château and *chais* from the INRA, and he has now renovated both. Classic wines were made here in '96, '97 and '98.

Château du Cruzeau

Owner: André Lurton. Red: 42ha. 20,000 cases.
CS 55%, Mer 43%, CF 2%.
White: 18ha. 10,000 cases. Sauv 85%, Sém 15%.

Another outpost of André Lurton's viticultural empire, this is the most important St-Médard-d'Eyrans *cru* and lies on the borders of that commune and Martillac. Acquired by André Lurton in 1973, the vineyard, on deep gravel, was entirely replanted by 1974.

Harvesting of the red grapes is by machine, while the white are hand-picked. The red is vinified in lined cement tanks and stainless steel vats at 28–30°C (82–86°F), then matured for a year in casks of which a third are new. The white is vinified in stainless steel and glass-lined steel vats at 16–18°C (61–64°F) and sees no new wood before bottling. The red wine is scented, full-bodied, fruity and supple, with the capacity for ageing but is also pleasant to drink after about three or four years. The white has a subtle aroma of spring blossom allied to a pleasant fruitiness of flavour. Compared with Rochemorin the red wine here is richer and finer, while the white emphasises its finesse and breed.

Château Ferran

Owner: Hervé Béraud-Sadreau. Red: 9ha. 5,300 cases.
Mer 60%, CS 30%, CF 10%.
White: 5ha. 2,800 cases. Sauv 60%, Sém 40%.

This property takes its name from Robert de Ferrand, proprietor during the 17th century and member of the Parlement de Bordeaux. In 1715 it changed hands and was run by the philosopher Montesquieu. The red and white wines are long-lived and need time for their sound fruit characteristics to develop.

Château de Fieuzal

Cru Classé. Owner: SA Château de Fieuzal.
Administrator: Gérard Gribelin. 35ha. Red: 12,000 cases.
CS 65%, Mer 25%, PV 5%, CF 5%. White: 9ha. 2,500 cases.
Sauv 50%, Sém 50%. Second label: l'Abeille de Fieuzal.

In 1945 a Swede, Erik Bocké, acquired this property which was then in ruinous condition, and restored it. In 1974 the present proprietor took over and has continued developments in the same vein.

The red wines are fermented in lined steel vats equipped with an electronic temperature-control system, and are then matured in casks, of which 60 per cent are new. They are well made: on the light side, but with elegance and a vivid fruity character. Since the '85 vintage there has been a marked filling-out, and recent wines show an extra dimension of concentration and depth of flavour that now puts them in contention with those of such leading *crus* such as Haut-Bailly and Chevalier. The Graves character is there, but is not too obtrusive. The reputation of this wine has grown steadily in recent years.

The change in the white wine has been even more dramatic. From 1985, it has been barrel-fermented under the supervision of Denis Dubourdieu, the white wine guru. They have become intensely scented and quite rich, and are now fetching some of the highest prices in Graves.

Château de France

Owner: Bernard Thomassin. Red: 28ha. 16,500 cases.
CS 55%, Mer 40%, CF 5%.
White: 3ha. 1,100 cases. Sauv 50%, Sém 30%, Musc 20%.

Situated just south of Léognan, this property was replanted and refurbished by Bernard Thomassin, who bought it in 1971. The white wine vineyards are still young, but some deliciously aromatic fruity wines have been made since '93. The reds are developing well, producing good vintages from '83 onwards.

This is certainly a property worth watching.

Château La Garde

Owner: Maison Dourthe. Red: 45ha, 25,000 cases.
CS 65%, Mer 35%. White: 5ha. 2,500 cases. Sauv 100%.
Second label: Château Naudin Larchay.

After belonging to Louis Eschenauer since 1926, this *cru* was sold to Dourthe in 1990. A substantial programme of development has been undertaken here in recent years. Not only has the red wine vineyard been expanded, but an elegant pure Sauvignon white wine has been introduced. The red wine has succulent juicy fruit and some complexity.

Château Haut-Bailly

Cru Classé. Owner: Robert G. Wilmers. Administrator: Jean
Sanders. Red: 28ha. 16,000 cases. CS 65%, Mer 25%, CF 10%.
Second label: la Parde de Haut-Bailly.

Today Haut-Bailly is regarded as one of the best red Graves properties, just behind Pape-Clément and often vying with Chevalier. The
soil is abundant in gravel and pebbles, mixed with sand and clay.

The wine is often lighter in colour and texture than the other
top red Graves, but the great feature is its harmony. It has both
richness and vinosity, reminiscent of La Mission but with less tannin and power; the bouquet is strikingly similar to Pape-Clément.
Thus the wines often develop quickly at first, yet keep well.

In 1998 the Sanders family sold to the present owner, an
American with strong Belgian links. Happily Jean Sanders still
oversees the winemaking, as he has since 1978. There were great
successes in '79, '81, '82, '83 and '85. Exceptionally concentrated
wines were made in '86. The '88, '89, '90, '93, '94, '95, '96 and '98
are all wines of great potential.

Château Haut-Bergey

Owner: Mme Garcin-Cathiard. Red: 17ha. 8,900 cases.
CS 70%, Mer 30%. White: 1ha. 600 cases. Sauv 70%, Sém 30%.

In 1991 Mme Garcin-Cathiard, sister of Daniel Cathiard of Smith-
Haut-Lafitte, bought this well placed Léognan vineyard. There
has been considerable investment in the *cuvier* and *chai*.

The first vintage of the new white wine was '91, and by the '94
vintage the wine, which was entirely fermented in barrel, was looking fine and distinguished. The reds now also seem more
polished, with better focused fruit and charm. This *cru* shows
considerable potential.

Château Haut-Brion

1er Cru Classé 1855. Owner: Domaine Clarence Dillon.
Red: 43ha. 16,000 cases. CS 50%, Mer 35%, CF 15%.
White: 2·7ha. 900 cases. Sém 55%, Sauv 45%.
Second label: de Bahans du Château Haut-Brion.

Haut-Brion is the only wine outside the Médoc to feature in the
1855 classification of red wines. In 1935 it was acquired by
Clarence Dillon, the American banker. Since 1979, Clarence
Dillon's grand-daughter Joan, the Duchesse de Mouchy, has been
president of the company, and her husband director-general. The
much-respected Jean Delmas succeeded his father as *régisseur* in
1961 and is now technical director. In 1960 this was the first of the
great *crus* to install stainless steel fermentation vats.

The essence of the Haut-Brion style today can be summarised
as elegance and harmony. The tannin, new oak (100 per cent
each year) and fruit seem to be in balance after the first few
months. This can give the wine the appearance of being ready to
drink early. I remember my disbelief at the forwardness of the '75
in 1979. But, while this wine is more forward and more enjoyable
than most leading wines of '75, there is also no doubting its ability to age well.

The great successes here in recent vintages are '82, '83, '85, '86, '88, '89 and '90. In the challenging 1990s, '91 is one of the few successes of the vintage, better than '92; '93 is one of the best wines of the vintage with '94 of similar quality. The '95, '96, '97 and '98 are all superb. Haut-Brion seems to be on a high at the moment.

The small quantity of white wine produced makes it a rarity, and most of it seems to go to the US. It appears to show its charm more quickly than the Laville, though the wine seems to go through a period of change while ageing.

Château Haut Lagrange

Owner: François Bouterny. Red: 12ha. 6,000 cases.
CS 50%, Mer 45%, CF 5%.
White: 3ha. 1,400 cases. Sauv 50%, Sém 45%, Sauv Gris 5%.
This new vineyard in Léognan has been created by François Bouterny who, after the sale of his family's neighbouring property, Larrivet-Haut-Brion, continued to advise there for a time.

The first vintage to be commercialised was '92, and I was pleasantly surprised to find a wine with such glorious fruit flavour, with length and body, from young vines in this vintage. It certainly bodes well for the future. The white, with its interesting use of Sauvignon Gris, was aromatic and complex.

Château Larrivet-Haut-Brion

Owner: Gerverson family. Administrator: Philippe Gerverson.
Red: 35ha. 17,800 cases. CS 55%, Mer 45%.
White: 10ha. 5,000 cases. Sauv 60%, Sém 35%, Musc 5%.
A famous old property in the central sector of Léognan, adjoining Haut-Bailly. It was called Haut-Brion-Larrivet until a lawsuit from Haut-Brion compelled a change. The Guillemaud family owned the property from 1941 and sold to the present owners in 1988.

This is a classic Graves with a fine colour and a spicy, delicate bouquet. Wines have finesse and age well. Usually they are as good or better than some of the red Crus Classés. The white wine has not been of the same standard, but with fermentation in cask from '87, better things can be expected. The '96 vintage saw a spectacular improvement with the involvement of Jean-Michel Arcaute (*see* Château Clinet). Both red and white wines are superb and show that this property is capable of moving up a class.

Château Laville-Haut-Brion

Cru Classé. Owner: Domaine Clarence Dillon.
White: 3·7ha. 1,100 cases. Sém 70%, Sauv 27%, Musc 3%.
The history of this tiny vineyard follows that of Château La Mission-Haut-Brion, where the wine is vinified, matured and bottled. The soil here is richer and less stony than that of La Mission or La Tour-Haut-Brion, and this contributes to the wines' remarkable keeping powers. The vinification is in cask and not *cuve* and takes place in an air-conditioned cellar. From 1961, the wines were bottled in the late spring after the vintage, but since the '85 vintage Jean Delmas has reverted to a longer cask maturation, bottling in the March of the second winter.

With Chevalier, this is the great example of classic white Graves. Full-bodied, its complex flavour and character evolves only gradually. The wines differ from year to year in weight and power, so the speed at which they evolve varies. These are long-lived wines: the '34 was still superb in 1989; and 'off' vintages such as '35 are a delightful surprise. After some austere vintages from '78 to '83, the wines are now richer and more harmonious; '84, '85, '86, '87, '88, '89, '90, '91 (only 12 casks were made) '92, '93 and '94 were all excellent, while '95 and '96 are exceptional.

Château La Louvière

Owner: André Lurton. Red: 35ha. 18,000 cases.
CS 64%, Mer 30%, CF 3%, PV 3%. White: 15ha. 7,500 cases.
Sauv 85%, Sém 15%. Second label: L de La Louvière.
This old property, which is a historical monument, has been largely restored and reconstructed by the dynamic André Lurton, who has owned it since 1965.

The white wine of Louvière has been notable for its outstanding finesse, delicacy and fruit since the '70 vintage at least. it certainly deserves to be Cru Classé. The red has made steady progress. The wines during the 1970s were vivid in colour, quite tannic but light-textured and had a tendency to be rather one-dimensional. However, the balance has recently improved. The '85 was better than a number of Crus Classés and the '86, more tannic but also opulent, was perhaps even finer. The '95 and '96 were outstandingly successful here. This is now a wine on a par with those of Pessac-Léognan's leading *crus*, and should feature in a new Graves classification.

Château Malartic-Lagravière

Cru Classé. Owner: Alfred Alexandre Bonnie. 15ha. Red: 8,300 cases. CS 50%, CF 25%, Mer 25%.
White: 4ha. 1,000 cases. Sauv 85%, Sém 15%.
This is a well-positioned vineyard on a high platform of gravelly soil, just southeast of the town of Léognan. Malartic, after remaining in the same family since 1850 (the Ricards – *see* Chevalier – then through marriage to Marlys), was sold in 1990 to the family Champagne firm of Laurent-Perrier then resold to the current owner in 1997. Since then major investments have been made to installations and vineyards. The red and white wines are vinified in stainless steel vats, the white at a temperature not exceeding 18°C (64°F). The red wines are matured in casks, of which a third are new, the white in one-year-old casks for about seven months.

The red wines have a marked Graves character without a lot of weight or flesh, but with a clean, fresh flavour and good fruit. There are signs of improvement under the new regime. The white wine is one of the most attractive of white Graves with an outstanding bouquet and real individuality. It develops quickly and for me is at its best in its youthful phase. In the 1990s a little Sémillon was introduced into what had been a 100 per cent Sauvignon wine, which should add complexity. A consistent wine.

Château La Mission-Haut-Brion

Cru Classé. Owner: Domaine Clarence Dillon.
Red: 27ha. 7,500 cases. CS 48%, Mer 45%, CF 7%.
Second label: La Chapelle de la Mission-Haut-Brion.

When the all-too-familiar problems of succession caused the Woltner heirs to put La Mission on the market in 1983 it was logical that their neighbours across the road at Haut-Brion should decide to buy. These two properties now constitute an oasis of vines surrounded by housing, much of it built on former vineyards between the two World Wars. Henri Woltner, who mas- terminded the vinification here from 1921 until his death in 1974, was responsible for installing between 1926 and 1950 a system of glass-lined steel vats to enable better control of the fermentation. La Mission was probably the first property in Bordeaux to ferment its red wines at around 28°C (82°F) as a consistent policy, and in 1987 the old *cuvier* was replaced by the latest stainless steel mod- els. The wine is matured in 100 per cent new casks. The gravel in the vineyard is of exceptional depth and results in low yields and great concentration of flavour.

The wine of La Mission is rich and powerful, whereas that of Haut-Brion is all finesse and delicacy. Clearly La Mission is a Premier Cru in all but name. Its price has yearly been edging closer to that of the Premiers Crus Classés, and since it has belonged to Domaine Clarence Dillon, the opening price has on occasion been only ten francs a bottle below that of the best of the Médoc.

The quality and individuality of this wine is outstanding. Always deep in colour, it is rich and concentrated in flavour with- out being uncomfortably tannic. It needs to evolve and lasts well. It also has a wonderful record for successes in 'off' vintages. Classic wines were made in '75 and '76; '78 and '79 were quite splendid; '80 was fine and '81, '82, '83, '85, '86, '88, '89 and '90 were all excep- tional. The '91, '93, '94, '95, '96, '97 and '98 were exceptional in these vintages. The second wine was introduced in '91.

Château Olivier

Cru Classé. Owner: GFA Château Olivier.
Administrator: Jean-Jacques de Bethmann.
Red: 30ha. 14,500 cases. CS 51%, Mer 41%, CF 8%.
White: 14ha. 6,000 cases. Sém 48%, Sauv 44%, Musc 8%.

For over 70 years this famous estate was farmed by Eschenauer, the *négociants*, and was their monopoly. Then in November 1981 the Bethmann family took the management back into their own hands and Jean-Jacques de Bethmann assumed responsibility for running the property. The distribution remained in Eschenauer's hands until 1987, but for only part of the crop. The vineyard was radically reconstructed in the early to mid-1970s with a view to increasing the size of the red vineyard and ensur- ing that the grape varieties were planted on the most favourable soils. After good efforts in '82 and '85, progress has been rather disappointing and many wines seem to suffer from too much new oak for their weight.

The white wine is what Olivier has always been known for. With the high proportion of Sémillon you must not expect the instant charm the Sauvignon gives in the first months of bottle-ageing, but the wines do become more interesting. The flavour is marked and individual with plenty of character. The '95 marks an important advance in quality.

Château le Pape

Owner: GFA du Château Le Pape. Administrator: Antony Perrin. 5ha. 3,000 cases. Mer 95%, CS 5%.

This property has a particularly attractive château, built in the style of the First Empire. Antony Perrin has been administrator for a comparatively short while and it will be interesting to see what changes he makes. An unusually small proportion of Cabernet Sauvignon is grown here, but the vines are young and the full impact of this *encépagement* is yet to be revealed.

Château Pape-Clément

Cru Classé. Owner: Montagne family. 30ha. Red: 13,000 cases. CS 60%, Mer 40%. White: 2·9ha. 900 cases. Sém 45%, Sauv 45%, Musc 10%. Second label: Le Clémentin du Pape-Clément.

The vineyard here has the longest continuous history of any in Bordeaux, having been first planted in 1300. This is a red wine château, although the white wine production has been expanded in the 1990s. The soil is sand and gravel and there are traces of iron. After traditional vinification, wine is matured in new oak.

The wines of Pape-Clément have a marvellous bouquet, intense with overtones of tobacco, and a supple, rich texture that enables them to be enjoyed relatively young. But after some wonderful vintages in the 1960s, Pape-Clément was disturbingly inconsistent for a number of years. After a good '75 came a string of small and often dilute wines. Even the '82 was disappointing. With the appointment of Bernard Pujols in 1985, however, and the completion of a new *cuvier* and re-equipped *chai*, Pape-Clément returned to its real form with the '85, and since then '86, '88, '89 and '90 have produced wines to set beside the great vintages of the 1960s. The '93 and '94 were excellent for the years and exceptional wines were made in '95, '96 and '98. In reputation Pape-Clément has overtaken Chevalier in recent vintages.

Château Picque-Caillou

Owner: Alphonse Denis. 20ha. 12,000 cases. Mer 40%, CS 40%, CF 20%. White: 0·8ha. 500 cases. Sém 50%, Sauv 50%.

This vineyard lies on gravelly and stony soil, surrounded by the sprawling suburbs of Bordeaux. The wines have a good reputation for being stylish, supple and full-flavoured. They usually evolve fairly quickly and also keep well. Wines of breed.

Château Pontac-Monplaisir

Owner: Jean Maufras. Red: 7ha. 4,500 cases. CS 50%, Mer 50%. White: 8ha. 3,000 cases. Sauv 60%, Sém 40%. Second label: Château Limbourg.

An old *cru*, dating back to the 1600s, this property is recorded on Cassini's map produced in the 18th century. The vineyards themselves are not the original ones as these were sold by the present owner and a supermarket now stands on its site. Much care and attention has been put into the winemaking and the results are elegant, scented reds with the character and breed typical of Graves; the whites are stylish with plenty of varietal Sémillon; the Limbourg whites have more Sauvignon character.

Château de Rochemorin

Owner: André Lurton.
Red: 47ha. 25,000 cases. CS 60%, Mer 40%.
White: 17ha. 9,000 cases. Sauv 90%, Sém 10%.
The name of this château is derived from 'Roche-Morine', indicating that it was a fortified palace at the time of the Moorish incursions from Spain in the 7th and 8th centuries. The energetic André Lurton bought this old property in 1973 and began replanting the vineyards (which had been replaced by forest) in 1974. The vines are on deep gravel on the highest ridge of Martillac. As at other Lurton properties, harvesting is mechanical for the reds and manual for the whites. Fermentation is controlled at 28–30°C (82–86°F) for the reds and 16–18°C (61–64°F) for the whites. The reds are matured for a year in cask, with one-third new wood, but the whites see no wood at all.

The red wines now show quite a spicy, aromatic Graves bouquet allied to elegance and breed, and are lighter and more marked by new oak than those of nearby Cruzeau. Even from '81 fine wines were being made here, and by the late 1980s they were filling out and moving into a higher gear. The white wine is different from that of Cruzeau. It has a less floral bouquet and more body, but is elegant, with a finish that is flinty and drier than that of Cruzeau. Now that the vineyard has gained maturity, the red wines especially have more structure and character.

Château de Rouillac

Owner: P Sarthou. 10ha. 5,600 cases. CS 75%, Mer 25%.
Once the only *cru* left in the commune of Canéjean (it lost this distinction when Château Séguin was replanted in 1987) Rouillac has an attractive château, built by the architect Baron Haussmann in 1869. The Sarthous are using the most up-to-date equipment for vinification and the vineyards have recently been replanted. The wines produced since their first vintage in '78 are well balanced and full of Graves character.

Château Le Sartre

Owner: GFA du Château Le Sartre. Administrator: Antony Perrin. Red: 18ha. 5,000 cases. CS 65%, Mer 35%.
White: 7ha. 1,400 cases. Sauv 65%, Sém 35%.
The Perrin family had to rebuild this property completely when they bought it in 1981: it had been much neglected since 1914. The early vintages so far have produced pleasing wines of character.

Château Smith-Haut-Lafitte

Cru Classé. Owner: Daniel and Florence Cathiard. Red: 44ha.
19,000 cases. CS 63%, Mer 26%, CF 11%. White: 11ha. 4,800
cases. Sauv 98%, Sauv Gris 2%. Second label: Les Hauts-de-
Smith-Haut-Lafitte.

A proprietor with the splendidly English name of George Smith
bought this *cru* in 1720 and added his name to that of the place-
name. The firm Louis Eschenauer owned the property from 1958
until 1991 when they sold to the Cathiard family. There has been
major investment here in the vineyards and buildings. In 1960 less
than six hectares were planted, and no white wine was made. Now
there are 55 hectares. A large underground cellar was built in 1974
to hold 2,000 casks, and all the vinification equipment was
renewed. Half the red wine is matured in new oak.

The wines have a pronounced character, aromatic and spicy.
Although there was an improvement with the introduction of
selection in '83, the dramatic turn around has been achieved under
the Cathiard ownership. After the difficult vintages of the early
'90s, a superb red wine was made in '95 with ripe harmonious
fruit. '96 seems to me to have more breed and length, while there
is a charming and delicious developing '97. For the whites, '94
proved to be a classic, one of the best of the vintage; '95 was richer
and very complex, '96 more opulent but benefited from the extra
acidity of the year, while '97 is tremendously scented and ripe, the
fruit flavours highlighted by the addition of Sauvignon Gris.

Alot of work has been done in the vineyards with the emphasis on traditional methods and lower yields. Michel Rolland
advises on the red wine, and Christophe Ollivier on the white.

Château La Tour-Haut-Brion

Cru Classé. Owner: Domaine Clarence Dillon.
Red: 4·9ha. 1,500 cases. CS 42%, CF 35%, Mer 23%.

This small property, adjoining La Mission, was purchased by the
Woltner brothers in 1933. The wines have been vinified at La
Mission since then, and under the Dewavrin administration
(1975–83) were treated as second wines. One of Jean Delmas'
first decisions was to restore its position as a *cru* in its own right.
The result is still a fine wine, certainly better than a number of
the other Crus Classés of Graves. It is full-bodied but less intense
than La Mission, and matures more quickly while ageing well.
Excellent wines were made in '85, '86, '88, '89 and '90. Good wines
were made in '93 and '94; excellent ones in '95 and '96.

Château La Tour-Martillac

Cru Classé. Owner: Jean Kressmann. Red: 28ha. 15,500 cases.
CS 59%, Mer 35%, CF 2%, Mal 2%, PV 2%.
White: 10ha. 5,000 cases. Sém 60%, Sauv 35%, Musc 5%.
Second label: Château La Grave-Martillac (red) 1,000 cases.

The name comes from a 12th-century tower, once the staircase of
a fort, the ruins of which were used in the building of today's farm
two centuries ago. In the 1870s, Edouard Kressmann, the founder
of the famous old *négociant* house, obtained the exclusivity of this

cru, and the family finally bought it in 1929. Ten hectares of pasture provide cattle manure for the vineyard. The grapes from the older vines are still fermented in the traditional wooden vats at 32–33°C (90–91°F), while the production from younger vines goes into lined steel vats which are water-cooled. Maturation is in casks of which a third are new. The second wine, Château La Grave-Martillac, is made from vines less than ten years old and *vin de presse*. It is sold only direct from the château. The white wine was vinified in stainless steel with automatic water-cooling until 1987 when, under Denis Dubourdieu's supervision, fermentation in cask was introduced. This has given the wines an extra dimension and lifted them to the upper echelons of white Graves.

I have found the red wine to have elegant fruit on the nose and a fine flavour with breed and length, but it is rather light-textured. The white wine is elegant and fresh with quite an original character. It has delicacy, real breed and a fine finish. This is high-class white Graves.

SOUTHERN GRAVES

Château d'Archambeau

Owner: Jean-Philippe Dubourdieu. Red: 13ha. 7,800 cases.
Mer 50%, CS 50%. White: 17ha. 10,000 cases. Sém 55%, Sauv 40%,
Musc 5%. Second label: Château Mourlet, Château La Citadelle.
The commune of Illats which adjoins Barsac, like those of Cérons and Potensac, can vinify its white wines either as Cérons or as Graves Supérieur. Here at d'Archambeau only small quantities of Cérons are now made, and the emphasis is on classic dry Graves. The Dubourdieu family have a formidable reputation as winemakers in Barsac and Graves, and Jean-Philippe, nephew of Pierre Dubourdieu of Doisy-Daëne fame, is no exception. The white wines are cold-fermented in lined metal and stainless steel vats, and bottled in the spring. The combination of Sémillon and Sauvignon produces wines of elegance and depth of character that are delicious within months of bottling but also keep and mature well.

The red wine is a more recent development, the first commercialised vintage from young vines being the '82. The wines have vivid fruit and immediate charm, and have added a little extra roundness and depth as the vineyard has matured.

Château Ardennes

Owners: François and Bertrand Dubrey.
Red: 42ha. 27,000 cases. Mer 50%, CS 40%, CF 10%.
White: 19·6ha. 12,500 cases. Sém 60%, Sauv 40%.
Both red and white wines are made at Château Ardennes, the red being rather better, with a violet perfume, good structure and the ability to age well (an unusual quality in wines of this area).

Château d'Arricaud

Owners: M et Mme Albert Bouyx.
Red: 12ha. 6,700 cases. CS 45%, Mer 55%.
White: 11ha. 5,600 cases. Sém 65%, Sauv 30%, Musc 5%.

An old property and the most important in the commune of Landiras, Château d'Arricaud was actually built by a former president of the Parlement de Bordeaux. Its wines are well made, the reds ideal for young drinking with a delicious fruitiness and plenty of charm; the whites elegant with good length.

Château Belon

Owner: Jean Depiot. Red: 11ha. 6,700 cases. CS 50%, Mer 50%.
White: 5ha. 3,300 cases. Sauv 45%, Sém 40%, Musc 15%.
This property in St-Morillon has been owned by the Depiot family since 1800. The wines produced here tend to be rather coarse, but some of the reds have an attractive spiciness.

Château La Blancherie and
Château La Blancherie-Peyret

Owner: F-C Braud-Coussié.
Red: 9ha. 4,600 cases. CS 60%, Mer 34%, CF 6%.
White: 11ha. 5,300 cases. Sém 55%, Sauv 40%, Musc 5%.
The commune of La Brède is famous for its Château of the same name where Montesquieu, the renowned 17th-century philosopher and historian, was born and lived. Today this is the most important wine-producing château of the commune. It also has a colourful history, for its proprietors at the time of the 1789 Revolution of were both guillotined! The white wines (sold under the La Blancherie label) are fermented at low temperatures, the reds (La Blancherie-Peyret) receive a long maceration and are aged in cask. The whites are fruity and vigorous in style. The reds have an arresting bouquet, redolent of tobacco and spice, and lots of flavour and character, but are supple and powerful at the same time, so that they can be drunk young yet can also age. This is an excellent *cru* producing well-made wines.

Château Brondelle

Owner: J N Belloc. Red: 25ha. 7,800 cases. CS 60%, Mer 40%.
White: 21ha. 5,600 cases. Sém 60%, Sauv 35%, Musc 5%.
Second label: Château La Croix-St-Pey.
Brondelle is in Langon, one of the most important winemaking communes in Graves, where the growers have profited much from the work on clonal selection carried out by the INRA. The wines produced, both the red and white, are attractive and worth looking out for.

Château Cabannieux

Owner: Mme Dudignac-Barrière.
Red: 15ha. 8,000 cases. Mer 50%, CS 45%, CF 5%.
White: 7ha. 3,500 cases. Sém 80%, Sauv 20%.
Second labels: Châteaux de Curcier and Haut Migot.
This property is in the highest part of the commune of Portets on well-drained, gravelly soil, with some traces of clay. It belongs to the same owners as the well-respected *négociant* firm of A & R Barrière. The red wines are given two to three weeks in contact with the skins for maximum extraction. Part of the crop is put in

cask, and a small amount of new wood is used. For the white there is a controlled low-temperature fermentation at below 20°C (68°F). The aim is to produce red wines with a pronounced Graves character, full-flavoured but soft and good for early drinking. The white has a small percentage of Sauvignon to give the early bouquet. Both enjoy a good reputation.

Château de Cardaillan

Owner: Comtesse de Bournazel. Red: 24ha. 5,000 cases.
CS 65%, Mer 35%.
White: 2·8ha. 1,700 cases (sold as M de Malle). GRAPES???

The de Bournazel family has a large property which is divided by the boundary between the Sauternes commune of Preignac and the Graves commune of Toulenne. The red wines of the Graves portion of the vineyard are sold as Cardaillan and the white as M de Malle. The red is early maturing, fruity and easy, while the white has a touch of distinction with aromatic fruit flavours and a nicely balanced acidity: a really well-made wine.

Château Cazebonne

Owner: Jean-Marc Bridet. Red: 15ha. 6,000 cases. CS 50%,
Mer 50%. White: 6·6ha. 4,300 cases. Sauv 60%, Sém 40%.

A property in St-Pierre-de-Mons producing red wines with plenty of fruit and colour but which are perhaps a bit firm. The whites are slightly more elegant with a pleasant crispness.

Château de Chantegrive

Owners: Henri and Françoise Lévêque. Red: 26ha. 13,500 cases.
CS 45%, Mer 45%, CF 10%. White: 38ha. 25,000 cases.
Sém 50%, Sauv 30%, Musc 20%. Second label: Mayne-d'Anice.
Other label: Cuvée Caroline

The Lévêques have steadily built up this property from modest beginnings. When I first visited Chantegrive there were only 15 hectares of vines, now there are over 50. The soil is white sand mixed with quartz pebbles.

Vinification at Chantegrive is carefully controlled at low temperatures for the whites. The white wines are fresh, delicious, fruity, aromatic and easy to drink. The Cuvée Caroline is fermented and aged in cask, an outstanding example of new-wave aromatic Graves style. The reds are aged for 18 months in casks, of which 30 per cent are new oak, in an underground cellar. They are fruity and supple but with some depth as well, the sort of easy-to-drink wines that deserve more attention than they currently receive.

Château Chéret-Pitres

Owner: Boulanger-Dulugat family. 11ha. 7,000 cases.
CS 50%, Mer 50%.

The Boulangers produce only red wines at Chéret-Pitres. They are most attractive, with plenty of distinctive Graves flavour. Their fruitiness makes them excellent for drinking young but some of the better vintages mature well and are worth keeping.

Château Chicane

Owner: Gauthier family. 6ha. 3,000 cases.
CS 55%, Mer 30%, Mal 15%.

In 1994 François Gauthier took over from his famous uncle, Pierre Coste. Red wines are produced for drinking young – at around two to four years old. They are light-bodied with a pleasing spicy nose and lots of fruit.

Domaine de Courbon

Owner: Jean Saunders, 5ha. 3,000 cases. Sauv 60%, Sém 40%.

Only white wines are vinified here; they are grown on soils of sand, gravel and clay which, being relatively near to Sauternes, produce wines that are richer and more full-bodied than those of the northern Graves regions. The proportions of Sauvignon and Sémillon used ensure that the wines are supple and fruity but also have good keeping properties.

Château Coutet

Owners: Marcel and Bertrand Baly.
White: 10ha. 5,000 cases. Sém 75%, Sauv 23%, Musc 2%.

The wines of the Château Coutet can be rather confusing. Dry wines made in Sauternes and Barsac are allowed only the Bordeaux Blanc AC and in 1977 the Baly family bought another château of the same name, the famous Barsac *cru* of Coutet, where it produces such wines. The family also owns property in Pujols-sur-Civon, a commune with Sauternes and Barsac on three sides of it, and is selling its Pujols *cru*, formerly known as Reverdon, as 'Vin Sec du Château Coutet' with the Graves AC. These wines, produced using cold fermentation, I find rather disappointing at present. Having a strong aroma of gooseberries they are surprisingly skeletal for wines with so much Sémillon.

Château L'Étoile

Owner: Domaines Latrille Bonnin. Red: 23ha. 8,000 cases. CS 70%,
Mer 15%, CF 15%. White: 12ha. 4,000 cases. Sauv 50%, Sém 50%.

Vinification at high temperatures produces reds that are rich in fruit and spice, balanced by body and tannin. They have plenty of ageing potential but are also delicious when young. The whites undergo cool fermentation and are macerated prior to this to enhance the wine's bouquet and fruit character. They are also most attractive for drinking young.

Château Ferrande

Owner: Héritiers H Delnaud. Administrators: Castel Frères.
Red: 30ha. 16,000 cases. Mer 34%, CS 33%, CF 33%.
White: 9ha. 5,000 cases. Sauv 60%, Sém 35%, Musc 5%.
Second label: Château Lognac.

This is the most important *cru* in the commune of Castres. Since the Delnaud family began their partnership with Marc Teisseire in 1955 the vineyard has been expanded and the facilities improved. Concrete and stainless steel vats are used for vinification and the red is matured in cask, with ten per cent new oak.

I have found the red deep in colour, having a lively and spicy bouquet with tobacco overtones. The flavour is frank and fresh, light-textured but full and fruity. This is an enjoyable wine which can be drunk with pleasure when three to four years old. The white has quite a pronounced Graves flavour. It is powerful and slightly earthy but fruity. It has its admirers, but for me it has less charm and breed than the red.

Clos Floridène

Owners: Denis and Florence Dubourdieu. Red: 5ha.
CS 80%, Mer 20%. White: 12ha. Sém 50%, Sauv 30%, Musc
20%. Second label: Second de Floridène.
Having already made a name at Château Reynon in the Premières Côtes, the Dubourdieus have chosen this site in Puyols/Ciron in the southern Graves to make white and red Graves. Nineteenth-century editions of *Bordeaux et ses Vins* show that Puyols produced the most reputed dry white wines in Graves at that time, when hardly any whites were made in Pessac-Léognan and most other white Graves were *demi-sec*. Certainly these wines have body and race, with a long flavour and a really dry finish. The reds are full of deliciously flattering supple fruit.

Château de Gaillat

Owner: Coste family. 11ha. 5,500 cases.
CS 65%, Mer 30%, Mal 5%.
The care Pierre Coste gives to vinification has resulted in some outstanding vintages. Wines are bottled usually in the June after the vintage to capture maximum fruit. An explosion of fruit on the nose followed by a taste of crushed fruit characterises these wines, which are delicious within 18 months of the vintage.

Château du Grand Abord

Owner: Marc and Colette Dugoua. Red: 15ha. 8,300 cases.
Mer 90%, CS 10%. White: 4ha. 2,000 cases. Sém 85%, Sauv 15%.
A property situated on the gravel soils of the plateau at Portets. The red wines are most attractive and for drinking young.

Domaine La Grave

Owner: M and Mme Van Quikelberg. 7ha. Red: 3,000 cases.
CS 50%, Mer 50%. White: 2ha. 900 cases. Sém 100%.
Peter Vinding-Diers acquired this property in 1980 and it was here that he produced his first wines. Both the reds and the whites are full in flavour, the reds tending to be rather tannic, but still having much elegance and a fine perfume.

Château Landiras

Owner: M and Mme Van Quikelberg. Red: 5ha. 2,200 cases.
CS 75%, Mer 25%. White: 15ha. Sém 80%, Sauv Gris 20%.
The château's history can be traced back to 1173: the ruins and moat of an ancient castle remain. The proprietor has built up a good reputation in Graves (*see* Château Rahoul) and is at present expanding this ancient *cru* to its full 40-hectare AOC allocation. A

new *cuvier* was completed in time for the '88 vintage and some stylish wines have been produced – the reds reflecting their Cabernet origins and the whites having plenty of classic Sémillon style and body enlivened by the spiciness of Sauvignon Gris. Sadly the property had to be sold in 1998.

Château Magence

Owner: Dominique Guillot de Suduiraut.
Red: 19·5ha. 10,000 cases. CS 43%, Mer 34%, CF 23%.
White: 14·5ha. 7,600 cases. Sauv 66%, Sém 34%.

One of the best-known properties in St-Pierre-de-Mons, the most important Graves commune lying to the southeast of Sauternes. It has been in the same family since 1800, but is fully up-to-date. Fermentation is in temperature-controlled stainless steel. This was one of the early classic modern white Graves, once entirely Sauvignon but now balanced with Sémillon: it has real finesse and style. The reds are also useful: supple yet slightly tannic.

Château Magneau

Owner: Henri Ardurats. Red: 14ha. 6,700 cases. Mer 50%, CS 35%, CF 15%. White: 26ha. 12,000 cases. Sauv 50%, Sém 30%, Musc 20%. Second label: Château Guirauton.

The white wines produced at this *cru* in La Brède are particularly good: they lack the coarseness of some Graves wines and are stylish and well made with plenty of fruit. The reds, attractive and with a distinctly pungent aroma, are mostly ready to drink when young. The Château Guirauton label is used only for white wines.

Château Millet

Owner: de la Mette family. Red: 15ha. 8,900 cases. Mer 60%, CS 30%, CF 10%. White: 7ha. 5,400 cases. Sém 70%, Sauv 30%.

The red, now more important than the white, is matured in cask. Wines not up to standard (such as the '77 and '80) are not bottled with the château name, but in general these are decent, fruity, early-maturing wines.

Château Montalivet

Owners: Pierre and Denis Dubourdieu, Robert Goffard. 7ha. Red: 4,000 cases. CS 50%, Mer 50%.

Pierre Coste is no longer involved in this well-reputed property, and the white vineyard has been incorporated into Denis Dubourdieu's Clos Floridène. This is attractive, vibrantly fruity early-drinking wine.

Château Le Pavillon-de-Boyrein

Owner: Société Pierre Bonnet et Fils. Red: 25ha. 11,000 cases. Mer 65%, CS 35%. White: 1,500 cases. Sém 80%, Sauv 20%. Second label: Domaine des Lauriers.

The best *cru* in its commune – Roaillon – this château produces wines similar in quality to many Crus Bourgeois of the northern Médoc. The red wines are the more pleasant, with a hint of *terroir* in the form of mineral and iron overtones.

Château Rahoul

Owner: Alain Thiénot. Red: 17ha. 10,000 cases.
Mer 60%, CS 40%. White: 12ha. 2,000 cases. Sém 100%.
Second label: Château Constantin.

This old property in Portets was bought by an Australian syndicate in 1978. The Australians brought in a young Danish oenologist, Peter Vinding-Diers, and invested in stainless steel and new oak. In 1982 they sold to another Dane, who in turn sold to the present owner, a merchant from Champagne. He took over the management when Vinding-Diers left in 1988 to run his own property (*see* Château Landiras). The vineyard is not in the best position (low-lying with some drainage problems) but the expertise of the winemaker has been successful.

One of Vinding-Diers' important contributions was the isolation of 'R2', a pure strain of yeast found in the vineyard. By eliminating the other yeasts he found it was possible to produce cleaner-tasting wines. The 'R2' has since been used as far afield as Australia. A proportion of new oak is used for the maturation of both red and white wines after low-temperature fermentations.

The white wines are elegant and long-flavoured, lacking only the complexity and depth of the best Graves further north. The reds, full of vivid spicy fruit, are at their most delicious when young. This is what investment in expertise and the best equipment can achieve. How much room for improvement there is at many better-known and better-placed vineyards!

Château Respide-Médeville

Owner: Christian Médeville. 7·5ha. Red: 3,000 cases.
CS and CF 65%, Mer 35%. White: 5·4ha. 2,500 cases.
Sém 50%, Sauv 45%, Musc 5%.

This *cru*, on the ridge of gravelly clay in Toulenne, has been built up by Christian Médeville of Château Gilette to earn its current high reputation. The white wines develop pleasingly; the reds are also charming for drinking when young.

Château de Roquetaillade-La-Grange

Owner: Jean Guignard. 30ha. Red: 16,500 cases. Mer 50%,
CS 25%, CF 20%, Mal 5%. White: 15ha. 8,200 cases. Sém 70%,
Sauv 20%, Musc 10%. Second label: Château de Carolle.

The splendid early-14th century château built by a nephew of Pope Clement V is regarded as the finest example of military architecture in southeastern France.

This property, on the hillsides to the east of the château, is actually unconnected with the château itself, which has no important vineyards. The owners (also of Château Rolland in Barsac) have raised the standard of the wines, winning a number of medals in Paris and a reputation as producers of one of the best red wines in southern Graves. The consistent reds have individuality and lovely mellow fruit on nose and palate – sometimes, as in '79, with an unmistakable hint of cherries, a fruit flavour unusual for Bordeaux. The white, quite full-bodied, has improved with better vinification, but is still rather unexciting.

Château St-Agrèves

Owner: Marie-Christiane Landry. Red: 12ha. 6,000 cases. CS &
CF 70%, Mer 30%. White: 4ha. 750 cases. Sauv 50%, Sém 50%.

The red wines produced at Château St-Agrèves are unusual for
this region in that they benefit from longer maturation than many
of their neighbours. They are attractive wines however and show
a good balance of fruit and tannin. The white wines are rather
more coarse in style than those from nearby *crus*.

Château de St-Pierre

Owner: Henri Dulac. 7ha. Red: 3,400 cases. CS 60%, Mer 40%.
White: 24ha. 10,600 cases. Sém 67%, Sauv 33%.
Second labels: Clos d'Uza, Château Les Queyrats.

An excellent property run in conjunction with Château Les
Queyrats by Henri Dulac. Reds and whites are made. The vine-
yard is on ridges of clay and limestone southeast of the
St-Pierre-de-Mons commune, the most important south of Sauternes.

   The wines are carefully vinified. The whites were some of the
first new-style Graves to emerge and have finesse and character.
The '82 won a gold medal in Paris. The reds are not as distinguished, but are vivid and quite generous, ageing well for this
area. A *cru* with a long record for consistency.

SICA Les Vignobles de Bordeaux

Red: 130ha. 54,000 cases. CS 55%, Mer 35%, CF 10%.
Participating châteaux: Camus, Cazebonne, Les Clauzots,
La Croix, Luderman La Côte, Magence, de Rolland, Toumilon
and de Cappes, Clos des Majureaux, Domaine de Quincarnon.

This is a group of producers pooling technical information and
facilities, especially bottling, in order to improve quality, and its
success provides a good example of the new dynamism which is
raising standards in the region.

Château Tourteau-Chollet

Owner: SC du Château. 46ha. Red: 13,400 cases; CS 52%,
Mer 48%. White: 10ha. 3,500 cases. Sauv 52%, Sém 48%.

The commune of Arbanat lies southeast of Portets: this is its most
important property. Since taking over in 1977 the owners have
steadily made improvements; now pleasant fruity reds (gold
label) and elegant dry whites (white label) are being made. A
property to watch. This is another part of the Mestrezat empire
(*see* Grand-Puy-Ducasse and Rayne-Vigneau).

Château Vieux Château Gaubert

Owner: Dominique Haverlan.
Red: 10ha. 6,000 cases. CS 50%, Mer 45%, CF 5%.
White: 3·6ha. 2,000 cases. Sém 60%, Sauv 30%, Musc 10%.

The present owner bought Château Pessan-St-Hilaire in 1981 and
has since then expanded the vineyards and enlarged the *chai*. In
1988 he bought this old property and has concentrated his efforts
here since then. He is a trained oenologist and makes attractive
wines. Both reds and whites show continual improvement.

Sauternes and Barsac

Sauternes is produced in five communes: Sauternes, Barsac, Fargues-de-Langon, Bommes and Preignac. Barsac is also an AC in its own right, and producers there can label their wines Barsac or Sauternes or (as many do) Sauternes-Barsac.

Traditional Sauternes is a luxury wine, and luxury wines have to be sold at luxury prices. If an article becomes unfashionable and can no longer command its former high prices, something has to give, and that is likely to be quality. This, in a nutshell, has been the dilemma facing Sauternes since the late 1950s.

The top red growth can expect to make 40 hectolitres per hectare in a good vintage, sometimes more, and seldom less than 30. At Yquem, the standard-bearer for Sauternes, over the past 30 years the average yield has been nine hectolitres per hectare, in contrast with 25 allowed by the appellation. On this basis, Yquem's price would need to be around four times that of Lafite or Pétrus to produce the same income, in fact it is in the region of two and half times that amount. Costs are also much higher because of picking methods (*see* page 35), and there are years when frosts, hail or rain during the vintage mean that the wine is not good enough to go out under the famous label of Yquem.

The result of all this has been that only a few Sauternes properties have been able to continue to make wines in anything approaching the traditional way. Whatever short-cuts may be possible with the aid of modern technology, there can be no substitute for botrytis or *pourriture noble* (noble rot). This is what gives Sauternes its distinctive bouquet and flavour, its complex range of fruit, flavours and finesse. The short-cut of picking ripe but unaffected grapes and then chaptalizing can produce only unsubtle sweet wines that may be quite elegant and fresh, but will never develop into anything of interest.

Fortunately, there are signs that there are now enough lovers of true Sauternes who are willing to pay the price for a certain quantity of this nectar, and enough dedicated proprietors with the financial strength to withstand the bad years. The 1980s and the mid '90s again produced great wines and a revival of interest.

One way of helping to cover costs is to produce a proportion of dry wine, or even red. Unfortunately, however good these may be, such efforts are hampered by the appellation system which will give only a simple Bordeaux AC to such wines (or Bordeaux Supérieur in the case of red wines). Ironically, in neighbouring Cérons, the producers of this sweet wine have the right to the Graves AC for their dry whites and reds. This has so far been denied to the growers of Sauternes, apparently quite illogically.

The dividing-line between success and failure is a fine one. There are now 11 Premiers Crus. Twenty years or so ago, only five of these were making wines that were up to standard. Since then the new owner of Guiraud has started to turn it around, and the Cordiers have reversed their policy at Lafaurie-Peyraguey. Most recently of all AXA bought Suduiraut which had been under-performing and Domaines Rothschild have secured the future of one of the best properties, Rieussec.

There are 14 Deuxièmes Crus, and of these there are probably eight owners who aim to produce quality wines to some extent, and only half of these make more than 2,000 cases. On the other hand, the vines of one of one of the Deuxièmes Crus, Myrat, were pulled up in 1976 but, happily, replanted in 1988. Doisy-Daëne has been the Deuxième Cru most dedicated to quality over the past 30 years. Improvements also came in the 1970s, with Nairac being transformed by Tom Heeter; more recently Pierre Perromat has leased d'Arche and the Guignard brothers have greatly improved their part of Lamothe. There are three unclassified growth that now make wines of classified quality: Bastor-Lamontagne, Raymond-Lafon and de Fargues.

Essentially Sauternes is a great dessert wine intended to be drunk at the end of a meal, and this clearly puts it into the special-occasions-only category. Of course it can be drunk as an aperitif; but it is not exactly designed to put an edge on your appetite, and the Bordelais habit of drinking it with a first course of foie gras hardly has a wide application.

A more likely way forward is through the new devices for keeping open bottles under nitrogen, which make it possible for restaurant diners to order a single glass of Sauternes at the end of a meal. If this practice becomes widespread the future of Sauternes will look brighter. But unless more people are prepared to pay more and drink Sauternes more often, then the future for even a small number of quality *crus* will remain limited.

Château d'Arche

2e Cru Classé. Owner: Bastit-St-Martin family.
Administrator: Pierre Perromat. 30ha. 2,200 cases.
Sém 80%, Sauv 15%, Musc 5%. Second label: Cru de Braneyre.
This old property has a château dating from the 16th century and a reputation going back to the 18th. After a rather undistinguished period, Pierre Perromat, (president of the INAO for 30 years) leased the property in 1981 and is determined to make classic Sauternes again. The traditional selections are now made in the vineyard again and, after fermentation in vat, the wine is matured for at least two years casks, one-third of which are new.

The first wines of the new regime seem well-balanced, with attractive fruit and sweetness and a certain fineness and breed. The vintages of '81 and '84 did well for these lesser years; '83 and '85 are also good wines, with the best vintages in '86, '88 and '90.

Château Bastor-Lamontagne

Cru Bourgeois. Owner: Crédit Foncier de France.
Administrator: Michel Garat. 50ha. 13,000 cases.
Sém 78%, Sauv 17%, Musc 5%.
Second label: Les Ramparts de Bastor.
This excellent *cru* is in Preignac, adjoining Suduiraut. It has for many years consistently produced excellent wines and is on the level of the Crus Classés, indeed better than some of them. The wines are carefully and traditionally made, with three years' cask-ageing and a small proportion of new wood. The result is rich,

luscious wine with the aroma and flavour of apricots and all the
stylishness of a top-rate Sauternes. Recently '83, '85, '86, '88, '89,
'90, '95, '96 and '97 have all been highly successful vintages.

Château Broustet

2e Cru Classé. Owner: Laulan family.
Administrator: Didier Laulan. 16ha. 3,000 cases. Sém 63%,
Sauv 25%, Musc 12%. Second label: Château de Ségur.

This small property is not well known, mainly because its production is small. From 1885 it belonged to the Fournier family,
although the vineyard was not replanted until 1900. Broustet was
sold to its present owners in 1994.

The wine is fermented in vat but matured in casks, of which
a small percentage is new. It has a fine perfume, is generous and
quite rich with pleasing individuality and breed. Often seemingly
clumsy when young, the wines age well.

Château Caillou

2e Cru Classé. Owner: J-B Bravo and Marie José Pierre. 13ha.
3,300 cases. Sém 90%, Sauv 10%. Second label: Petit Mayne.

A little-known property because the wine is all sold by *vente
directe* to private customers, so this is a place to visit if you have
your car and room in the boot! The present owner has run the
property since 1969 and keeps stocks of old vintages; I have memories of a wonderful bottle of '20. The wines are carefully made,
with fermentation in vat and maturation in casks, of which a
small percentage is new, for up to three years. The wines have
the reputation of being light, elegant and fruity and '96 and '97
seem to mark an improvement.

Château Climens

1er Cru Classé. Owner: SCEA du Château Climens.
Administrator: Bérénice Lurton. 29ha. 5,600 cases. Sém 100%.
Second label: Cyprès de Climens.

For many, Climens is the region's best wine after Yquem – not
that the two can really be compared. The emphasis here is on elegance, breed and freshness: Climens does not generally attempt
to compete with Yquem's lusciousness. Since 1971 the property
has belonged to the Lurton family. In 1992 Lucien Lurton handed
over to his two daughters Brigitte (who ran it in the 1980s) and
Bérénice, who has been in charge during the 1990s. The soil is red
sand and gravel over limestone. After settling for 24 hours in vat,
the juice is fermented in casks, of which 25 per cent are new, and
matured for about two years before bottling.

The wines here are remarkably consistent in a region where
it is not always easy to make good Sauternes. They are rather
closed at first and usually need a minimum of ten years before
they begin to give of their best. The qualities here are balance,
freshness, elegance and liquorousness in the great years, which
make it a long-lived wine. Surprisingly acceptable light wines
were made in '72 and '77, years not noted for Sauternes at all; '71,
'75 and '76 are also outstanding wines for their vintages. The '78

is without botrytis but elegant; '79 is light but fine and can be drunk now; the '80 and '81 are also both fine but the '82 is no more than average. Since 1983, the wines seem to have moved into another gear with a succession of outstanding wines: '83, '85, '86, '88, '89 and '90, placing Climens second only to Yquem as Sauternes' quality *cru*. The '91 is one of the few good wines of this vintage, and fine wines were made in '94 and '95, great wines in '96, '97 and '98.

Château Coutet

1er Cru Classé. Owner: Marcel Baly. 38ha. 7,000 cases.
Sém 75%, Sauv 23%, Musc 2%.
Other label: Château Coutet Cuvée Madame.

The name of Coutet is always linked to that of Climens, the other great wine of Barsac. Generally Coutet is less powerful and often a little drier than Climens, which also tends to have more finesse in the great years. For 30 years the property was well run by the Rolland-Guy family, who sold in 1977 to Marcel Baly. Production methods are traditional, with fermentation in casks, of which a third are new, and two years in cask before bottling.

Of the early vintages, the '71 is fine and the '73 one of the few fine wines in this mixed year. The last two of the old regime were superb: '75 a classic in a year when many wines were clumsy and unbalanced; '76 is perfumed, beautifully balanced but lighter. The '79 is elegant but rather dry; '83 is better, while in '88, '89, '90, '95, '96 and '97 Coutet really returned to top form. Look out for the remarkable Cuvée Madame, made in minute quantities.

Château Doisy-Daëne

2e Cru Classé. Owner: Pierre Dubourdieu.
15ha. 6,000 cases. Sém 100%.
Second labels: Vin Sec de Doisy-Daëne, Château Cantegril.

Once the three Doisys were one, and when they split up in the 19th century the first owner of this part was an Englishman called Deane, which has become corrupted to Daëne. Its present owner, Pierre Dubourdieu, is a great innovator, being one of the first to make a dry wine in Sauternes in 1962.

The vinification methods here have been developed over a number of years and are special to Doisy-Daëne. Juice is fermented in vat at not more than 18°C (64°F); after 15 to 21 days when the balance between alcohol and sugar is judged correct, the temperature is lowered to 4°C (39°F) and the wine is sterile-filtered into new casks. Arresting the fermentation in this way much reduces the amount of sulphur needed. The process is repeated for the final *assemblage* in the following March, and the wine is sterile-filtered again a year later.

All this gives Doisy-Daëne a freshness and elegance that I find delightful. The wines seem light to start with but mature and keep well, developing great finesse. The '83 is elegant but '86 is finer, with '88, '89 and '90 proving exceptional. Then '95, '96, '97 and '98 are all excellent. This wine is finer than several Premiers Crus.

Château Doisy-Dubroca

2e Cru Classé. Owner: Louis Lurton. 3·3ha. 500 cases.
Sém 100%. Second label: La Demoiselle de Doisy.

This small property has been run in conjunction with Climens for nearly 70 years. The vinification and maturation all take place at Climens with exactly the same care as the Premier Cru.

The wines, as at Climens, are remarkably consistent. In style they are light and elegant and take time to evolve in bottle, but can be drunk young.

Château Doisy-Védrines

2e Cru Classé. Owner: Pierre Castéja. 25ha. 1,500 cases.
Sém 80%, Sauv 17%, Musc 3%.
Second label: Château La Tour-Védrines.

This property contains the original Védrines château and *chai*. Pierre Castéja's family have inherited the property through several marriages since 1840, and he himself comes from an old family of proprietors. He also ran the *négociant* firm Roger Joanne. The wines are traditionally made with fermentation and maturation in casks, of which 75 per cent are new.

There is a strong contrast between this and the other Doisys, which both concentrate on elegance and delicacy. Védrines is fuller and richer, but to my mind lacks the breed and stylishness of the others. Of some good wines in the 1980s, '89 was exceptional and '96 and '97 continued this trend. There is a red La Tour-Védrines, but another wine, Chevalier Védrines, is a Joanne brand unconnected with this property.

Château de Fargues

Cru Bourgeois. Owner: Comte Alexandre de Lur-Saluces.
13ha. 1,000 cases. Sém 80%, Sauv 20%.

This tiny vineyard lies on the extremity of the commune of Fargues and of the Sauternes AC, and has belonged to the Lur-Saluces family for over 500 years. Under the present owner, Comte Alexandre de Lur-Saluces, the production of red wine has been abandoned in order to concentrate on producing the best possible Sauternes. Winemaking is identical to that at Yquem, with fermentation and maturation in new casks.

The wines, most of which are sold in the US, combine lusciousness and elegance with great breed and finesse. The '67, '71, '75, '76, '80, '81, '83, '85, '88, '89 and '90 are all great successes here, the '76 being finer than the '75 for me. This wine is of the standard of a top Premier Cru, and the price is high – indeed higher than the Premiers Crus – at approximately half that of Yquem.

Château Filhot

2e Cru Classé. Owner: Comte Henri de Vaucelles. 60ha.
10,000 cases. Sém 50%, Sauv 45%, Musc 5%.

There are many beautiful properties in Sauternes, and this is one of the finest, an imposing late-18th-century mansion set among woods and fields. The wine is fermented in glass-fibre vats and also matured in them: no wood is used. At its best this is a wine of individuality and great fruit but not necessarily great sweetness, except in extraordinary years. The high proportion of Sauvignon and the practice of keeping in vat contribute to this tendency. Yet I cannot help feeling that the full potential here is not being realised. The '83, '86, '88, '89 and '90 yielded raisin-like botrytized wines.

Château Gilette

Owner: Christian Médeville. 4·5ha. 500–600 cases.
Sém 94%, Sauv 4%, Musc 2%.

This is a curiosity among the wines of Sauternes. Situated just outside the village of Preignac, it belongs to the Médeville family of Château Respide-Médeville in Graves.

The soil here is sandy with a subsoil of rocks and clay. Between three and seven pickings are made, with the earliest being of single berries affected by botrytis. Each picking is vinified separately with temperatures controlled at 24–25°C (75–77°F) during the first days of fermentation, and brought down to 20°C (68°F) for the remainder. The result is several different *cuvées* with differing characteristics, and normally two separate wines are made in each vintage. After the fermentation the wines are kept in small concrete vats, some for at least 20 years. The theory is that the large volume gives a mature flavour and bouquet while preserving fruit and freshness, so that the maturation process is slower than in a bottle. In 1985 I was able to taste the '55 and '59 bottled in 1981, and the '49 and '50 bottled only six to seven years after the vintage. I thought the early bottlings were clearly superior to the later ones. In particular the '55 and '59 lack the bouquet and balance of the '49 and '50. In addition the '55 and '59 had great sweetness and concentration but rather lacked complexity. The '49 seemed the finest wine of all, and I preferred the '55 to the '59. So, while this system means you can find an old vintage more easily, the result may not be as good as that achieved by earlier and more conventional bottlings.

Château Guiraud

1er Cru Classé. Owner: SC Agricole.
Administrator: Frank Narby. 100ha. 16,000 cases. Sém 65%,
Sauv 35%. Dry white: Sauv 100%.
Second labels: 'G' Château Guiraud (Bordeaux Sec), Le
Dauphin de Château Guiraud (Sauternes).

This famous old property received a shot in the arm when it was bought by the Narby family from Canada in 1981. Hamilton Narby, followed by his father in 1988, brought in an excellent *régisseur*, Xavier Planty, in 1983 and imposed the highest traditional standards for making classic Sauternes. A shortage of money had reduced Guiraud to maturing its wines in vat instead of cask, after a cask-fermentation. Now 45 per cent new wood is used for maturation. A dry white wine is also made.

I remember this as a light, elegant wine which was less luscious than most Sauternes, but extremely fine in vintages such as '54, '55 and '62. Part of this distinctive character comes from the high proportion of Sauvignon. Now signs of this old distinction are returning. The successes of the new regime began with the '83, followed by '85, with the '86 even better than the '83. Good wines were also made in '88, '89 and '90.

Château Guiteronde

Owner: GFA du Hayot. 45ha. 10,000 cases.
Sém 70%, Sauv 20%, Musc 10%.

A well-known *cru* in Barsac, where André du Hayot makes some excellent wine. The '83 and '85 were fine vintages here, with all the finesse and breed typical of wines from this property. A wine to look out for, offering good value for money.

Clos Haut-Peyraguey

1er Cru Classé. Owner: Jacques Pauly. 15ha. 3,000 cases.
Sém 83%, Sauv 15%, Musc 2%. Second label: Haut-Bommes.

A single *cru* at the time of the 1855 classification, Peyraguey was divided in 1878. This is the smaller part with just a tower built in the manner of the older, grander one at Lafaurie. Jacques Pauly has been in charge since 1969. The fermentation is in vat, then the wine spends six months in vat and about 18 months in cask. The wines are light, they can be quite fine, but can also be inconsistent. The '86 showed an improvement, the '88 and '90 are outstanding; the '94 above average and '95, '96, '97 and '98 excellent.

Château Les Justices

Owner: Christian Médeville. 17ha.
White: 8·5ha. 2,000 cases. Sém 88%, Sauv 10%, Musc 2%.
Red: (Bordeaux rouge) 5·6ha. 2,600 cases. CS 58%, Mer 42%.

This property, run by the same owners as Gilette, has belonged to the family since 1710. The harvesting and vinification are basically the same but the wines are bottled after only four years in small vats. The wine is marketed in a more conventional manner.

The '71 is superb, with a concentration of sweetness, a strong perfume and a lovely ripe fruitiness. It was perfection at nearly 14 years of age. The '80 and '81 are both good, the '80 elegant with length and charming fruit and the '81 having more richness and concentration. Good results were obtained in '88, '89 and '90.

Château Lafaurie-Peyraguey

1er Cru Classé. Owner: Domaines Cordier. 38·5ha. 6,000 cases.
Sém 90%, Sauv 5%, Musc 5%.

After Yquem, the château is the most spectacular in Sauternes, with its 13th-century fortifications and 17th-century buildings. It has been carefully run by the Cordiers since 1913.

Recently the winemaking policy has changed: Sauvignon has been dropped from 30 to five per cent of the blend, and Sémillon increased from 70 to 90 per cent. In 1967 a new system was introduced whereby the wines were kept in glass-lined vats under nitrogen after fermentation in cask. The resulting wines became light and one-dimensional, lacking the distinction of a top Sauternes. Now however the winemaking has returned to more traditional ways and wines are matured in casks, of which a third are new. This, combined with the change in the vineyard, promises well for the future.

Much more interesting wines were made in '79, '80, '81 and especially '83. The '84 is delightful, one of the best of the vintage. The '86 was finer than '83, with '88, '89 and '90 following the same pattern of excellence. They have a honeyed bouquet, elegant fruit and breed, and will certainly be worth waiting for. Since then '94, '95, '96, '97 and '98 all produced good to excellent results.

Château Lamothe
2e Cru Classé. Owner: Guy Despujols. 7·1ha. 2,000 cases.
Sém 85%, Sauv 10%, Musc 5%.
Another divided property. Lamothe used to belong to the same owners as Château d'Arche. Then in 1961 half the property, including the château and half the cellars, was sold to the Despujols family. Now wines are fermented in tanks and matured partly in tank, partly in cask. The result is a rather light and dry-ish commercial Sauternes, which is decent but no more. A fine '86 followed by a good '96, however, may mark the beginning of better things.

Château Lamothe-Guignard
2e Cru Classé. Owners: Philippe and Jacques Guignard. 17ha.
3,200 cases. Sém 90%, Musc 5%, Sauv 5%.
Lamothe as a single property belonged to the owners of d'Arche. In 1961 they sold part of the property to the Despujols family and continued to sell the wines from their portion as Lamothe-Bergey. In 1981 the Guignards bought Lamothe-Bergey and substituted their name for Bergey. The same family owns Château Rolland.

The newly-named château's first vintage '81, has elegance and ripeness, length and finesse, delectable fruit and moderate sweetness. This was followed by fine wines in the vintages of '83, '86, '88, '89, '90, '94, '95, '96, '97 and '98.

Château Liot
Owner: J David. 20ha. 4,500 cases.
Sém 85%, Sauv 10%, Musc 5%.
Once bottled by Harveys of Bristol, these well-made wines are sold under the château label only in good vintages – the rest is sold in bulk. The '88, '89 and '90 were particularly good vintages at this property as were '97 and '98.

Château de Malle
2e Cru Classé. Owner: Comtesse de Bournazel. 27ha.
4,000 cases. Sém 75%, Sauv 23%, Musc 2%. Second labels:
Château Ste-Hélène, Chevalier de Malle (white Graves, 3,000 cases), Château de Cardaillan (red Graves, 6,000 cases).
This beautiful property has a 17th-century château. The vineyard is partly in Sauternes and partly in Graves. Fermentation is in cask as well as vat, and maturation follows a similar pattern. The wine has great elegance and charm and is of a light style, only

moderately liquorous. It can be drunk young (at three or four years) but in good years gradually opens up in bottle and repays keeping. The '89 and '90 vintages produced the finest wines I have ever seen here, much richer and more exotic than usual.

Château Menota
Owners: M et Mme Noël Labat. 28ha. 7,500 cases.
Sém 50%, Sauv 50%.

A stunning 16th-century château at which some attractive wines are made. With plenty of classic Sauvignon elegance, the wines are stylish but rather one-dimensional.

Château Myrat
2e Cru Classé. Owner: Comte de Pontac. 22ha.
Sém 88%, Sauv 8%, Musc 4%.

In 1975, the proprietor of this 17th-century château pulled up all his vines as he was no longer able to afford to run the property. Fortunately his successor was able to begin replanting them just before the planting rights expired in 1988. The first dry wine was made in '90, from 50 per cent Sémillon, 30 per cent Sauvignon and 20 per cent Muscadelle. The first Sauternes was made in '91, the vines yielding only three hectolitres per hectare of rich-textured honeyed botrytized juice. After a succession of difficult vintages, '96 really showed what can be achieved here, combining opulent fruit with real finesse.

Château Nairac
2e Cru Classé. Owner: Nicole Heeter-Tari. 16ha. 2,000 cases.
Sém 90%, Sauv 7%, Musc 3%.

Tom Heeter, a young American, came to work at Château Giscours to learn about wine, and in the process he carried off the daughter of the house. His father-in-law Nicolas Tari then spotted that Nairac, in the commune of Barsac, was for sale: the couple finally took possession in 1972. With Professor Peynaud's guidance, Tom Heeter set out to make Barsac in a traditional way, using only wood (65 per cent new) to ferment and mature the wines. However, like Pierre Dubourdieu, he wanted to reduce the use of sulphur. He did not go to the extremes used at Doisy-Daëne, but by using vitamin C, an anti-oxidant, he had much success. Following their divorce (the '86 was Tom Heeter's last vintage), Nicole has shown equal dedication and the '88, '89 and '90 are as good or better than any-thing that went before. '96 and '97 continue this trend. The care of the winemaking has quickly won admirers for Nairac. The wines are not normally liquorous, but are powerful and rich under the influence of new oak. The most successful years here before '86 were '76, '79, '80 and '82. A wine to watch out for.

Château Rabaud-Promis
1er Cru Classé. Owner: GFA Rabaud-Promis.
Administrator: Philippe Dejean. 33ha. 5,000 cases.
Sém 80%, Sauv 18%, Musc 2%.
Second labels: Domaine de l'Estremade, Château Bequet.

Rabaud was a single property until 1903 when it was divided (*see* Sigalas-Rabaud), and this part, two-thirds of the original property, was bought by Adrien Promis. The château dates from the 18th century and is built in a fine hilltop position. The properties were reunited in 1929, but divided again in 1952. The Deuxième Cru Château Peixotto is now also incorporated into Rabaud-Promis.

The grapes, contrary to the tradition in Sauternes, are crushed before going into the presses, and the fermentation and maturation are carried out in cement vats. Improvements came with a new generation of administration and now some casks are used. The '83 was a fine stylish wine; '86 was powerfully botrytized; and the '88 set new standards of excellence, reviving memories of past glories, and was followed by splendid wines in '89 and '90.

Château Raymond-Lafon

Cru Bourgeois. Owner: Marie-Françoise Meslier.
Administrator: Pierre Meslier. 18ha. 2,000 cases.
Sém 80%, Sauv 20%. Second label: Château Lafon-Laroze.
This property belonged to Yquem's former *régisseur*, Pierre Meslier, who has handed the running of the property to his children. Pierre Meslier gave the well-placed vineyard the same meticulous care he gave to neighbouring Yquem. The wine is matured in cask with up to a third in new oak: the results are well up to Cru Classé standards: fine, perfumed, and luscious. Fine wines were made in '75, '76, '79, '80, '81, '82, '83, '84, '85, '86 and '87. The '88, '89 and '90 reached new heights. In the difficult '78, with little or no botrytis, a particularly successful wine was made.

Château de Rayne-Vigneau

1er Cru Classé. Owner: SC du Château. Administrator: Jean Pierre Angliviel de la Beaumelle. 79ha. 16,500 cases (incl 4,000 cases dry). Sém 83%, Sauv 15%, Musc 2%. Dry wine: Rayne Sec.
The wines of Rayne-Vigneau enjoyed a great reputation in the 19th and early 20th centuries. Until 1961 the property belonged to the Pontac family, which still owns the château. In 1971 it was bought by the group that owns Château Grand-Puy-Ducasse and a number of other châteaux. The properties are run and the wines distributed by Mestrezat. The Sémillon and Sauvignon are pressed separately here, because some of the Sauvignon is also used for the dry wine (although most of this is made from less-ripe grapes picked earlier). The fermentation is in vat, then the wine goes into casks (20 per cent are new) for maturation. The property is now well run again, but the yields were too high at first and the wines tended to be correct but rather dull and uninspired – frankly commercial wines. The '76 is the best of this period, but things began to improve with the '83 and '85. The '86, '88, '89 and '90 have maintained this progress.

Château Rieussec

1er Cru Classé. Owner: SA Château Rieussec. 75ha.
8,000 cases. Sém 89%, Sauv 8%, Musc 3%. Second labels: Clos Labère, Château Mayne des Carmes, 'R' de Rieussec (dry).

This property is superbly placed on the highest hill in Sauternes after Yquem. The vineyard is in the commune of Sauternes, but the estate buildings are in Fargues. The soil here is particularly gravelly. Rieussec has always been regarded as one of the finest *crus* in Sauternes, producing wines of great individuality with an outstanding bouquet and great concentration of flavour, but also marked elegance and less lusciousness than some. In 1971 it was acquired by Albert Vuillier who determined to use the most traditional methods and produced wines that have been adored by some and disliked by others. In 1984 he sold to Domaines Rothschild and some time afterwards Charles Chevallier came from Lafite to run the property. The fermentation is in vat, then maturation is partly in large oak *foudres* (vats) and partly in casks, of which 50 per cent is new.

After making a classic Rieussec in 1971, Albert Vuillier mostly made heavily botrytized wines, deep in colour, often with that dry nose and aftertaste associated with botrytis which in excess has the effect of cutting the sweetness at the finish owing to high volatile acidity. For this reason I dislike the '75 in spite of its obvious concentration. The '76 is opulent and attractive but I think slightly unbalanced and therefore was at its best when young. The '83 was Albert Vuillier's last and best vintage.

Under the new regime there has been an acceleration of success. A lovely fresh, ripe '85 was followed by a concentrated '86 with real breed and finesse, then great wines were made in the three outstanding vintages of '88, '89 and '90. Very fine wines were also made in '95, '96, '97 and '98.The dry wine 'R' de Rieussec was made in a rather alcoholic and heavy style that required bottle-age, but a new lighter fresher style, designed for early drinking, was introduced after the '92 vintage.

Château de Rolland

Cru Bourgeois. Owners: Jean and Pierre Guignard. 16ha.
3,600 cases. Sém 80%, Sauv 15%, Musc 5%.
This *cru* in Barsac is also a good restaurant and hotel, the only place to stay if you want to be in the middle of the Sauternes vineyards. The owners are also the proprietors of the excellent Château Roquetaillade-La-Grange in Graves. The wines enjoy a good reputation at Cru Bourgeois level. Wines are vinified and matured in casks bought from Yquem.

Château Romer-du-Hayot

2e Cru Classé. Owner: André du Hayot. 16ha. 4,000 cases.
Sém 70%, Sauv 25%, Musc 5%.
This *cru* deserves to be more widely known. The vineyard adjoins de Malle on the edge of the commune of Fargues. For some years the ownership has been divided between the du Hayot and Farques families, but since 1977 the Farques portion has been leased to the du Hayots, so that the property is now run as one, although there are two owners. The wine is both fermented and matured in vat, and bottling is done early. André du Hayot is producing excellent wines, of their sort, with limited resources both

here and at Guiteronde in Barsac (where the wines are actually made). There is an emphasis on fruit and freshness. Only in years such as '76 is there much sweetness, but the wines always seem well balanced and most attractive. Both '79 and '80 are successes, the '79 fuller and richer; '88 and '89 are both fruity and stylish.

Château St-Amand

Owner: Louis Ricard and Mme Faccheti-Ricard. 19ha.
4,500 cases. Sém 85%, Sauv 14%, Musc 1%.
Second label: Château La Chartreuse.

Traditionally made and elegant, some fine Cru Bourgeois wines are produced at this property in Preignac. They are more commonly sold in England under the Château La Chartreuse label. The '80, '81, '83 and '90 are especially good vintages, though all are stylish and reliable.

Château Sigalas-Ribaud

1er Cru Classé. Owner: Héritiers de la Marquise de Lambert
des Granges. Administrator: Domaines Cordier.
13ha. 2,500 cases. Sém 85%, Sauv 15%.

This *cru* formed part of the old property of Rabaud, which was divided in 1903. From 1929 to 1952 the properties were reunited. Yields are low and the traditional *trie* (selective picking of the ripest grapes) is made four or five times. Fermentation is in vat, as is maturation. I have found the wines perfumed, elegant and quite delicate, yet liquorous and with real breed. For me the best and most typical vintages here have been the especially fine '67 and the '71, '75 and '81. The '83 and '86 follow the same lines.

In January 1995 the proprietors entered into a management contract with Domaines Cordier, so that the property will now benefit from the expertise which has taken its neighbour Lafaurie-Peyraguey to the top of the Sauternes hierarchy in recent vintages. The '95 and '96 showed that the new management can produce even more finely honed wines.

Château Suau

2e Cru Classé. Owner: Roger Biarnés. 8ha. 2,000 cases.
Sém 80%, Sauv 10%, Musc 10%.

Probably the least known of the Crus Classés. The vineyard is in Barsac, but the present owner vinifies the wine at his other property in Illats. Much of the wine is sold by *vente directe* in France. The wine is fermented in vats and then in used casks. The reputation is for rather ordinary, dull wines with an unbalanced sweetness and lacking breed but the '88 is delicate and fine.

Château Suduiraut

1er Cru Classé. Owner: AXA-Millésimes.
Administrator: Jean-Michel Cazes. 90ha. 12,000 cases.
Sém 80%, Sauv 20%.
Second label: Castelnau de Suduiraut.

This famous old *cru* adjoins Yquem and is partly in the commune of Sauternes and partly in that of Preignac. The Fonquernie family bought the property, with its lovely 17th-century château, in 1940 and slowly nursed it back to quality and fame. In 1992 some members of the family sold a majority shareholding to AXA. This is normally the most liquorous and intensely rich wine after Yquem, and when at its best is also one of the best Sauternes. The juice ferments in vats after a careful selection in the vineyard, and is then matured in casks, of which 35 per cent are new. But Suduiraut did go through a bad patch when there was little or no selection and virtually no cask-ageing. This affected the vintages from '71 to '75 inclusive.

The best Suduirauts are pale gold in colour, the bouquet is exquisitely perfumed and penetrating and the flavour rich and vigorous, distinctive, honeyed, with great finesse and breed. In good years the wines usually have five degrees Baumé or more of unfermented sugar (*see* page 161 Yquem). The '70 was one of the best examples of its vintage and '76 produced a classic wine to stand beside the '59, '62 and '67. There were good but not out-standing wines in '79 and '80. During the 1980s the wines have generally had less residual sugar than in the great vintages of the 1950s and 1960s, so one is left with an impression of alcohol at the finish. The '83, '86, '88, '89 and '90 were the best years. '97 and '98 seem closer to the classic balance of the 1960s.

Château La Tour-Blanche
1er Cru Classé. Owner: Ministère de l'Agriculture.
Administrator: J-P Jausserand. 30ha. 5,600 cases. Sém 77%,
Sauv 20%, Musc 3%. Second label: Mademoiselle de St-Marc.
The *cru* was placed at the head of the Premiers Crus in 1855 and since 1910 has belonged to the state, now being run as an agricultural school. Until recently its reputation was far from what it should have been, and there were Deuxièmes Crus and indeed unclassified wines that were better.

The wine is fermented in vat and then matured in cask with 25 per cent new wood. In 1988 a degree of cask fermentation was introduced, just in time to take full advantage of the three great vintages of '88, '89 and '90 – which is one of the great wines of that year and certainly the greatest wine from this property in modern times. This is the culmination of some years of effort which are now restoring the famous *cru* to its rightful place among the finest of the Premier Crus. Again fine wines were made in '94, '95, '96, '97 and '98.

Château d'Yquem
1er Grand Cru Classé 1855. Owner: LVHM.
106ha. 6,500 cases. Sém 80%, Sauv 20%.
Second label: 'Y' (Bordeaux Blanc, 2,000 cases).
In 1855, when the great sweet wines of Sauternes and Barsac were classified, Yquem was placed in a category of its own as the sole Premier Grand Cru, as distinct from the Premiers Crus. Its unique position has remained unassailed ever since.

This is not only the greatest Sauternes, it is also the supreme dessert wine in the world. Since 1593 only two families have owned it. The continuity of ownership lasted for 400 years, as the Lur-Saluces married the last de Sauvage heiress in 1785. Alexandre de Lur-Saluces succeeded his uncle in 1968. In 1999 Alexandre de Lur Saluces lost his long battle to retain his independence, but remains to guide this unique *cru* into the next millennium. The château is a superb fortress commanding fine views over the region. The vineyard is rotated, so that although there are 102 hectares under vine, only about 80 are actually producing the *grand vin*; the rest are young vines.

The picking is carefully controlled, using only skilled workers, mostly from the 57 full-time estate workers, who go through the vineyard a number of times (anything from four to 11) selecting only overripe and botrytized berries. The aim is to pick at not less than 20 degrees and not more than 22 degrees Baumé. This produces the most balanced wines, which ferment to between 13·5 and 14 per cent, leaving between four and seven degrees Baumé unfermented sugar. The pressing is traditional and the musts are fermented in new oak, maturing in cask for three years prior to bottling. Yquem can never be sampled, even by its buyers. A dry wine, 'Y' or Ygrec, is made in some years. It has quite a honeyed nose, and is full-bodied and fairly rich.

Yquem is the quintessence of Sauternes, with its colour turning gradually to pale gold, its intense honeyed bouquet, and the wonderful lusciousness and elegance of the flavour itself. It is always a privilege to drink this wine. One should not attempt to drink it before ten years of age, and it has a special charm of freshness for another decade after that. In the greatest years it can continue almost indefinitely.

Wines at their peak now are '67 (a great year), '70 (very fine), '71 (a great wine), '73 (a good lesser vintage), '75 and '76. Years now drinking well, although still improving, are '80 and '81 (very good) and the '82 (exceptional for the year). The '83 (a massive slow developer), '84 (exceptional for the year), '85 (made in small quantity but excellent) and '86 (potentially the greatest Yquem for many years) and '87, which is remarkable for the year. The '88 promises to rival '86; '89 is even richer while '90 is an elixir. The '91 is remarkable.

St-Émilion

What strikes one about St-Émilion as a district, compared to the other great regions, especially Médoc or Graves, is its small and compact nature. One can walk straight out of the cramped mediaeval streets of St-Émilion and find all but one of the Premiers Crus Classés of the *côtes* just a few minutes' walk away.

St-Émilion covers 5,000 hectares and is divided among 1,000 different *crus*, of which only a small proportion are actually classified. The 330 members of the Union des Producteurs cooperative own 1,150 hectares. Another notable feature is the small size of the properties themselves. The average area of the 13 Premiers Grands Crus Classés is a bare 20 hectares, that of the Grands Crus Classés is less than ten hectares. Compare this with the vineyard sizes in Médoc.

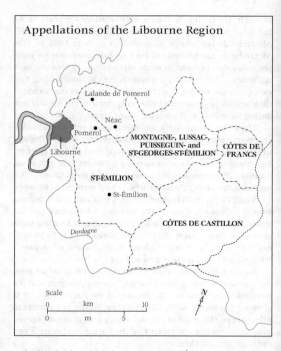

Appellations of the Libourne Region

Lalande de Pomerol

Néac

Pomerol

Libourne

MONTAGNE-, LUSSAC-, PUISSEGUIN- and ST-GEORGES-ST-ÉMILION

CÔTES DE FRANCS

ST-ÉMILION

St-Émilion

CÔTES DE CASTILLON

Dordogne

Scale

0   km   10

0   m   5

N

A further fundamental characteristic of St-Émilion is its complex variety of soils. For practical purposes these can be divided into three groups. First, the limestone plateau (*plateau calcaire*) and the *côtes* and *pieds de côtes*, the hillsides and lower slopes. There is also an important element of clay in these soils. This covers the area around the town of St-Émilion, where all but two of the Premiers Grands Crus Classés are found. The second group is the *graves et sables anciens*, an area of gravel mixed with sand, but sand of an old wind-blown variety as distinct from the more recent alluvial kind. This is a small area near the border with Pomerol, where a succession of gravelly slopes covers about 60 hectares in a sea of sandy soils. Cheval-Blanc and Figeac dominate, and nearly all the other *crus* here are classified. The third soil type is the *sables anciens*, the area of sandy soils of the type already described. There are a number of good, attractive classified *crus* in this area, which lies between the first two.

In terms of appellation and geography, divisions are as follows.

1   The Grands Crus Classés: allowed by a system of classification under the control of the INAO that is subject to revision every ten years. In fact the original system of 1954 was revised in 1969 and the second revision came in 1985. This reduced the number of classified wines from 12 to 11 in the Premiers Grands Crus Classés, and from 72 to 63 in the Grands Crus

Classés. The third revision of 1996 increased the Premiers to 13 restoring Beau-Séjour-Bécot and promoting L'Angélus, while the Grands Crus Classés were again reduced.

2 The Grand Crus: comprising some 200 *crus* that have to submit samples annually for tasting.

3 Wines bearing the simple St-Émilion appellation.

Geographically, although the best wines are to be found in the commune of St-Émilion itself, eight communes which come within the ancient jurisdiction of the Jurade de St-Émilion are also entitled to the appellation. The best wines come from St-Christophe-des-Bardes, St-Laurent-des-Combes, St-Hippolyte and St-Étienne-de-Lisse. The remaining four – St-Pey-d'Armens, Vignonet, St-Sulpice-de-Faleyrens and Libourne – are mostly on low-lying sandy soil or terraces of newer gravel and sand.

There was a time when St-Émilion was said to tend its vines better than anywhere else but to be less skillful at winemaking. There has been a great improvement in this direction with many new *chais* and *cuviers* being built. Only the problems involved in commercialising so many small properties remain to be solved.

Château L'Angélus

1er Grand Cru Classé B. Owner: de Boüard de Laforest family.
Administrators: Hubert de Boüard de Laforest and Jean
Bernard Gressé. 26ha. 8,000 cases. Mer 50%, CF 45%, CS 5%.
Second label: Carillon de L'Angélus.

This is one of the most important estates on the St-Émilion *côtes*. Before buying L'Angélus in 1924, the de Boüard de Laforest family owned Château Mazerat, which they later incorporated, together with several other properties, into L'Angélus. The vineyard is on the lower slopes of the *côtes*, to the west of St-Émilion. There is a large modern *chai* and cask-maturing was introduced in 1980 – between half and two-thirds new oak is used. Before this the wines saw no wood at all.

The wines are characterised by perfume and rich flattering fruit, but tend to lack depth. Prior to '83 many of these wines lacked concentration and needed to be drunk young. Since then they have had more solidity, while retaining their crunchy fruit and richness. The '79 and '82 marked a big step forward, followed by '85 and '86. But then '89 and '90 added an extra voluptuousness, which was repeated in the '95.

My only note of caution is that the high percentage of new oak can tend to mark the wines. In 1996, efforts to upgrade the wines were rewarded by elevation to Premier Cru status. Prices have soared.

Château L'Arrosée

Grand Cru Classé. Owner: François Rodhain. 10ha.
4,000 cases. Mer 50%, CS 35%, CF 15%.
Second label: Les Côteaux du Château L'Arrosée.

The vineyard is well sited on the *côtes* above the cooperative and below Tertre-Daugay, southwest of the town. The name means 'watered by springs'. The balance of the wine comes from its position: the *haute de côte* giving body and power, the *milieu de côte* providing the richness, and the *pied de côte* contributing finesse.

This is classic St-Émilion, rich, luscious, but with great depth, flavour and personality. Not easy to find, but well worth the effort.

Château Ausone
1er Grand Cru Classé A. Owner: Héritiers Vauthier.
Administrator: Alain Vauthier. 7ha. 2,250 cases.
Mer 50%, CF 50%.

Named after the Roman poet Ausonius in the 18th century, this château has the remains of an important Roman villa nearby which may well have belonged to the poet himself.

It was only in the 1890s that Ausone was recognised as the first wine of the St-Émilion *côtes*, a position previously held by its larger neighbour Belair. During the 1950s and 1960s Ausone did not live up to its Premier Cru status, although in 1955 it had earned its placed alongside Cheval-Blanc at the head of the new classification. In 1975 a new *régisseur*, Pascal Delbeck, arrived and took full control in 1976. Since then Ausone's reputation has soared. In 1995 a long-running battle between Mme Dubois-Challon and the Vauthier family ended when the Vauthiers gained control of the management and in 1996 they bought her out. There has been a notable change of style in the '95 and '96 vintages which are more supple, sensuous wines, due to doing the malolactic fermentation in cask.

The essence of Ausone is the combination of delicacy and finesse with power, so that the concentration of complex perfumes on the nose is both lively and beautiful, while the sensation of multi-layered flavours on the palate is remarkable. The wines take longer to mature than other St-Émilions and have an ability to age which is unrivalled on this side of the river.

Since the massive '75 there has been a fine '76, a great '78, a great '82 (opulent and concentrated), a softer yet exotic '83, a top-quality '85 and a complex, densely rich '86. The '89 and '90 are two fascinating wines that will need, but surely repay, plenty of patience.

Everything seems set for Ausone to become the new Pétrus in terms of extraordinary wines produced in small quantities. Let us hope that wine-lovers as well as collectors get a look-in.

Château Balestard-la-Tonnelle
Grand Cru Classé. Owner: GFA Capdemourlin. Administrator:
Jacques Capdemourlin. 10·6ha. 5,000 cases. Mer 65%, CF 20%,
CS 10%, Mal 5%. Second label: Les Tournelles de Balestard.

This estate lies at the limit of the *plateau calcaire*, to the east of St-Émilion and across the road from Soutard. A third of the maturation is in new wood, a third in one- or two-year-old wood and the remainder in *cuves*.

The wines here are consistent and most attractive, archetypical St-Émilion which is big, luscious and full-bodied; easy to drink yet lasting longer than one might expect. The '82 shows concentration with a rich meaty structure and will probably be ready early. The '83 is high in extract and tannins, '85 is an opulent early-developer, and the '86 has real concentration with ripe, elegant tannins. The '89 and '90 are opulent beauties that make a wonderful pair. '95 and '98 are excellent wines.

Château Beau-Séjour-Bécot
1er Grand Cru Classé B. Owners: Michel, Gérard and Dominique Bécot. 16·5ha. 8,000 cases. Mer 70%, CS 15%, CF 15%. Second label: Tournelles des Moines.

This *cru* was classified in 1955 as a Premier Grand Cru, and in 1985 was demoted amidst much controversy. The demotion seems to have been because Bécot added the vineyards of La Carte and Trois Moulins to the original ten hectares of Beau-Séjour which he bought in 1970, although the merger was not effected until 1979. The vineyard is on the *plateau calcaire* and the fermentation is in stainless steel; 90 per cent new wood is used. There are fine underground cellars for maturation in bottle.

The style of the wines here is different from that of the other Beauséjour, more fleshy and rich, but with less tannin and style. They are attractive, easy-to-drink wines but do sometimes lack distinction. Under Gérard and Dominique's management a great effort has been made to improve the wines and restore this *cru* to its former position. This was rewarded in the 1996 revision of the classification. Excellent wines were made in '95, '96, '97 and '98.

Château Beauséjour (Duffau-Lagarrosse)
1er Grand Cru Classé B. Owner: Duffau-Lagarrosse. Administrator: Jean-Michel Fernandez. 7ha. 3,000 cases. Mer 60%, CF 25%, CS 15%. Second label: Le Croix de Mazerat.

The least-known of the Premiers Grands Crus, partly because about half of its tiny production is sold direct to private customers. Beauséjour was a single property until 1869 when it was divided between two daughters. One married a doctor from St-Émilion, and this part of the property now belongs to her heirs. Long vatting here gives the wine breed and stylish fruit, but perhaps rather too much tannin for wines that are light in body.

At one time this wine owed its classification to the vineyard site and a long tradition of respectable wines, because until recently it was good but not brilliant. However, after a rich '82 with real 'race', '85 again had concentration and the '86 was even more impressive, combining elegant fruit with rich concentrated fruit and tannins. The '88, '89, '90, '95 and '96 follow the same line of improvement. Now a wine of distinction.

Château Belair
1er Grand Cru Classé B. Owner: Mme Dubois-Challon, 13ha. 5,000 cases. Mer 65%, CF 35%.

Belair adjoins Ausone and its owner was until 1996 also co-owner of Ausone. Pascal Delbeck, an outstanding *régisseur*, has made a great difference to consistency and quality since 1976. The main difference between Belair and Ausone is that, while Ausone is wholly on the *côtes* , the vineyard of Belair is divided between the *côtes* and the plateau above it. Having been made and kept in the Ausone cellars for many years, the wines of Belair returned to their own cellars in 1976, and the old wooden fermentation *cuves* were replaced by stainless steel vats after the '80 vintage.

Today Belair is nearly always one of the best of the Premiers Grands Crus B group. The wines tend to be a little richer and more fleshy than Ausone, without quite the same intensity, but with real finesse and great vigour. The '75 is firm and still backward; '76 is charming and lightweight, for drinking now, while the '78 gets better all the time; '79 is outstanding. The wines of '82, '83, '85 and '86 are exceptional. The '89, '90, '93, '94, '95 and '96 vie with each other in their dense concentration and inscrutable power.

Château Bellefont-Belcier
Grand Cru. Owner: SC BJL. Administrator: Louis Mitjavile.
13ha. 5,900 cases. Mer 83%, CF 10%, CS 7%.
A good *cru* in St-Laurent-des-Combes, on the *côtes* and their lower slopes. The wines have a reputation for being robust and supple. Louis Mitjavile has run the property since 1994.

Château Bellevue
Grand Cru Classé. Owner: SC du Château (M L Horeau).
Administrator: René de Coninck. 6ha. 3,500 cases.
Mer 68%, CF 16%, CS 16%.
The vineyard lies on the limestone plateau and *côte* just to the west of Beauséjour. It must be one of the least-known of the Grands Crus today. It has the misfortune to have one of the commonest names in Bordeaux: there are 23 properties at present using it, several of which are in the St-Émilion region. This Château Bellevue is an old property and has belonged to the same group of connected families since the 17th century.

For the '88 vintage a proportion of new oak was used for the first time, and from being a rather anonymous pleasant wine, one began to see the breed and style one would expect from a vineyard in this position. This was one of the 39 *crus* of St-Émilion that represented the region at the Paris Exhibition of 1867.

Château Belregard-Figeac
Grand Cru. Owner: Pueyo family. 5ha. 2,500 cases. Mer 68%,
CF 25%, CS 7%. Second wine: Château la Fleur Garderose.
The Pueyo family have owned this small property since the late 19th century. The vineyard is partly on sandy gravel in the Libourne commune, and partly on deep sand on the Figeac plateau. This is a meticulously made wine with hints of cherries and violets, and a fresh crispness to the fruit. Not rich and showy, rather elegant and fine. The first Grand Cru vintage was the admirable '89. '95, '96 and '97 are all good examples.

Château Bergat
Grand Cru Classé. Owner: Héritiers Castéja.
Administrator: Philippe Castéja. 4ha. 1,500 cases.
Mer 50%, CF 40%, CS 10%.

This is one of the smallest and least-known of the Grands Crus Classés. It lies to the east of St-Émilion at the edge of the plateau and *côtes*, overlooking the valley of Fougabaud. The property is farmed by Émile Castéja from nearby Trottevieille and distributed by his firm Borie-Manoux.

In 1984, the '79 was scented and full on the nose with a distinctive spicy character on the palate, full-flavoured and still quite tough, promising a good wine in 1986 or 1987. A bottle of Bergat should always be worth investigating.

Château Berliquet
Grand Cru Classé. Owners: Vicomte et Vicomtesse Patrick de Lesquen. 9ha. 4,200 cases. Mer 67%, CF 25%, CS 8%.
An old *cru*, superbly placed on the *plateau calcaire* and the *côtes*, adjoining Magdelaine, Canon and Tertre Daugay. Dense, textured, powerful and quite tannic wines were made from 1985 onward. Then Patrick de Lesquen called in Patrick Valette to help him and '97 and '98 mark a great improvement. The potential is at last being unlocked.

Château Cadet-Bon
Grand Cru Classé. Owner: Société Loriene.
Administrators: Marceline and Bernard Gans. 6·5ha.
2,500 cases. Mer 70%, CF 20%, CS 10%.
This small property, north of the town on the *plateau calcaire* and *côtes*, lost its status as a Cru Classé in the 1985 revision after producing poorly made wines for some years. But in 1986 the present owners acquired it and determined to make wines worthy of the vineyard. The attractive new label sets the tone of the new regime.

The '88 is spicy and aromatic, a big concentrated wine; the '89 is a classic St-Émilion with a lovely richness and lots of glycerol, power and tannin, while '90 is more supple but with gloriously concentrated fruit. The seriousness of the selection and winemaking come through in the fine '92 and lovely '97. Not surprisingly such wines are rapidly creating a reputation for themselves and already appear on some of the best wine lists in France. These efforts were rewarded in 1996 with promotion to Grand Cru Classé.

Château Cadet-Piola
Grand Cru Classé. Owner: Alain Jabiol. 6·8ha. 3,000 cases.
Mer 51%, CS 28%, CF 18%, Mal 3%.
Second label: Chevaliers de Malte.
Cadet-Piola lies to the north of St-Émilion on the *plateau calcaire* and *côtes* at their culminating northern point. The present owner bought it in 1952 and runs it in conjunction with another Grand Cru Classé, Faurie-de-Souchard. Vinification is in glass-lined vats and is carefully controlled. Maturation is in cellars quarried under the vineyard, and 50 per cent of the wood used is new.

The wines are certainly marked by their grape varieties. They need patience compared with many St-Émilions, being tightly knit and austere to start with, but with the structure and style of a wine of some distinction. However, they are rather short on charm.

Château Canon

1er Grand Cru Classé B. Owner: Chanel Inc.
Administrator: David Orr. 18ha. 8,000 cases.
Mer 55%, CF 45%. Second label: Clos de J Kanon.

This is a beautifully placed property, with 13 hectares of its vineyard in a walled *clos* on the plateau just outside the walls of St-Émilion, and an elegant little 18th-century château. The remainder of the vineyard is on the *côtes*. The wines are matured in as much as 40 per cent new wood.

The wine is classic, beautifully perfumed, with great length of flavour, and can be almost silky in texture. There is an inner concentration of tannin and rich fruit that opens out only slowly. The wine always has immense breed, elegance and style. It is usually one of the top St-Émilions, but one you must wait for. The '75 is a long-term classic. The '85 is compact and fruity – a lovely wine – and '86 achieves the balance of power and finesse that is the hallmark of previous owner Eric Fournier's achievements here. Sadly in 1996 the Fournier family had to sell, fortunately to Chanel, so David Orr and John Kolassa, the highly successful Rauzan-Ségla team, promise a bright future.

Château Canon-la-Gaffelière

Grand Cru Classé. Owner: Comte von Neipperg. 20ha.
14,000 cases. Mer 55%, CF 40%, CS 5%.
Second label: Côte Mignon la Gaffelière.

This property lies on the road which runs from the Libourne–Bergerac road to St-Émilion, at the southern foot of the *côtes* on flat, sandy soil. This owner took over in 1971, but the real changes occured from 1985 onwards when Stephan von Neipperg took over from his father. The evolution has been almost continuous, from stainless steel to a return to wooden vats (since the '97 vintage), malolactic fermentation in barrel, *élevage* on the lees, bottling without filtration. In the late '80s and early '90s the wines often seemed too oaky, now they are richer, denser, textured and more harmonious. Stephan Neipperg is very much his own man and has found his own path by experimentation and experience. These are now very rewarding wines.

Château Cap-de-Mourlin

Grand Cru Classé. Owner: Capdemourlin family.
Administrator: Jacques Capdemourlin. 14ha. 6,000 cases.
Mer 60%, CF 25%, CS 12%, Mal 3%.

During the 1970s and until after the '82 vintage, this historic property was divided between two parts of the Capdemourlin family. Its wines were made and bottled separately, but used identical labels, the one difference being that one bore the name of Mme Jean Capdemourlin, the other that of her nephew Jacques, who also owns Balestard.

Generally I have found the wines vinified by Jacques Capdemourlin to be superior during this period, and he is now responsible for the reunited whole. A third of the wood used for maturation is new. The vineyard is north of St-Émilion on the lower *côtes*. This is a classic St-Émilion, perfumed and fruity on the nose and with a generous, almost unctuous flavour, supported with a good structure. Jacques Capdemourlin made excellent wines in '82, '83, '85, '86, '88, '89, '90, '95, '97 and '98. The future of the reunited property looks promising.

Château Cardinal-Villemaurine
Grand Cru. Owner: J F Carille. 10ha. 5,000 cases.
Mer 70%, CF and CS 30%.
A domaine on the *plateau calcaire* just to the east of the town, with extensive underground cellars. The wines tend to be firm, tannic and a shade austere. They take time to mature. The '70, '75, '76, '79, '81 and '82 are fine examples.

Château Carteau Côtes Daugay
Grand Cru. Owner: Jacques Bertrand. 17ha. 9,000 cases.
Mer 70%, CF 25%, CS 3% and Mal 2%.
This is a consistently reliable Grand Cru. The '95 was very perfumed with delicious open-textured flattering fruit at three years of age, yet with the potential to improve, as older vintages testify.

Château Le Castelot
Grand Cru. Owner: J Janoueix. 9·5ha. 4,000 cases.
Mer 70%, CF 20%, CS 10%.
The vineyards are situated on the sandy plains of St-Sulpice-de-Faleyrens. The sand, gravel and iron traces give these wines noticeable *terroir* with an initially strong impact that usually softens as the wine ages. Careful vinification, using 20 per cent new oak, is carried out by Paul Cazenave, *maître de chai* for all the Janoueix properties as well as Château Canon. Once matured the wines are consistently delicious. Certainly a reliable property.

Château Chauvin
Grand Cru Classé. Owner: Mesdames Ondet. 12·5ha.
6,000 cases. Mer 70%, CS 20%, CF 10%.
Second label: Chauvin Variation.
This *cru* lies in what misleadingly used to be called the St-Émilion Graves. It is the most southeasterly of this group of *crus*, east of Ripeau and south of Corbin. The soil is sandy and 45 per cent of the casks for maturation are new. The wines are typical of this area near the Pomerol border, rich and dense in texture, quickly becoming mellow and unctuous in flavour, but with a touch of coarseness. I have always found this to be an attractive wine.

Château Cheval-Blanc
1er Grand Cru Classé A. Owner: SC du Château Cheval-Blanc.
Administrator: Pierre Lurton. 36ha. 12,000 cases.
CF 60%, Mer 37%, Mal 2%, CS 1%. Second label: Petit Cheval.
St-Émilion's two greatest wines, Ausone and Cheval-Blanc, are at opposite ends of the appellation and on quite different soils. Cheval-Blanc, the most famous of all, is a large property for the region, on the border with Pomerol. Its reputation goes back to

the '21 vintage, and was strengthened by the legendary '47. The soil is gravel and sand, but clay and sandstone with traces of iron are also present. The high proportion of Cabernet Franc at the expense of Merlot is an unusual feature. In 1956 the vineyard was seriously affected by the February frost and took some time to recover. The vinification is in vat, with refrigeration available; 100 per cent new oak is used for maturation. In 1989 Jacques Hébrard retired, having successfully run the property on behalf of his wife's family since 1972. After a hiatus, the family appointed Pierre Lurton, who has been responsible for the marked improvement at Clos Fourtet in recent years. In 1998 the Fourcaud-Lussac heirs ended an ownership which had began with the creation of the *cru* in the 1830s, by selling to Albert Frère (a Belgian businessman) and Bernard Arnault (of LVMH fame, but in his personal capacity).

The wines are famous for their powerful enveloping bouquet, which is rich and often spicy, and their full, mellow, almost unctuous flavour. It is a particular quality of this *cru* that in ripe years the wines can be drunk young. This happened with the famous '47, which was delectable when a mere six or seven years old. At this stage the sheer animal vigour and stunning beauty of the wine is matched only by Pétrus, just across the border in Pomerol. Of course the wines keep and develop well according to the individuality of each year, but the early exuberance is not to be missed and Cheval-Blanc does not age as well as Ausone and some other wines of the *côtes*, becoming lacy and frail when over 40 years old. Great vintages from this property are '64, '66 and '70; other major years are '75, '78, '79 and '81, all of which are delicious to drink now. Of the more recent vintages the '82 is probably the best since '47, and the '83 is also fine. The '85 is a bull's eye, with that opulence bordering on sweetness of the greatest years, and '86 is dense-textured with the style to suggest a great wine. The '88, '89 and '90 also promise great things and '93 and '94 are elegant, stylish wines that make the best of these vintages. The '95 is fine classic Cheval-Blanc. '98 promises to be a great wine. There is no '91 Cheval-Blanc, as it is being sold as Petit Cheval.

Château Clos-des-Jacobins
Grand Cru Classé. Owner: Domaine Cordier. 8·4ha.
4,800 cases. Mer 55%, CF 40%, CS 5%.
The wines here have always been consistent and attractive, but recent vintages have been more concentrated and impressive.

The '82, '83, '86, '88, '89 and '90 are excellent with great richness and opulence. This is certainly one of the best *crus* in this section of St-Émilion.

Château La Clotte
Grand Cru Classé. Owner: Héritiers Chailleau. 3·7ha.
1,200 cases. Mer 70%, CF 30%.
This tiny vineyard is beautifully placed on the edge of the *plateau calcaire* and the *côtes*, just outside the walls of St-Émilion to the east. It is farmed by Éts J-P Moueix which takes three-quarters of

the crop in return for running the vineyard and making the wine (using 25 per cent new wood). The remainder of the crop is kept by the owners, who sell most of it in their popular restaurant, Logis de la Cadène, in St-Émilion.

The wines have real finesse and delicacy, and are fresh and supple with a lovely bouquet in the best style of the *côtes* wines. Owing to the small quantities involved, Éts J-P Moueix sell these wines on an exclusive basis in the US and UK.

Château La Clusière

Grand Cru Classé. Owner: M and Mme Gerard Perse. 3ha.
1,700 cases. Mer 70%, CF 20%, CS 10%.

This tiny vineyard forms a small enclave high on the Côte de Pavie, among the vines of Pavie and under the same ownership and management.

This vineyard belonged to the Vilette family which sold to the Perses in '97. The wines were sound but unexciting. Judging by what has happened at Pavie, one can expect improvements.

Château Corbin

Grand Cru Classé. Owner: Domaines Giraud. 12·7ha.
7,000 cases. Mer 70%, CF 24%, Mal 6%.

A good example of the curse of duplicated names in St-Émilion. In this area of St-Émilion near the Pomerol border there are five adjoining properties, all with Corbin in their names, all Grands Crus Classés, two of them belonging to the Giraud family, to say nothing of others in Montagne-St-Émilion and Graves.

One-third new wood is used in the maturation, and the wines have a reputation for being rich and supple, characteristic of this area of sandy soils near Pomerol.

Château Corbin-Michotte

Grand Cru Classé. Owner: Jean-Noël Boidron. 6·7ha.
3,000 cases. Mer 65%, CF 30%, CS 5%.
Second label: Les Abeilles.

There is a double confusion of names here. This is one of five adjoining Grands Crus Classés with the name Corbin and one of two adjoining Michottes. This one lies immediately to the south of Croque-Michotte, east of La Dominique. The soil is sandy with some clay in the subsoil, contains iron traces, and has some surface gravel. Since acquiring this property in 1959, Jean-Noël Boidron has carried out many improvements, and the *chai* was entirely rebuilt in 1980. Twenty per cent of the wine is matured in new wood, rotated with wine held in stainless steel vats.

I am always impressed with this wine. The rich, plummy texture, fat and full and mellow in the mouth, is typical of the best wines from this corner of St-Émilion near Pomerol.

Château Cormeil-Figeac

Grand Cru. Owner: Héritiers R & L Moreaud. 10ha.
5,500 cases. Mer 70%, CF 30%.
Second label: Château Haut-Cormey.

A good vineyard on the sandy soils southeast of Château Figeac. Wood maturation is carried out in 100 per cent new oak. The wines are scented, supple and full-flavoured with lots of vibrant fruit: delicious for early drinking.

Château Côte-Baleau
Grand Cru. Owner: Société des Grandes Murailles. 17ha.
7,500 cases. Mer 60%, CF 25%, CS 15%.

This *cru* was classified in 1969 but lost its position in 1985. It is on the lower slope of the *côtes* and on sandy soils, north of the town, adjoining Château Laniote. The wines of both Grandes Murailles and Clos St-Martin are actually made and kept here. It is hard to say what was behind the thinking that demoted this *cru* and Grandes Murailles but retained Clos St-Martin. My own comparative tastings suggested that this was the best of the properties.

The wines have plenty of structure and richness of flavour, and require some ageing.

Château Coudert
Grand Cru. Owner: Jean-Claude Carles. 14ha. 7,000 cases.
Mer 50%, CF and CS 50%.

This *cru*, in the commune of St-Christophe-des-Bardes, makes stylish wines that are long on the palate and have some breed.

Château Coudert-Pelletan
Grand Cru. Owner: Jean Lavau et Fils. 6·5ha. 3,600 cases.
Mer 70%, CF 15%, CS 15%.

A château producing classic St-Émilion with style and marvellous ageing potential. The '70, at over 15 years old, was still splendid.

Château La Couronne
Grand Cru. Owner: Mähler-Besse. 9ha. 5,000 cases.
Mer 65%, CS 20%, CF15%.

This *cru* in St-Hippolyte was bought by the Bordeaux *négociants* Mähler-Besse (who are also shareholders in Château Palmer) in 1992. The improvements they have made enabled the owners to gain the Grand Cru appellation. I found the '95 deliciously ripe with easy flattering fruit, yet also body and depth.

Château La Couspaude
Grand Cru Classé. Owner: Vignobles Aubert. 7ha. 3,000 cases.
Mer 60%, CF and CS 40%.

A property on the *plateau calcaire* immediately to the east of the town, between Villemaurine and Trottevieille. It lost its place in the classification in 1985, but regained it in 1996. Eighty per cent new oak is used, but the wine is attractively fruity and stylish and well worth looking out for.

Château Couvent-des-Jacobins
Grand Cru Classé. Owner: Mme Joineau-Borde. 10ha.
4,400 cases. Mer 65%, CF 30%, CS 5%.
Second label: Beau-Mayne.

This old property originally belonging to the Dominican friars was added to the classification in 1969. The house and *chai* are in the old town of St-Émilion, while the vineyard nestles beneath the eastern ramparts of the town on the edge of the *plateau calcaire* and on sandy soils. Secular owners took over in the 18th century and the present family has been here since 1902.

This is a traditionally made wine, with one-third new wood used for the maturation. In recent vintages I have found the wines to be consistent, well made, with a beautiful flavour and firm finish, quite taut and well structured. There is a distinctive blue-black label. The wine is distributed by Dourthe Frères.

Château Croque-Michotte
Grand Cru. Owner: Mme Rigal. 14ha. 6,500 cases.
Mer 70%, CF 30%.

This *cru*, on the northwest of St-Émilion, borders on Pomerol. It has been in the same family since 1890. One-third new wood is used. The wine seems to be consistently well made in a robust if slightly rustic style. The '78 is ripe and attractive, drinking well, and the '79 is massive and dense with backbone and tannin. The '81 is tannic and robust with a fine finish; the '83 rich and complex and the '85 has a lively opulent flavour of plums. The wine is above average in terms of quality and consistency, yet lost its classification in 1996, partly because of its reasonable prices.

Château Curé-Bon
Grand Cru Classé. Owner: SA Loriene. Administrators:
Marceline and Bernard Gaus. 4·4ha. 1,500 cases.
Mer 80%, CF 20%.

This is a well placed vineyard on the *plateau calcaire*, a part of which forms the base of an old quarry. Its neighbours are Ausone, Belair and Canon. Maturation is in cask with 50 per cent new wood. The wines have a good reputation and tend to be quite firm in spite of the high proportion of Merlot, but they are also fleshy and generous with a distinctive bouquet, denoting breed. The present owners took over in 1992, and the wines are already showing an improvement, with lovely pure fruit flavours coming through.

Château Dassault
Grand Cru Classé. Owner: SARL Château Dassault.
Administrator: André Vergriette. 23ha. 13,000 cases.
Mer 65%, CF 30%, CS 5%.

This was one of eight *crus* added to the classification in 1969. Formerly known as Château Couperie, it was renamed in 1955. Vinification is in stainless steel with maturation in wood, of which 50 per cent is new oak.

The style of the Dassault wines is uncomplicated, full-flavoured and supple, with charm and breed. They reflect careful vinification and *élevage* and are most consistent. Pleasant middle-of-the-road wines.

Château La Dominique
Grand Cru Classé. Owner: Clément Fayat. 22·5ha.
10,000 cases. Mer 75%, CF 15%, CS 5%, Mal 5%.
Second label: St-Paul de la Dominique.
This *cru* has always had the capacity to make exceptional wines, but was not consistent until the present owner took over in 1969.

The wines now are an impressive blend of fruit, ripeness and tannin which come together to produce remarkable opulence and power-packed flavour, placing them at the forefront of the Grands Crus Classés. '82, '83, '85, '86, '89 and '90 are all exceptional, while '93, '94, '95, '96, '97 and '98 are great successes for these vintages.

Château Faugères
Grand Cru Classé. Owner: Corinne Guissey.
20ha. 8,300 cases. Mer 70%, CF 25%, CS 5%.
Second label: Château Haut-Bardoulet.
When a new generation of the family took over in 1987, they transformed the property with new drainage of the vineyard, replanting of vines, installation of stainless steel vats, selection parcel by parcel, use of 50 per cent new oak and château-bottling of all wine. The excellence and fame of these new wines quickly spread and they are now widely exported. They are rich and powerful but with unmistakable style and breed. The splendid '90 vintage showed the potential of the property which actually straddles the boundary of St-Étienne-de-Lisse and St-Colombe in the Côtes de Castillon appellation. *See under* Cap de Faugères.

Château Faurie-de-Souchard
Grand Cru Classé. Owner: Jabiol-Sciard family. 11·5ha.
6,000 cases. Mer 65%, CF 26%, CS 9%.
The name is not to be confused with that of the neighbouring Petit-Faurie-de-Soutard. Previously this property also had the prefix 'Petit', but this has been dropped. The vineyard is on the plateau and *côtes* northeast of the town. Fermentation is in concrete vats and maturation is by rotating the wine between casks (of which a third are new) and vats. Although there is much more Merlot here than at Cadet-Piola, there are some similarities of style, especially a lack of flesh and tightness of flavour. There seems to be a lack of consistency and charm about these wines at present.

Château de Ferrand
Grand Cru. Owner: Baron Marcel Bich. Administrator: Jean-Pierre Palatin. 30ha. 17,800 cases. Mer 70%, CF 15%, CS 15%.
This is the most important property in St-Hippolyte, situated on the *plateau calcaire*. Not less than 50 per cent and sometimes 100 per cent new wood is used for the maturation. The aim is to produce rich, tannic wines that are suitable for ageing.

Château Figeac
1er Grand Cru Classé B. Owner: Thierry de Manoncourt.
39ha. 17,500 cases. CS 35%, CF 35%, Mer 30%.
Second label: La Grange Neuve de Figeac.

This fine old property is the remnant of a much larger estate, which in the 18th century included Cheval-Blanc and several others that now incorporate the name of Figeac. As with Cheval-Blanc, some two-thirds of the vineyard is on gravel and the remaining third on sandy soil. A fine new *chai* with a large underground section is the latest improvement here.

Under Thierry de Manoncourt (who was in charge from 1947 to the early '90s) the consistency and quality of winemaking has been of a high order. The similarities and differences between Figeac and Cheval-Blanc are always fascinating. The size of the vineyards and composition of the soils are strikingly similar, but the *encépagement* is notably different. Here an important role is given to Cabernet Sauvignon, while at Cheval-Blanc the Cabernet Franc reigns supreme. As a result, for all their similarities, Figeac seldom matches Cheval-Blanc for sheer weight and opulence of flavour, although it sometimes approaches it and occasionally (as in '53 and '55) can even surpass it. The '82, '83, '85, '86, '88, '89, '90, '95 and '98 are superb wines. Now Thierry de Manoncourt's son-in-law Eric d'Aramon manages the property.

Château La Fleur

Grand Cru. Owner: Lily Lacoste. 6·5ha. 3,000 cases.
Mer 92%, CF 8%.
This is a good vineyard northeast of Soutard on sandy soils. The owner is better known as co-proprietor of Pétrus and owner of Latour à Pomerol. The fleshy, rich wines are full of easy fruit and charm.

Château Fleur-Cardinale

Owner: Claude and Alain Asséo. 9ha. 4,500 cases.
Mer 70%, CF 15%, CS 15%.
Situated on the clay-chalk soils of the *côte* at St-Étienne-de-Lisse, this *cru's* wines are traditionally vinified and matured in oak, but need time to soften before drinking at their best.

Château Fleur-Cravignac

Grand Cru. Owner: Lucienne Beaupertins. 7.5ha. 3,000 cases.
Mer 70%, CF 20%, CS 10%.
Several recent tastings have shown Fleur-Cravignac to be an excellent Grand Cru. The '95 was rich and solid with plenty of substance, depth and harmony. Just what one looks for in a good St-Emilion.

Château La Fleur-Pourret

Grand Cru. Owner: AXA-Millésimes.
Administrators: Jean-Michel Cazes and Gilbert Xans.
4·5ha. 2,500 cases. Mer 50%, CS 50%.
A property created by the grandfather of Bruno Prats in the 19th century, combining two *crus*; Clos Haut-Pourret and Château La Fleur. Now owned by AXA. The La Fleur-Pourret wines have an unusually high proportion of Cabernet Sauvignon in their blend.

Château Fombrauge

Grand Cru. Owner: Bordeaux Château Invest. 52ha.
26,000 cases. Mer 70%, CF 15%, CS 15%.

An important *cru* in St-Christophe-des-Bardes, situated partly on
the *plateau calcaire* and partly on the north-facing *côte* and its
lower slopes. In 1987 it was sold to its present owner, a Danish
consortium. The wines are matured in cask with 40 per cent new
oak used. This *cru* has a long-established reputation in the UK for
producing consistent, reliable wines that are rich and fleshy.

Château Fonplégade

Grand Cru Classé. Owner: Armand Moueix. 18ha. 10,000
cases. Mer 60%, CF 40%. Second label: Clos Goudichaud.

These are firm rather than tannic wines that require time to show
their style and finesse. This is a consistent and reliable wine, without the richness and charm of some, but rewarding to keep: solid
and dependable, if lacking flair.

Château Fonroque

Grand Cru Classé. Owner: GFA Château Fonroque.
Administrators: Éts J-P Moueix. 16ha. 8,000 cases.
Mer 90%, CF 10%.

The style here tends to be robust, and these are quite firm wines
that need ageing to show at their best – not the flamboyant, early-
drinking style at all. Tannic and solid, the wines are consistent
and age well.

Clos Fourtet

1er Grand Cru Classé B. Owners: Lurton brothers (André,
Dominique, Lucien, Simone). 19ha. 8,500 cases.
Mer 72%, CF 22%, CS 6%. Second label: Domaine de Martialis.
The reputation of this château was in decline until 1973 when
extensive improvements were made and the proportion of Merlot
increased. There are distinct similarities of style between Clos
Fourtet and its neighbour Canon. The wines tend to be tightly
knit and slow to evolve, but recently richer and more open-
textured than of old. The '85, '86, '88, '89, '90, '93, '95, '96, '97 and
'98 are particularly good, having extra concentration and richness
allied to a lovely flavour. This is certainly a château with the
potential to improve its standing still further.

Château Franc-Grâce-Dieu

Grand Cru. Owner: Germain Siloret. Administrator: Eric
Fournier. 8ha. 3,500 cases. Mer 52%, CF 41%, CS 7%.
Until Eric Fournier from Premier Grand Cru Château Canon took
over the farming and management here in 1981, the property was
called Guadet-Franc-Grâce-Dieu. It was decided that this was rather
a mouthful and the Guadet was dropped. Vinification is now in
stainless steel with maturation in cask. I found Eric Fournier's first
vintage, the '81, had finesse and style with intense, vibrant young
fruit – better frankly than some Crus Classés – and the improvement during the 1980s has been impressively built upon since.

Château Franc-Mayne

Grand Cru Classé. Owner: Georgy Fourcroy and associates.
7ha. 3,000 cases. Mer 72%, CF 14%, CS 14%.

This *cru* lies northwest of St-Émilion, just off the St-Émilion–Pomerol road, and is on the *côtes*. In recent years the proportion of Cabernet Franc has been increased, at the expense of the Cabernet Sauvignon, in order to produce less tannic and more elegant wine. AXA took over in 1987 and then sold in '96 to a group of Belgians headed by Belgian *négociant* Georgy Fourcroy. They have brought in Michel Rolland and have invested in the cellars and the vineyard. The first wines are very concentrated and rich.

Château La Gaffelière

1er Grand Cru Classé B. Owner: Comte Léo de Malet-Roquefort.
22ha. 10,500 cases. Mer 65%, CF 30%, CS 5%.
Second label: Clos La Gaffelière.

The reputation of La Gaffelière is mixed. It can produce marvellously perfumed, supple, rich and fleshy wines, but in the past they have been inconsistent, lacking the backbone and breed of some of the best *crus* on the *côtes* and plateau. The signs now are that there is more consistency and a high standard of winemaking.

The '82 is reminiscent of the '47 with its dense, almost jammy concentration. The '83 is particularly successful, rich and complex with real 'race', and the '85 and '86 have benefited from increased selection, summer pruning of bunches and longer maceration, their concentration and structure much improved – a pattern which continued with the '88, '89, '90, '94, '95 and '97. A wine of enormous charm, which perhaps needs a degree of richness to give of its best, and one to watch.

Château La Gomerie

Grand Cru. Owner: Gerard and Dominique Bécot. 2.5ha.
750 cases. Mer 100%.

I do not usually list properties with such a miniscule production, but this has become a trophy wine in a very short time, and is getting around. I first tasted it in Sweden! It belongs to the Bécots of neighbouring Beau-Séjour-Bécot, but sells for a higher price, due to the tiny quantities. Although this is a new-wave wine in terms of malolactic in cask and 100 per cent new oak, the old vines do give it a natural concentration which makes the '95 delicious with rich, ripe fruit and harmony with no sign of excessive oak. Whether it is worth the money, only the buyers and the market can decide.

Château La Grâce-Dieu-Les-Menuts

Grand Cru. Owner: Audier and Pilotte families. 13ha.
6,500 cases. Mer 65%, CF 30%, CS 5%.

The name Grâce-Dieu comes from a Cistercian grange which was secularised in the 17th century and subsequently divided.

Some new casks have been introduced for the maturation, and the reputation of this *cru* is improving. It lies northwest of St-Émilion on the Libourne road, in the sector of sandy soils. The wines tend to be light-textured – suitable for young drinking.

Château Grand-Barrail-Lamarzelle-Figeac

Grand Cru. Owner: Association E Carrère. 19ha. 8,400 cases.
Mer 80%, CF 15%, CS 5%.

The Carrère family bought the property in the disastrous year of 1956. Ten per cent new wood is used for the maturation and the wines have a reputation for being supple, fruity and early-maturing. Given the position of the vineyard, one wonders if the full potential has yet been realised: in 1996 it lost its Grand Cru status. The château has now been converted into a luxury hotel, providing a rare opportunity to stay in a working vineyard.

Château Grand Corbin

Grand Cru. Owner: Alain Giraud. 13ha. 7,500 cases.
Mer 68%, CF 27%, CS 5%.

The history of this property echoes that of Château Corbin, which shares the same ownership. It lies on sandy soils between Corbin and Grand-Corbin-Despagne. Maturation is in casks, of which one-third are new.

The reputation of this *cru* is for producing wines that tend to be blander than those of Corbin.

Château Grand-Corbin-Despagne

Grand Cru. Owner: Despagne family. 26·5ha. 12,500 cases.
Mer 75%, CF 20%, CS 4%, Mal 1%.

The wines have a reputation for being rich and fleshy, but sometimes rather dilute and rustic. Cru Classé status was lost in 1996.

Château Grandes Murailles

Grand Cru Classé. Owner: SC du Château. 2ha. 1,000 cases.
Mer 70%, CF 30%.

This tiny vineyard adjoins Clos Fourtet where the *plateau calcaire* begins to fall away to the *côte*. There is a curious situation here. The wine is made and kept at the cellars of Baleau, the largest of the three properties owned by this company, but Grandes Murailles and Baleau lost their classified status as a result of the 1985 revision (in 1996 this property regained it).

I have found these wines rich and opulent in style, and quick to mature.

Château Grand-Mayne

Grand Cru Classé. Owner: Jean-Pierre Nony. 19ha. 9,500 cases.
Mer 72%, CF 23%, CS 5%. Second label: Les Plants du Mayne.

This old domaine with its beautiful mansion, dating in part from the 15th century, is one of the finest buildings in the vicinity of St-Émilion. It lies on the western *côte* and its lower slopes. Stainless steel vats replaced the traditional wooden ones in 1975. Maturation is in casks, 80 per cent of which are new.

The wines here seem to have got better and better. '88, '89 and '90 have been exceptionally rich and fine, while the remarkable quality of the '92, '93, '94, '95, '96, '97 and '98 confirm this improvement. A wine that seems to have moved up a notch.

Château Grand-Pontet

Grand Cru Classé. Owners: Bécot and Pourquet families.
14ha. 6,500 cases. Mer 70%, CF 15%, CS 15%.

This château, at the foot of the *côtes*, lies just outside St-Émilion on the Libourne road. From 1965 to 1980 it belonged to Barton & Guestier, who completely modernised the property. One of the two present partners also owns nearby Beau-Séjour-Bécot.

Under the new management rich, vibrant, flattering wines of character are now being made. The '90, '95 and '96 are very successful.

Château Guadet-St-Julien

Grand Cru Classé. Owner: Robert Lignac. 6ha. 2,000 cases.
Mer 75%, CF 25%.

Generally this is an attractive, supple wine, showing unmistakable class and maturing quickly. But there can also be a touch of iron in its soul.

Château Haut-Badette

Owner: J-F Janoueix. 4·5ha. 3,000 cases. Mer 90%, CS 10%.

The wines are of better quality than many of Grand Cru status: charmingly perfumed with an abundance of fruit and body, combining the fruit and qualities of a young-drinking wine with the ability to mature well. The '95 vintage was especially good here.

Château Haut-Corbin

Grand Cru Classé. Owner: A M du Bâtiment et Travaux
Publics. Administrator: Philippe Dambrine. 7·6ha. 4,000 cases.
Mer 67%, CS 33%.

This small property near the border with Montagne-St-Émilion lies north and east of the other Corbin properties on sandy soil. It was the only *cru* in this part of the appellation to be upgraded to Grand Cru Classé in 1969. The wines are matured in cask, but no new wood is used. Since new management took over in 1986 there has been a dramatic improvement, with rich, meaty wines in '86, '88, '89 and '90. Serious wines were also made in '93, '94 and '95.

Château Haut-Gueyrot

Owner: Jean-Claude Gombeau. 6·3ha. 3,900 cases.
Mer 85%, CF 15%.

This small vineyard on the lower slopes and plain of St-Laurent-des-Combes produces consistently attractive, rich, fruity, quite luscious and typical wines, usually delicious after three years.

Château Haut-Pontet

Grand Cru. Owner: Limouzin Frères. 5·2ha. 2,500 cases.
Mer 75%, CF and CS 25%.

This small *cru* is on the lower slopes of the *côte* north of St-Émilion. The consistently well-made wine is distinctive, rich and full-flavoured with a good backbone.

Château Haut-Sarpe

Grand Cru Classé. Owner: J-F Janoueix. 11·5ha. 5,600 cases.
Mer 70%, CF 30%.

Tastings of a number of recent vintages over a period of years have confirmed this as a wine of character and breed. The '89 and '90 are powerful and dense-textured.

Château Jean-Faure

Grand Cru. Owner: Michel Amart. 17ha. 9,500 cases.
CF 60%, Mer 30%, Mal 10%.

This *cru*, lying on sandy soils between Cheval-Blanc and Ripeau, belonged to Ripeau for many years and the properties were run together until the present owner bought it in 1976. The wine is distributed by Dourthe Frères. The *cru* lost its classified status in the revision of 1985. The aim is to produce full-bodied but elegant wines. My limited experience of them is that they are either tough and ferrous or soft and lacking in personality and style.

Château Lamarzelle

Grand Cru Classé. Owner: Carrière family. 13ha. 5,800 cases.
Mer 80%, CF 20%.

In the revision of 1996 this *cru* retained its place while its sister *cru*, Grand-Barrail-Lamarzelle-Figeac, lost its position. Neither wine has been outstanding in recent years, but with Dourthe distributing this wine, the attention to quality may have proved decisive – and there is more gravel in the vineyard here. Ten per cent new oak is used in the ageing. This seems to be one of the few properties near to Figeac not to hyphenate its name!

Château Laniote

Grand Cru Classé. Owner: Freymond-Rouja family. 5ha.
2,600 cases. Mer 70%, CS 20%, CF 10%.

This is not a big beefy St-Émilion but it has great finesse. It is perfumed and intense with a long, refined and beautiful flavour and real 'race'. It has a most enchanting texture, lush and silky, which makes the wine exciting.

Château Laplagnotte-Bellevue

Grand Cru. Owner: Henri and Claude de Labarie. 6ha.
2,500 cases. Mer 70%, CF 20%, CS 10%.

Claude de Labarie, *née* Fourcaud-Lussac, was one of the principal shareholders of Cheval-Blanc, and since she and her husband bought this small property in St-Christophe-des-Bardes in the late 1980s, the reputation of the *cru* has grown. The '90 has lovely crushed-fruit aromas with clean, crisp, fresh fruit flavours. Already delicious when three years old, it has the capacity to mature for some years.

Château Larcis-Ducasse

Grand Cru Classé. Owner: Jacques Olivier Gratiot. 11ha.
5,000 cases. Mer 65%, CF 25%, CS 10%.

The wines here have been noted for their breed and charm, but have sometimes been rather light. Recent vintages have shown a marked improvement in consistency and quality. Lovely rich wines were made in '89 and '90.

Château Larmande

Grand Cru Classé. Owner: Le Groupe Mondiale.
Administrator: Marc Dworkin. 25ha. 12,500 cases. Mer 65%,
CF 30%, CS 5%. Second label: Le Cadet de Larmande.

This fine property lies north of St-Émilion looking towards St-Georges. It marks the end of the *côtes* and the beginning of the sandy soils. The last decade has been one of progress here. The vineyard has been enlarged and the proportion of Merlot increased at the expense of Cabernet Franc and, to an even greater extent, Cabernet Sauvignon. A new *cuvier* equipped with stainless steel fermentation vats was built in 1975. Sixty per cent new oak is now used. This wine has won many accolades, and consistently does well in blind tastings. The bouquet tends to be perfumed, full and vibrant, the wine rich, full-flavoured, quite spicy and with depth, harmony and style. The wines are rather heavily marked by oak in all but the most luscious years.

Château Laroque

Grand Cru Classé. Owner: Beaumartin family.
Administrator: Bruno Sainson. 58ha. 12,500 cases.
Mer 87%, CF 10%, CS 3%. Second label: Les Tours de Laroque.

This large property is in the commune of St-Christophe-des-Bardes where it occupies an exceptional site on the *plateau calcaire* and *côte*. The château itself is one of the grandest in the St-Émilion area, built in the time of Louis XIV and having a 12th-century tower as a reminder of the feudal domaine. The improvements date from 1982 when Bruno Sainson was brought in to manage the estate. He identified 27 of the 58 hectares that could produce wines of top quality. Buildings and cellars were renovated and some plots were replanted. Yields are strictly controlled, grapes hand-picked and sorted before fermentation and 40 per cent new oak is used for the ageing. Then there is a further strict selection for the Laroque label, the rest being sold under the Les Tours de Laroque *marque*.

All this work was crowned by promotion to Grand Cru Classé in 1996, the first time this has been granted to a property whose vineyards are wholly outside the St-Émilion commune. Lovely rich, concentrated wines are now being made in years like '94, '95, '96, '97 and '98.

Château Laroze

Grand Cru Classé. Owner: Georges Meslin. 27ha. 13,000 cases.
Mer 59%, CF 38%, CS 3%.

The wines here are characterised by their fresh, clean, up-front fruit. They are perfumed, supple and easy to drink, maturing quite quickly (over three to five years) and usually at their best at around five to eight years. These are delicious, flattering, fruity wines sold at reasonable prices.

Château Magdelaine
1er Grand Cru Classé B. Owner: Éts J-P Moueix. 11ha.
5,000 cases. Mer 90%, CF 10%.

The hallmark of Magdelaine is its great delicacy, breed and refinement of flavour. There was an exceptionally attractive '75 and fine wines were made in '78, '79, '81, '82, '83, '85, '86, '88, '89, '90, '94, '95, '97 and '98. The personality of the *cru* is interesting because it is more charming than straight plateau wines such as Canon, but less fleshy and more elegant than a lower *côtes* such as La Gaffelière. For me this is certainly one of the most rewarding wines of the St-Émilion *côtes*.

Château Magnan La Gaffelière
Grand Cru. Owner: GFA du Clos de la Madeleine. 7.8ha.
3,500 cases. Mer 65%, CF 25%, CS 10%.

In 1995 at a blind tasting of '45s, this wine outperformed some of the most illustrious Premiers Grands Crus. We all wondered if the *cru* still existed. In fact, it was bought, along with Clos de la Madeleine, by a group of enthusiasts in 1992, and the '95 proved to be one of the outstanding wines in a large tasting organised for me by the Syndicat in 1999. This is a wine full of character and luscious Merlot fruit.

Château Matras
Grand Cru Classé. Owner: Mme Véronique Gaboriaud-Bernard.
10ha. 5,000 cases. Mer 33%, CF 33%, CS 33%, Mal 1%.

If you stand on the promontory at Tertre-Daugay and look across the *côte* northwards, you will see a battery of tanks standing beside some modest buildings. This is Matras. It lies southwest of the town and occupies a hollow on the *côtes* and the lower slope. The proprietor is an oenologist. Ageing is in 35 per cent new casks.

I found both the '79 and '81 had an unpleasantly marked iron taste and were tough and charmless. The impression was that all was not well with the winemaking, especially as the site is so good. However a fine '90 showed that things have improved.

Château Mauvezin
Grand Cru. Owner: Pierre Cassat. 4ha. 4,500 cases.
Mer 60%, CF 30%, CS 10%.

This small vineyard lies east of St-Émilion at the limits of the *plateau calcaire*, between Haut-Sarpe and Balestard-la-Tonnelle. Since the present owner took over in 1986 there has been much replanting, and the yields have increased accordingly. A high percentage of new wood is used in the maturation. The many gold medals won by this *cru* attest to the quality of its wines.

Château Monbousquet
Grand Cru. Owner: M et Mme Gérard Perse. 30ha.
17,000 cases. Mer 50%, CF 40%, CS 10%.

When the property was run by Alain Querre, these were attractive, rich, supple wines with a distinctive character, sometimes a hint of tobacco on the nose and a strong, rather earthy flavour.

They lacked the ultimate breed of the best St-Émilions, but were nevertheless highly enjoyable wines. Now the new owner has transformed both *chai* and wines, using the pre-fermentation cold maceration and 100 per cent new oak to make opulent, dense-textured, plummy, fruity wines, much to the new taste. The first vintage was '93. Michel Rolland is consultant oenologist.

Château Mondotte

Grand Cru. Owner: Comte Stephen von Neipperg. 4.5ha. 2,000 cases. Mer 80%, CF 20%.

This small vineyard is just to the east of Troplong-Mondot and it is only recently that Stephen von Neipperg has found that he can make more remarkable wines here than at his Grand Cru Classé, Canon-la-Gaffelière. 100 per cent new oak is now being used and a new *cuverie* with wooden vats was completed in time for the '98 crop. '96 is the first vintage of the new Mondotte with its small yield of 30hl/ha, and '97 and '98 are in the same vein. One finds truffles, black cherries, liquorice, together with complexity and a very special and marked character, unctuous fruit with very rich tannins. There is no doubting the quality of these wines, but the prices are something else!

Château Montlabert

Grand Cru. Owner: SC Civile. Administrator: Montagu Curgon. 13ha. 7,800 cases. Mer 55%, CF 32%, CS 13%.

This property lies on sandy soils northwest of St-Émilion near Figeac. The wines have good concentration and lovely rich luscious fruit with good structure.

Château Moulin du Cadet

Grand Cru Classé. Owner: Éts J-P Moueix. 5ha. 2,300 cases. Mer 90%, CF 10%.

A small property on the *plateau calcaire*, north of St-Émilion and adjoining the Moueix property of Fonroque. The wines bear the hallmarks of the impeccable care that Éts J-P Moueix take of all the properties they own or farm. Recently 25 per cent new wood has been introduced to the cask maturation. The wines are little known because of the small production, but I have been impressed by their perfume, breed and elegance. They can be rather finer than those at neighbouring Fonroque, but less powerful and robust.

Château Moulin-St-Georges

Grand Cru. Owner: Alain Vauthier. 8ha. 3,500 cases. Mer 70%, CF 20%, CS 10%.

Very stylish wines are produced at this property; past vintages have shown the ability to age well, also being pleasant to drink when young. Alain Vauthier's family are owners of Ausone. The '95 is one of the best Grand Cru wines of the year.

Clos L'Oratoire

Grand Cru Classé. Owner: Comte Stephan von Neipperg. 10ha. 5,000 cases. Mer 75%, CF 25%.

This property lies northeast of the town where the lower slope of the *côte* gives way to the sandy soils, close to the border with St-Christophe-des-Bardes. It is run with the larger Château Peyreau which is an unclassified Grand Cru. One-third new casks are used for the maturation.

These are rich, concentrated wines, Merlot in style with a good depth of flavour; what one thinks of as a typical St-Émilion. They develop quite quickly. In 1990 the new owner brought to L'Oratoire all the attention to detail he shows at Canon-la-Gaffelière, and the wines are now more consistent.

Château Palais-Cardinal-La-Fuie

Grand Cru. Owner: Gérard Frétier. 20ha. 7,000 cases.
Mer 50%, CF 35%, CS 15%.

This *cru* is situated in the commune of St-Sulpice-de-Faleyrens. It produces wines that are pleasant to drink young but which age rather rapidly in years of high production.

Château Patris

Grand Cru. Owner: Michel Querre. 12·3ha. 6,700 cases.
Mer 88%, CF 8%, CS 4%.

This *cru*, on sandy soils of the little valley of Mazerat, just at the southwest base of the *côte* of St-Émilion, is run with the same care as the owner's *cru* in Pomerol, Château Mazeyres. Two-thirds of the wine is matured in casks, of which 25 per cent are new; the rest in vats. Perfumed, supple wines of good repute are made.

Château Pavie

1er Grand Cru Classé B. Owner: M and Mme Gérard Perse.
35ha. 15,000 cases.
Mer 55%, CF 25%, CS 20%.

This is the largest vineyard on the *côtes*, and is splendidly placed on a long, south-facing slope southeast of St-Émilion.

In 1998 the present owners, having already bought Pavie-Decesse from the Valette family, finally acquired the Valette's largest and finest vineyard. During the 1980s, under Jean-Paul Valette's guidance, Pavie was the most improved *cru* among the Premiers, with outstanding wines being made in '82, '83, '85, '86, '88, '89 and '90. Although many improvements were made during this period, Jean-Paul Valette always worked under the restraints that beset members of family concerns who have to answer to shareholders not involved in the company. Thus he inherited concrete vats that were too large, but was unable to change them. When I passed by the property during Vinexpo 1999 the whole place resembled a building site. New installations, including a new barrel cellar, were under construction, and parts of the vineyard had been pulled up. Obviously all these changes will take time to work through to the wine. What I can report is that fears that Pavie would simply become a more expensive Monbousquet appear unjustified by the '98 vintage here, which has more concentration and oak without losing its distinctive character. Watch this space!

Château Pavie-Decesse

Grand Cru Classé. Owner: M et Mme Gérard Perse.
9ha. 4,500 cases.
Mer 65%, CF 20%, CS 15%.

This is fine classic *côtes* wine, with power and breed. Sometimes one is more conscious of the tannin than with Pavie because the wine has less opulence and fat. Yet sometimes – as in '82 – it can actually have more alcohol. All this was during the Valette period which ended in '97.

In 1997 the property was sold to the Perses of Monbousquet. The fact that the '97 here outshone the Pavie made by the Valettes, just prior to bottling bodes well for the future of both. But prices here have been adjusted upwards, though, with a vengeance!

Château Pavie-Macquin

Grand Cru Classé. Owner: Corre family.
Administrator: Nicolas Thienpont. 14·5ha. 6,400 cases.
Mer 70%, CF 25%, CS 5%.
Second label: Les Chênes de Macquin.

The property is named after Albert Macquin who was a pioneer of the processes used to graft European vines onto American rootstocks to combat the phylloxera.

This *cru* is situated on the plateau above the Côte de Pavie, and between Pavie, Troplong-Mondot and the town. The wines are elegant and pleasant, of good average quality, and are sold at reasonable prices, have moved up a scale in the '90s and are now richer and fruitier with more oak. '95 is superb. The hand of Nicolas Thienpont of Vieux Château Certan has been most beneficial.

Château Petit-Faurie-de-Soutard

Grand Cru Classé. Owner: Mme Françoise Capdemourlin.
Administrator: Jacques Capdemourlin. 8ha. 3,500 cases.
Mer 60%, CF 30%, CS 10%.

Until 1850 this formed part of Soutard. It lies in a fine position on the *plateau calcaire* and the *côtes*.

This is a stylish wine with real breed and finesse. Because of the soil here, with its high limestone content, the wines are less luscious but have more structure and are perhaps finer than at Balestard.

Château Pipeau

Grand Cru. Owner: Pierre Mestreguilhem. 35ha. 15,000 cases.
Mer 80%, CF 10%, CS 10%.
Second labels: Château Reynaud, Château Barbeyron.

Pierre Mestreguilhem's aim at Pipeau is to produce wines with body and suppleness, and which mature well. The resulting wines are often superior to some Crus Classés. The yield here spans the three communes of St-Laurent-des-Combes, St-Hippolyte and St-Émilion on a variety of soils. Thirty per cent new oak is used.

Château de Pressac

Grand Cru. Owner: Jacques Pouey. 33ha. 13,000 cases.
Mer 50%, CF 30%, CS 20%.

A fine feudal château overlooks this *cru*, which is situated on the chalky soils of the plateau in St-Étienne-de-Lisse. It was here in the late 1730s that the Auxerrois or 'Noir de Pressac' grape was introduced to Bordeaux. Now better known as the Malbec, it was an important contributor to the wines of this region. At this château, wines with a fine reputation are produced, using traditional methods of vinification and 30 per cent new oak.

Château Le Prieuré

Grand Cru Classé. Owner: Baronne Guichard. 5ha.
2,000 cases. Mer 60%, CS 30%, CF 10%.
Second label: Château l'Olivier.

This property on the *plateau calcaire* is on high ground, on a site set apart between Trottevieille and Troplong-Mondot. The owner also has an important property in Lalande de Pomerol, as well as Château Siaurac and Château Vrai-Croix-de-Gay in Pomerol. Château Le Prieuré once belonged to the Franciscan house in St-Émilion, the Cordeliers. One quarter new wood is used in the maturation. I have found the wines to be attractive, elegant, and on the light side: good breed but not above average.

Château Quercy

Grand Cru. Owner: Apelbaum-Pidoux. 6ha. 2,800 cases.
Mer 70%, CF 25%, CS 5%.

The present owners, a Swiss famiy, bought this property in Vignonet in 1988. The combination of old vines, hand harvesting, 30 per cent new oak and meticulous care at every stage comes through in this attractive open-textured wine.

Château Quinault

Grand Cru. Owner: A and F Reynaud. 12ha. 4,600 cases.
Mer 70%, CF 20%, CS 10%.

This *cru*, now surrounded by the urban sprawl of Libourne, was saved from the developers by Dr Alain Raynaud and his wife Françoise (of Château La Croix de Gay) when they acquired it in 1997. With its old vines and special microclimate they believe exceptional wines can be made here, and have begun auspiciously with the '97 vintage.

Château Ripeau

Grand Cru Classé. Owner: Françoise de Wilde. 15·5ha.
8,000 cases. Mer 60%, CF 30%, CF 10%.

A fine, important *cru* on the sandy soils near the border with Pomerol, southeast of Cheval-Blanc and La Dominique. Since the present owners took over in 1976 they have considerably expanded the *cuvier* and *chai*.

Unfortunately, I have not been encouraged the few times I have tasted Ripeau recently.

Château Rozier

Grand Cru. Owner: Jean Saby. 16·5ha. 9,000 cases.
Mer 65%, CF and CS 35%.

Rozier is a *cru* in the St-Laurent-des-Combes commune producing
appealingly fruity, characterful wines which age well.

Château St-Georges-Côte-Pavie

Grand Cru Classé. Owner: Jacques Masson. 5·1ha. 2,500 cases.
Mer 60%, CF 40%.

A small, well-placed *cru* on the western end of the Côte de Pavie
and its lower slope. La Gaffelière is on the other side, and there
are views across to Ausone. The fermentation is in stainless steel,
and maturation is in cask. The wines are notable for their delicious easy fruit and marked character and breed. They are
high-toned and flavoured and delightful to drink when four to
seven years old. Though delicious when drunk young, however,
they lack the concentration needed for ageing.

Clos St-Martin

Grand Cru Classé. Owner: SC des Grandes Murailles. 1·4ha.
800 cases. Mer 70%, CF 30%.

Three *crus* – this one, Grandes Murailles and Côte Baleau – were,
until 1985, all managed together, with the wine made and kept
at Côte Baleau. In 1985, however, the other two *crus* lost their
Grand Cru Classé status in a revision of the classification system,
and since then the proprietors have made a determined effort to
improve matters. Clos St-Martin now has separate facilities, and
the '86 consequently showed a big step forward in quality, with a
bouquet full of vivid, scented fruit; breed, elegance and balanced
tannins. This improvement has been maintained.

Château Sansonnet

Grand Cru. Owner: François d'Aulan. 7ha. 3,300 cases.
Mer 60%, CF 20%, CS 20%.

This *cru* is on the *plateau calcaire* east of St-Émilion on its eastern
culminating point, and just north of Trottevieille. There is clay
mixed with limestone here, on rocky subsoil. The wine is matured
in cask. These are firm wines which are not particularly
rich or luscious and need time to unfold and develop. In 1996
the Cru Classé status was lost. In 1999 the property was bought
by François d'Aulan, the former owner of Champagne Piper
Heidsieck. So, without a doubt, this *cru* should soon be on
the way back.

Château La Serre

Grand Cru Classé. Owner: Bernard d'Arfeuille.
Administrator: Luc d'Arfeuille. 7ha. 3,500 cases.
Mer 80%, CF 20%. Second label: Menuts de La Serre.

This is a wine with structure, depth of flavour and a finely perfumed bouquet, a wine of individuality, highly typical of the
plateau surrounding St-Émilion. La Serre is a solid, reliable Grand
Cru Classé of good quality: not a high-flyer but thoroughly worthy.

Château Soutard

Grand Cru Classé. Owners: Comte François et Comtesse
Isabelle des Ligneris. 22ha. 10,000 cases. Mer 70%, CF 30%.
Second label: Clos de la Tonnelle.

The aim at Soutard is to make traditional, long-keeping wines and the result is uncompromising and requires patience. My own feeling is that sometimes the fruit and natural charm of St-Émilion are unnecessarily sacrificed and that often the wines would benefit from earlier bottling and a lighter touch – but these are matters of taste. The stylishness comes through, but the wines often seem lean and ungrateful. They are hard to judge in cask because the *assemblage* is effected shortly before bottling.

Château Tertre-Daugay

Grand Cru Classé. Owner: Comte Léo de Malet Roquefort.
16ha. 6,500 cases. Mer 60%, CF 40%.
Second label: Château de Roquefort.

The property was in an appalling state of neglect when Comte Léo de Malet-Roquefort bought it in 1978. From then until the reconstruction of the *cuvier* and *chai* in 1984 the wines had to be made and kept at La Gaffelière. This property now receives the same care and attention as the Premier Grand Cru, but with a third new wood used for the maturation.

Tertre-Daugay has the potential to be one of the best of the Grands Crus Classés. The wines are gloriously perfumed and spicy on the nose with tannic rich, ripe fruitiness well matched to give a fine, powerful, complex flavour and stylish breed.

Château Tertre-Rôteboeuf

Owner: François Mitjavile. 5·7ha. 2,800 cases. Mer 80%, CF 20%.

The name derives from the oxen which were once used to plough the steep slopes: exposed to the hot sun as they worked, the oxen roasted in the heat – hence 'roast beef.' François Mitjavile has been the proprietor since 1978, and by late harvesting and long vatting he aims to produce serious wines that age well. His wines have great individuality, with a lot of oak but retaining plenty of fruitiness and structure. This is now something of a cult wine, commanding high prices.

Château La Tour-Figeac

Grand Cru Classé. Owner: Otto Maximilian Rettenmaïer.
Administrator: Otto M Rettenmaïer. 13·5ha.
6,000 cases. Mer 60%, CF 40%.

This property lies on the border with Pomerol and was part of Figeac until 1879. Three years later the two La Tour-du-Pin-Figeacs were also hived off.

This is a powerful yet stylish wine, rich and scented on the nose, with real length of flavour, marked by elegant breed. The new owners are improving the wines yet further. Otto Maximilian, the son of the family, took over management in 1994 and produced a delicious '95. '96, '97 and '98 have continued to enhance the reputation of this excellent *cru*.

Château La Tour-du-Pin-Figeac

Grand Cru Classé. Owner: Héritiers Marcel Moueix.
Administrator: A Moueix. 9ha. 4,000 cases.
Mer 60%, CF 30%, Mal and CS 10%.
These are powerful, robust, full-flavoured wines of style which
have consistently come out well in blind tastings in recent years.
Together with its neighbours, La Tour-Figeac and La Dominique,
this is one of the outstanding *crus* in this area adjoining Pomerol,
and indeed stands with them among the top Grands Crus Classés.

Château La Tour-du-Pin-Figeac (Giraud-Bélivier)

Grand Cru Classé. Owner: GFA Giraud-Bélivier.
11ha. 5,500 cases. Mer 75%, CF 25%.
This property is not nearly as well known or as well reputed as its
neighbour of the same name, owned by the A Moueix firm of
Château Taillefer, though they shared a common history until
1882. The Girauds bought the property from the Béliviers in 1972,
but this still hasn't resulted in wines worthy of its excellent site.

Château Troplong-Mondot

Grand Cru Classé. Owner: Claude Valette.
Administrator: Christine Valette. 30ha. 11,000 cases.
Mer 80%, CF 10%, CS 10%. Second label: Mondot.
This is one of the most important properties in St-Émilion on the
côte and plateau. It should be one of the best St-Émilion *crus* and
if sites play a part should be challenging for a position as a
Premier Grand Cru. But until recently the full potential was not
realised in terms of consistency and quality. Then, for the marvellous '86, 50 per cent new oak was used and all the wines were
kept in cask instead of rotating between cask and vat. 80 per cent
new oak is now used. This vintage proved a watershed. The '88,
'89, '90, '94, '95, '96, '97 and '98 have produced wines that are
increasingly on a level with the Premiers Crus Classés. This has
all been the work of the owner's daughter, Christine Valette.
Before this the best vintages were '70, '78, '79, '82 and '83.

Château Trottevieille

1er Grand Cru Classé B. Owner: Castéja family. Administrator:
Philippe Castéja. 10ha. 4,500 cases. Mer 50%, CF 45%, CS 5%.
This is the only Premier Grand Cru to be owned by a Bordeaux
négociant. The vineyard is set apart from the other Premiers on
the plateau to the east of St-Émilion, somewhat below Troplong-
Mondot. The soil is a mixture of limestone and clay. The
reputation of Trottevieille has been disappointing in recent years,
and does not correspond with some of the rich, concentrated
wines I recall before the 1956 frost. Too often the wines were
either coarse and dull or disappointingly diluted.

Then Philippe Castéja introduced 80 per cent new oak for the
'85 vintage, and began producing much more concentrated wines.
The difference between '82 and '83 on the one hand, and the '85,
'86 and '88 on the other, is marked. But sadly, it's performance
since then has been patchy.

Union des Producteurs de St-Émilion

Members: 360. Director: Jacques Baugier. 950ha. 550,000 cases.
There is no other cooperative in Bordeaux that produces as much
high-quality wine as this one, lying just at the southern foot of the
côtes, between the town and the Libourne–Bergerac road. In 1985
it saw one of its 330 members, Château Berliquet, become a
Grand Cru Classé (*see* Château Berliquet).

There are four important wines, all entitled to the Grand Cru
status, which are sold under trademarks:

Royal St-Émilion This is made from properties on the plain. The
wine is full, robust and open-textured with a certain coarseness typical of its origins, but attractive.

Côtes Rocheuses As the name implies, this comes from properties in the *côtes* area. This takes longer to develop its richness,
and has more power. Some 120,000 cases are made.

Haut Quercus *Quercus* is the Latin for oak. This brand was
launched in 1978, and the wine is aged in new oak. At present
2,500 cases, all in numbered bottles, are produced annually.
The wines have real intensity and are quite tannic with a classic flavour. They take time to mature.

Cuvée Galius This is a special selection of cask-aged wines. The
first vintage was '82, and it was selected at a 1984 blind tasting
for the Trophée des Honneurs as one of the 12 best wines.

The quality of these branded wines is often superior to that of
many small *crus* made at the property, and certainly more
saleable. It is a valuable source of good, typical, sound St-Émilion.
In addition, a large number of château wines are individually
made and bottled under their respective labels. They are labelled
mis à la propriété.

Château Valandraud

Owner: Jean-Luc Thunevin. 2·5ha.
Mer 75%, CF 20%, Mal 5%. 700 cases.
You may wonder why I thought it appropriate to include a *cru*
producing only 700 cases. It is simply because its wines are now
selling at prices above those of the Premières Grands Crus
Classés. This is an extreme example of the new fashion for bou-
tique *crus* in St-Emilion and Pomerol. You create a new *cru* out of
bits and pieces, dress it up in massive new oak, and wheel it out
as a super *cru*. The vineyard here consists of 65 ares (0.65
hectares) in a good position on the *côtes* next to La Clotte, with the
remaining 1·9ha near Monbousquet on the plain, with sand and
some gravel; not a great position.

There is some 40 year-old Merlot, some Cabernet Franc and a
touch of Malbec. The wines are put into 100 per cent new oak
then, at their first racking, into another lot of 100 per cent new
oak. The result is spicy, prune-like aromas and dense thick tex-
tures, impressive if rather on one note: the handling has produced
something which smothers any sense of origin or *terroir*.

One knows how it has been vinified and handled but not
where it might come from – this is a dangerous course for
Bordeaux to follow.

Château Vieux Sarpe

Grand Cru. Owner: J-F Janoueix. 6·5ha. 4,000 cases.
Mer 70%, CF 20%, CS 10%.

A property run in conjunction with Château Haut-Sarpe – also owned by the Janoueix family – producing wines with their own distinct character. Excellent fruit structure and balance enable them to age particularly well.

Château Villemaurine

Grand Cru Classé. Owner: Robert Giraud. 7ha. 3,800 cases.
Mer 70%, CS 30%.

The name is derived from *Villa Maure*, Moorish city, the name given to the place where the Saracens camped in the eighth century.

Great efforts are being made to improve the quality here, and there is certainly potential, though whether it is appropriate to have so much Cabernet Sauvignon must be open to question. The '82 is perfumed and rich with an attractive spicy and complex flavour; long, with a taste of cinnamon.

At this stage Villemaurine seemed to using high extraction and masses of new wood and producing rather one-dimensional wines. But now 45 per cent new wood is being used and the wines of the '90s are lighter and fruitier.

Château Yon-Figeac

Grand Cru Classé. Owner: Vignobles Germain. 25ha.
13,000 cases. Mer 34%, CF 33%, CS 33%.

This large vineyard lies northwest of St-Émilion on the road to Pomerol, between Laroze and Grand-Barrail-Lamarzelle-Figeac on sandy soil. The Lussiez family were owners here for four generations before selling to their distributors.

The wines have one-third new oak and have been noted for their consistency and typical attractive characteristics for many years. They tend to be scented, soft, rich and full-flavoured, with a nice underlying firmness.

The St-Émilion Satellites

Outside the St-Émilion appellation to the north and northeast lie the so-called St-Émilion Satellites. While they have been excluded from the straightforward St-Émilion AC, they have the right to add the name St-Émilion to their own communal names. Some of these wines are in fact superior to St-Émilions produced from the plain of the Dordogne, and there is a much higher proportion of large domaines than in St-Émilion and Pomerol. Many of the small owners are members of the cooperatives of Montagne, Lussac and Puisseguin. The Satellite communes are as follows:

Montagne-St-Émilion The small communes of St-Georges and Parsac were joined to Montagne in 1972, but some growers in St-Georges continue to exercise their option of using the St-Georges-St-Émilion appellation. The AC now covers around 1,500 hectares of vineyard. The soils are *plateau calcaire* but with more clay than in St-Émilion.

Lussac-St-Émilion Here there are around 1,350 hectares of vines, on the *plateau calcaire* of the type found in St-Émilion and St-Christophe-des-Bardes. But below these are the *côtes* of 'sables du Perigord' which are less favourable for viticulture. This is the most northerly of these appellations.

Puisseguin-St-Émilion This lies northeast of St-Émilion with around 700 hectares of vines. There is a large *plateau calcaire* and its *côtes*, which provide good viticultural land.

Châteaux Belair-Montaiguillon and Belair St-Georges

Owners: Nadine Pocci and Yannick Le Menn. 10ha.
4,700 cases. Mer 75%, CF and CS 20%, Mal 5%.

This excellent *cru* is situated on one of the highest points in the commune of St-Georges, facing south towards St-Émilion on limestone and clay soils. Delicious wines are now being made here. They are full of rich, supple fruit and have a marked character – comparable to the best St-Émilion Grands Crus. Since the '88 vintage, two separate wines have been made. The Belair St-Georges is a selection from the oldest vines, aged in cask with some new oak. This wine is slower-developing, so needs longer ageing than the Belair-Montaiguillon, which sees no wood but has lots of fruit.

Château Bel-Air

Owner: Robert Adove. 16ha. 10,000 cases. Mer 70%, CF 30%.

A *cru* at the most northerly part of the region, in the commune of Puisseguin. Some attractive wines of good fruit and substance are produced here.

Château Calon

Owner: Jean-Noël Boidron. Montagne vineyard: 31·5ha.
18,000 cases. Mer 70%, CF 15%, CS 13%, Mal 2%.
St-Georges vineyard: 5ha. 2,600 cases.
Mer 80%, CF 10%, CS 10%.

Some cause for confusion here! This is basically one property with land in two communes, Montagne and St-Georges. The label is the same but both appellations are used, although the whole production could now be sold as Montagne. The owner also owns Château Corbin-Michotte, whose wines have a good reputation. These are dependable well-made wines.

Château Faizeau

Owner: SC du Château.
Administrators: Chantal Lebreton and M Alain Raynaud.
10ha. 5,000 cases. Mer 85%, CS 10%, CF 5%.

This vineyard is in a single piece on the hill of Calon at the highest point of the Montagne appellation. The old family property has been controlled since 1983 by the administrators, who are also owners of La Croix de Gay in Pomerol.

The quality of the '93 with its rich, supple, flattering fruit, the result of a selection of old vines, is exemplary, and shows that the best Montagne wines are often better than the St-Émilions from the plain.

Château de la Grenière

Owner: Jean-Paul Dubreuil. 10ha. 5,500 cases.
Mer 55%, CS 30%, CF 15%. Second label: Château les Noves.
This property in Lussac-St-Émilion makes solid well-structured wines with plenty of rich fruit. To judge by the excellent '89 when tasted in late 1995, it may also age well.

Château Guibeau-La Fourvieille

Owner: Bourlon family. Administrator: Henri Bourlon.
41ha. 23,000 cases. Mer 70%, CF 15%, CS 15%.
Second labels: Le Vieux Château Guibeau,
Châteaux La Fourvieille and Les Barrails.
Situated on the limestone plateau near Puisseguin, the wines of this large *cru* are of good quality – on a par with the St-Émilion Grands Crus even – and reflect the attention to detail shown by the Bourlon family, who have invested much in restoring and modernising this property.

Château Laroze-Bayard

Owner: Laporte family. 21ha. 13,000 cases. Mer 70%, CF 15%,
CS 15%. Second label: Château le Tuileries-de-Bayard.
An old property in the hamlet of Bayard, which has been owned by the Laporte family since 1700. *Cuve*-matured wines, rich in colour and fruit, are produced here. They are well structured with good body.

Château des Laurets

Owner: SA Château des Laurets. Administrator: Henri Bourlon.
72ha. 40,000 cases. Mer 70%, CF 22%, CS 8%.
Second labels: Châteaux La Rochette and Maison-Rose.
This is Puisseguin's most important property and one of the largest in the St-Émilion Satellites. The vineyards are on the *plateau calcaire* and the *côtes* south of Puisseguin and in adjoining Montagne-St-Émilion, so both appellations are used. These are well-reputed robust and attractive wines. Since 1995 it has been run by Henri Bourlon of Château Guibeau-La Fourvieille, so improvements can now be expected.

Château du Lyonnat

Owner: GFA des Vignobles Jean Milhade. 45ha. 25,000 cases.
Mer 50%, CF 50%. Second label: Château La Rose-Peruchon.
This is one of the largest and best-known domaines of the St-Émilion Satellites. It lies to the east of Lussac on the *plateau calcaire*. This is reliable, fairly light-textured, stylish wine which nevertheless keeps quite well. The standard is comparable to a good St-Émilion Grand Cru.

Château Macquin St-Georges

Owner: François Corre. Administrator: Denis Corre. 13ha.
7,500 cases. Mer 70%, CF 15%, CS 15%.
Second label: Château Bellonne St-Georges.
This well-known *cru* is situated on hillside sites near St-Georges.

The wines are bottled and distributed by Éts J-P Moueix (*see also* Château Pavie-Macquin). Fine, attractive, luscious wines are made here: Macquin St-Georges wines are are up to good St-Émilion Grand Cru standards.

Château Maison-Blanche

Owners: Gérard and Françoise Despagne. 32ha. 15,000 cases.
Mer 80%, CF 20%. Other label: Château La Rose Corbin.
Second label: Les Piliars de Maison-Blanche.

This important domaine is on the *côte* to the west of Montagne. The wines are richly perfumed and attractive for early drinking. The *négociants* Parrot have exclusive distribution for the Château La Rose Corbin. This wine has a slightly different emphasis to the main *cru*, having 65 per cent Merlot, and spending six months in cask. Again, the wine is most attractive.

Château Mayne-Blanc

Owner: Jean Boucheau. 15ha. 9,400 cases.
Mer 60%, CS 30%, CF 10%. Other label: Cuvée St-Vincent

One of the best *crus* in Lussac-St-Émilion which has been in the same family for many generations. Only vines of eight years and older are bottled under the château name, and vines of 20 years and older are put in one-third new casks under the name Cuvée St-Vincent. The '89 Mayne-Blanc is deliciously robust with a rich layered fruity texture.

Château Montaiguillon

Owner: Amart family. 26ha. 16,500 cases. Mer 40%, CS 30%, CF 30%.

One of the most reliable and attractive wines in Montagne-St-Emilion. Whenever I have found it on a wine list it has been a safe bet. Solid, fleshy, attractive wines with body and good fruit are consistently made.

Château de Musset

Owner: Patrick Valette. 7·5ha. 4,500 cases. Mer 70%, CS 20%, CF 10%.

Situated in the commune of Parsac, now absorbed into that of Montagne, this old *cru* has attracted deserved attention since Patrick Valette, son of Jean-Paul Valette of Château Pavie, began to run the property. If he can obtain the richness and concentration allied to charm which he achieved in the '92, what will he be able to do in better years? Certainly a *cru* to watch.

Château la Papeterie

Owner: Jean-Pierre Estager. 10ha. 5,000 cases. Mer 70%, CF 30%.

This good property lies at the crossroads of four appellations: Pomerol, Lalande de Pomerol, St-Émilion and Montagne-St-Émilion, the vineyard being in Montagne. The owner also has a well-reputed Pomerol *cru*, Château la Cabanne. The '90 was most attractive in 1997 with lovely supple fruit and good structure, and no sign of the dilution which affects some wines in this vintage.

Les Productions Réunies de Puisseguin et Lussac-St-Émilion

770ha. 400,000 cases. Mer 70%, CF and CS 30%.

Wines from this cooperative of 150 members are mostly sold under two separate labels, one for each of the two communes. Lussac accounts for about 75 per cent of the production and Puisseguin for the rest. There are also 21 *crus* that are vinified here separately and marketed under their own château labels.

Château Rocher Corbin

Owner: Durand family. 9·5ha. 5,000 cases.
Mer 80%, CF 15%, CS 5%.

Confusingly the château is called Rocher Corbin, but the label on the bottle says 'Vieux Château Rocher Corbin'. The vineyard is situated on the west side of the *'tertre' de Calon*, in Montagne. The '90 has real depth and concentration of spicy fruit and is a most impressive wine.

Château de Roques

Owner: Michel Sublett. 25ha. 12,000 cases.
Mer 60%, CF and CS 40%. Second labels: Châteaux
Vieux-Moulin, des Aubarèdes and Roc du Creuzelat.

The name comes from Jean de Roques, a former proprietor and close acquaintance of Henri IV. Some delicious wines are made: comparable to good Grand Cru St-Émilions.

Château Roudier

Owner: Jacques Capdemourlin. 30ha. 15,000 cases.
Mer 60%, CF 25%, CS 15%.

This fine and important property is on the *côte* (limestone and clay) facing south towards St-Émilion. The proprietor also owns Balestard-la-Tonnelle and manages Capdemourlin. The wines are of a high standard and have a marvellously rich, gamey flavour. Easily up to the best St-Émilion Grand Cru standard.

Château St-André-Corbin

Owner: Robert Carré. 19ha. 8,000 cases. Mer 77%, CF 23%.

A *cru* of comparable quality to the St-Émilion Grands Crus, producing charming wines which have spiciness, fruit and a good balanced structure. For some years now the vineyard has been managed and the wines sold by J-P Moueix.

Château St-Georges

Owner: M Desbois-Pétrus. 50ha. 25,000 cases.
Mer 60%, CS 20%, CF 20%. Second label: Puy-St-Georges.

This is certainly one of the most spectacular properties in the whole region, with a palatial château built in 1774 by Victor Louis, architect of the Grand Théâtre, in the purest classical style. Its vineyards are on south-facing *côtes* looking towards St-Émilion. These are elegant but well-constructed wines that have a considerable life-span. Half the maturation casks used each year are of new oak. If this were in St-Émilion it is hard to think it would not be a Grand Cru Classé. As it is the wine has a great reputation, especially in France, where much is sold by mail-order.

Château Teyssier
Owner: Family Durand-Teyssier. Administrator: Dourthe-Kressmann. 25ha. 9,000 cases.
Mer 75%, CF/CS 25%.
Rather confusingly this property straddles two appellations, Montagne- and Puisseguin-St-Emilion. Since 1995 Dourthe-Kressmann has been responsible for the management and commercialisation of the wines. Very fruity, rich wines are now being made, but there is a tendency to over-extract.

Château Tour-du-Pas-St-Georges
Owner: Mme Dubois-Challon. 15ha. 8,000 cases.
Mer 50%, CF 35%, CS 15%.
This property lies on south-facing slopes of limestone and clay in St-Georges. It is now farmed by Mme Dubois-Challon, so the gifted Pascal Delbeck, *régisseur* of Belair, is making the wine. The results are excellent.

La Tour Mont d'Or
118ha. 72,000 cases. Mer 75%, CS 15%, CF 10%.
A cooperative of 60 members in Montagne-St-Émilion producing well-reputed wines in the classic style of the St-Émilion Satellites. Three individual labels, Châteaux Palon Grand Seigneur, La Tour Mont d'Or and Baudron, are also vinified here.

Château Tour Musset
Owner: Henri Guiter. Administrator: Maurice Guiter. 30ha. 15,000 cases. Mer 50%, CS 50%.
Some unusual wines are produced at this *cru* near Parsac. They are tannic with a strong, fruity flavour, probably derived from the high proportion of Cabernet Sauvignon. These are wines that age well.

Château des Tours
Owner: Marne et Champagne. 52ha. 34,000 cases.
Mer 34%, CF and CS 33%, Mal 33%.
Second label: Château La Croix-Blanche.
This is the largest domaine in Montagne and also has the most imposing 14th-century château. The vineyards are on the *côte* east of Montagne, facing St-Émilion. The *chai* is modern and well equipped to handle the large production. There is storage capacity for over 80,000 cases. The present owners bought the property, which forms the flagship of their Bordeaux group in 1983. Their offices are also here. Unfortunately, things have rather marked time here but in 1998 a fresh start was made. There is the possibility, and hopefully now the will, to make very good wines here.

Pomerol

This is easily the smallest of the great red wine districts of Bordeaux. It measures four by three kilometres and covers only about 760 hectares. It produces on average around 32,000 hectolitres of wine per year, which is roughly comparable with St-Julien in the Médoc. But the complexity of the Pomerol soils gives these wines an individuality and originality that sets them apart, enabling them to produce some of Bordeaux's most remarkable wines.

The best Pomerols are more intense, richer, denser and more tannic than most St-Émilions. Although the Merlot is even more predominant here than in St-Émilion, because of the clay and generally cold soils, many wines go through a stage in early maturity when they can look remarkably like Médocs, which shows how soil can change the character of grape varieties. The majority of wines become enjoyable to drink when four to seven years old, but a few top growths will take longer. The best vintages keep well. The '55, '64 and '70 are still excellent.

There is no classification in Pomerol, nor will there be, since there is no desire for one locally. After Pétrus, universally acknowledged as *hors classe*, the following wines are recognised as the leading ones, in alphabetical order: Certan-de-May, La Conseillante, L'Eglise-Clinet, L'Évangile, La Fleur-Pétrus, Gazin, Lafleur, Latour à Pomerol, Petit-Village, Trotanoy and Vieux Château Certan.

Château Beauregard
Owner: Crédit Foncier de France. 16ha. 7,800 cases. Mer 60%, CF 30%, CS 10%. Second label: Benjamin de Beauregard.

This counts as a large property by Pomerol standards and has a fine château dating from the 17th and 18th centuries. A replica was erected on Long Island, New York, for the Guggenheims in the 1920s – an unusual compliment for a Bordeaux château – and is called Mille-Fleurs. In 1991 the Clauzels sold to Crédit Foncier de France (*see* Bastor-Lamontagne page 147)

The vineyard is on the high plateau of Pomerol, with some sand mixed with the gravel. This is a well-run and well-reputed *cru*; 25 per cent new wood is used for its maturation. While not among the leading dozen *crus* of Pomerol, it is a good wine in the second flight, rich and full-flavoured. It develops quite quickly and has real breed and charm.

Château le Bon-Pasteur
Owner: Dupuy-Rolland. Administrator: Michel Rolland. 7ha. 4,000 cases. Mer 75%, CF 25%.

This *cru* is right on the Pomerol–St-Émilion border in the north-west of the appellation, between Gazin and Croque-Michotte. Since the present owner took over this property it has established quite a reputation for itself in the US. But the wines were rich and enticing before that – I recall a splendid '70. Now 35 per cent new wood is being used for the cask-maturation.

The wines are extremely attractive, supple and rich.

Château Bonalgue

Owner: Pierre Bourotte. 6·5ha. 2,500 cases.
Mer 80%, CF 20%. Second label: Château Burgrave.

This château was built in 1815 by Antoine Rabioun and is situated on the sand and gravel soils of the plateau, in the south of the appellation. The Bourotte family has owned this property since 1926 and produces some attractive wines. Fermentation takes place in modern stainless steel vats and a high proportion of new oak is used for maturation. The wines have ample fruit and weight to balance the oak flavours, but need five to seven years before they drink at their best.

Château Bourgneuf-Vayron

Owner: Xavier Vayron. 9ha. 4,000 cases. Mer 90%, CF 10%.

A property on the western side of the high plateau of Pomerol as it slopes away in that direction. Here the gravelly soils are mixed with sand. This is a good *cru* placed by Alexis Lichine in the third category of Pomerols. The wines tend to become supple and enjoyable quite quickly and lack the concentration of the leading wines, while showing definite breed.

Château La Cabanne

Owner: Jean-Pierre Estager. 10ha. 5,000 cases.
Mer 92%, CF 8%. Second label: Domaine de Compostelle.

La Cabanne is situated on the high terrace of Pomerol, on soils of gravel and clay, which overlie an iron-pan or *crasse de fer*. Jean-Pierre Estager bought this property in 1966 and has since modernised the *cuvier* and *chai*, installing vats of lined concrete and stainless steel. Care is taken that the grapes are fully matured and that as much tannin as possible is extracted from them to balance the high proportion of new oak used. The results are reliable wines with concentrated fruit character. They are not yet widely known but their reputation is growing.

Château Certan-de-May

Owner: Mme Odette Barreau-Bader. 5ha. 2,000 cases.
Mer 70%, CF 25%, CS 5%.

This minute vineyard is typical of a number of properties at the heart of Pomerol's high plateau, its size combined with the devotion of its owners creates something individual and personal. Originally part of Vieux Château Certan, the soil here has clay mixed with the predominant gravel. It lies in the area, close to Cheval-Blanc, where nearly all the best Pomerols are to be found. In recent vintages this *cru* has re-emerged from the shadows and has rapidly taken its place again among the leading wines of the district. Twenty-five per cent new oak is used for the maturation.

The wines have an opulence, richness and power that are reminiscent of Trotanoy rather than of Certan-de-May's more compact neighbour, Vieux Château Certan. The '82, '83, '85, '86, '88, '89, '90, '95 and '98 are splendid wines. Certainly this is a wine to snatch up when you can.

Château Certan-Giraud

Owner: J-P Moueix. 7·5ha. 4,300 cases.
Mer 80%, CF 20%. Part of crop sold as Certan-Marzelle.
Second label: Clos du Roy.

With neighbours such as Pétrus and Vieux Château Certan, this small *cru* on the best gravel mixed with clay in the heart of the Pomerol high plateau should be among the region's top wines but it has yet to equal its illustrious neighbours – though it still offers value for money. Now all new wood is used for the maturation. In 1999 J-P Moueix bought the property so the potential should now be realised in full.

Château Clinet

Owner: Éts G A M Audy. Administrator: Jean-Michel Arcaute.
9ha. 4,400 cases. Mer 75%, CS 15%, CF 10%.

This *cru*, belonging to Libourne *négociants* Audy, is near the church of Pomerol on the high plateau with its gravelly soil mixed with sand. For years there was too much Cabernet Sauvignon in the vineyards here and the wines were tough and charmless. Then Jean-Michel Arcaute took over the management of all Audy's vineyards in the mid-1970s.

First he increased the Merlot and reduced the Cabernet then, in '85, in consultation with oenologist Michael Rolland, he changed his pattern of working, going for late-picking (maximum maturation), selection of grapes prior to vinification, long vatting and the use of plenty of new oak. The difference has been dramatic, with '86 easily the best Clinet I have ever tasted, followed by the fine example of '87, and the classic wines of '88, '89 and '90. My only caveat is the policy here of very late bottling. Wines that look marvellous in the cask can get dry – this happened to the '96. This is now one of the rising stars of Pomerol.

Clos du Clocher

Owner: Éts J-B Audy. 6ha. 2,600 cases.
Mer 80%, CF 20%. Second label: Esprit de Clocher.

Established in 1931 by Jean-Baptiste Audy, this is now a well-known and reliable *cru*, its wines being vinified with much care and attention to detail. Blending or *assemblage* is carried out by Michel Rolland of Château Le Bon Pasteur.

Château la Conseillante

Owner: Héritiers Louis Nicolas. Administrator: Bernard
Nicolas. 12ha. 5,000 cases. Mer 65%, CF 30%, Mal 5%.

This is one of the best two or three wines in Pomerol after Pétrus, year after year. Added to the consistency is the strong personality of the wine. It combines concentration and breed on the nose with a superb flavour of real originality, an unctuous yet fine centre, and great persistence of flavour. Its neighbour L'Évangile is clearly from the same stable, but at present is less consistent and tends to be more massive but less fine. On the other side there are similarities with Petit-Village as the wine improves. The outstanding vintages here are '70, '75, '76, '79, '81, '82, '83, '85, '86,

'88, '89 and '90. Lesser years such as '73, '77 and '80 have still provided some delicious bottles. Recently '93, '94, '95, '97 and '98 were all among the best Pomerols of each vintage.

Château La Croix

Owner: SC J Janoueix. 10ha. 5,000 cases. Mer 60%, CF 20%, CS 20%. Second label: Château Le Gabachot.

These are well-balanced attractive wines that are enjoyable after four or five years, yet also keep well, acquiring delicacy and spicy complexity. The '71 was keeping well and had fined down (developing a lovely flavour, mellow but with a good backbone) when 14 years old. If you can sort this château from all the others in Pomerol with 'Croix' their names, it is a wine worth looking out for.

Château La Croix-de-Gay

Owner: Noël Raynaud. 12ha. 6,500 cases. Mer 80%, CS 10%, CF 10%. Cuvée Prestige: Château La Fleur de Gay.

This property is on the northern borders of the plateau of Pomerol where the predominantly gravelly soils mingle with sand. For the maturation 50 per cent new wood is used. This is stylish, charmingly fruity, aromatic wine which is rich and solid in top years such as '95 and '98.

Château La Croix-du-Casse

Owner: Éts G A M Audy. Administrator: Jean-Michel Arcaute. 9ha. 5,300 cases. Mer 70%, CF 30%. Second label: Domaine du Casse.

La Croix-du-Casse is under the same management as Château Clinet but produces wines of a totally difference style. Benefiting from the gravel soils and underling iron-pan, they are attractively perfumed, full-flavoured and have a delicious fruit quality.

Château La Croix-St-Georges

Owner: SC J Janoueix. 5ha. 4,000 cases. Mer 95%, CF 5%. Second label: la Fleur Tropchaud.

This property is run in conjunction with Château le Croix, the main differences in their wines being derived from the variations in the *terroirs* of their respective vineyards. La Croix-St-Georges is situated on the plateau and therefore is based mainly on gravel. The wines have both suppleness and finesse.

Domaine de l'Église

Owners: Philippe Castéja and Mme Peter Preben Hansen. 7ha. 3,500 cases. Mer 90%, CF 10%.

Not surprisingly this vineyard is near the church, on the high plateau. The soil is deep gravel with traces of iron deposit which gives the wines a certain brilliance and depth of colour. The Castéjas bought the property, whose wine they had distributed for many years, in 1972. The wines tend to be light in style yet fine, perfumed and elegant. With the '86 vintage, however, Philippe Castéja began making much more concentrated wines using new oak for the maturation casks – a third being new each year. This is good second-tier Pomerol.

Clos L'Église

Owner: M and Mme Garcin-Cathiard. 6ha. 2,800 cases.
Mer 57%, CF 43%. Second label: La Petite Église.

This small vineyard lies near the church on the high plateau
where the predominantly gravelly soil is mixed with sand. This
well-run property (acquired in 1997 by the present owner) has
undergone a transformation since the Garcin-Cathiards of Haut-
Bergey bought it. Gone are the stainless steel vats put in in 1983,
replaced by small 60hl wooden vats. In 1997 a marvellous wine of
exquisite quality (23hl/ha) was the result. There is little doubt
that this can be a top Pomerol.

Château L'Église-Clinet

Owner: Denis Durantou. 5·5ha. 1,700 cases. Mer 80%, CF 20%.
Second label: La Petite Eglise.

This small vineyard has for many years been farmed by the
Lasserre family of Clos René. It is near the church on the high
plateau. The soil is mainly gravelly mixed with sand. An important point here is that the vines are older than in most Pomerol
domaines because they were not pulled up after the 1956 frost
but left to recover, which most of them did. Wines are carefully
made and 30 to 50 per cent new wood is used for the cask maturation. Their reputation has long been high amongst devotees.
This is classic rich, supple and fruity Pomerol, but in the last
decade has become one of Pomerol's most sought-after *crus*.
Unfortunately this is a wine that takes some finding.

Château L'Enclos

Owner: SC du Château L'Enclos. Administrator: Hugues
Weydert. 9·5ha. 4,400 cases. Mer 90%, CF 9·5%, Mal 0·5%.

This good *cru* lies on the opposite side of the N89 Libourne–
Périgueux road from the main vineyards of the high plateau of
Pomerol. The soil is predominantly sandy, but there is an important gravelly outcrop here, at the neighbouring Clos René, and
further away at Moulinet. The wines are well made and of high
quality in the second tier of Pomerol. I have memories of a wonderful '29. Today the style of the wines is rather similar to that of
Close René: dense-textured, succulent and fruity, drinkable quite
young but also having the capacity to age. This is fine classic
Pomerol which is thoroughly reliable and enjoyable.

Château L'Évangile

Owner: Domaines Rothschild.
14·8ha. 4,500 cases. Mer 65%, CF 35%.

This is one of the leading *crus* of Pomerol, situated near the edge
of the high plateau adjoining La Conseillante and Vieux Château
Certan. The predominantly gravelly soil is mixed with some clay
and sand, the feature responsible for the unique quality of Pétrus
(where the vineyard is almost entirely clay and gravel). The style
of the wines most resembles that of La Conseillante, but has a different emphasis owing to the high proportion of Merlot, the
presence of clay in the soil and the fact that only 20 per cent new

oak is used here for the maturation. The submerged cap system of vinification is used and results in high colour extraction. The wines tend to be more massive and chewy in texture, yet sometimes lack the firmness of La Conseillante.

In 1990 all the shareholders except Mme Ducasse sold to Domaines Rothschild, which now distributes the wine, but Mme Ducasse ran the property until 1999 using Michel Rolland as consultant oenologist. There have in the past been some inconsistencies but the recent record is impressive. The '82 is luscious and ripe and '83 big and firm; '85 is generous and fine, but the '86 shows some dilution. The '87 is good for the year and the '88 is also fine; '89 and '90 are exceptional wines; '93 was one of the outstanding wines of this vintage, and '94 is no less fine. The '95, '96, '97 and '98 are exceptional, placing L'Evangile among the top *crus* in Pomerol. The future of this property looks bright indeed.

Château Feytit-Clinet
Owner: Ind Chasseuil. Administrator: Éts J-P Moueix. 6·3ha. 3,000 cases. Mer 85%, CF 15%.
A property on the northwestern edge of the plateau where the predominantly gravelly soil is mixed with sand. It is entirely run by the highly efficient Moueix organisation presided over by Christian Moueix and his oenologist Jean-Claude Berrouet. While the wine is all plummy fruit on the nose, the flavour is more elegant than one expects, with good length and a firm finish. An excellent second-tier Pomerol and naturally, from such a stable, most consistent.

Château La Fleur-de-Gay
Owner: Raynaud family. 1·75ha. 1,000 cases. Mer 100%.
The Raynaud family has set this vineyard aside for Merlot. Benefiting from deep gravelly soils, the wines are full of flavour and concentrated fruit. Vinification is monitored by Michel Rolland and Pascal Ribéreau-Gayon and is carried out at fairly high temperatures. These special wines are of a very high quality.

Château La Fleur-Pétrus
Owner: SC du Château. Administrator: Jean-Pierre Moueix. 13·8ha. 6,500 cases. Mer 80%, CF 20%.
One of the leading *crus* of Pomerol, situated just across the road from Pétrus, but on quite different soil. Here the soil is stony with large gravel but no clay or sand. In recent years the reputation of this wine has steadily grown, and this is now one of the flagships of the Moueix empire and almost certainly the finest Pomerol on purely gravelly soil, all the others except for Latour à Pomerol having some clay in their make-up. A third of the wood used here for maturation is new. The wines are gorgeous, perfumed, powerful and elegant on the nose, with great complexity, richness and power of flavour which is so obviously of the highest quality. They are consistently good. Lovely examples were the '82, '83, '85 (quite exceptional), '86, '88, '89, '90, '95 and '98. Not as massive as most of the other leading *crus*, but there is no doubting the breed

and beauty of this wine. In 1994 four hectares were purchased from the adjoining vineyard at Le Gay and have added an extra dimension to the wine.

Château Le Gay

Owner: Marie Robin. 4ha. 1,000 cases. Mer 50%, CF and CS 50%.
This *cru* lies on the northern side of the high plateau on gravelly soils, near to the owner's other *cru*, Lafleur. For many years its wines have been exclusively distributed by Éts J-P Moueix, but the Robin sisters ran the properties themselves. However, since the death of Thérèse Robin the Moueix team has taken over the management of both properties.

Le Gay has always produced big, dense, firm-textured wines that age well, as bottles of '64 and '66 still demonstrate. Now things can only get better and no doubt the wines will be poilished up a little and show some consistency. In 1994 half the vineyard was sold to neighbouring La Fleur-Pétrus.

Château Gazin

Owner: Étienne de Bailliencourt. 24ha. 8,000 cases.
Mer 85%, CF 10%, CS 5%.
This is the largest of the leading Pomerols, situated on the north-eastern corner of the high plateau on gravelly soils. In the late 1960s a portion of the vineyard adjoining Pétrus, with the same clay in the soil, was sold to Pétrus. Only a small percentage of new oak is used for the maturation in cask.

I find Gazin a difficult wine to assess. It is undeniably rich and opulent with an extraordinarily vivid and forceful character when young. There is a touch of coarseness but this perhaps is merely a part of a highly extrovert personality that demands attention. There has been a shortage of money here, due to inheritance problems, but from '85 onwards greater concentration and more style have been achieved. The '85 is concentrated, rich and firm, the '86 is rather austerely tannic while the '88 has a lovely rich aftertaste and is stylish, the '89 and '90 are both impressive indeed, while '93 is one of the successes of the year. Excellent wines followed in '94, '95, '96, '97 and '98. It is good to see this distinguished *cru* returning to form.

Château La Grave

Owner: Christian Moueix. 8ha. 4,000 cases. Mer 85%, CF 15%.
This small vineyard has been the personal property of Christian Moueix of Éts J-P Moueix since 1971. The firm owns a number of properties and farms and manages many others, with Christian Moueix heading the team. The property is on gravelly soil on the middle plateau in the northwest of Pomerol, just before the Libourne–Périgueux road. The name used to be something of a handicap, the words 'Château La Grave' appearing in large characters on the label, with 'Trigant de Boisset' in smaller ones underneath: now this has been simplified.

For maturation in cask 25 per cent new oak is used. The wine is quite rich, tannic and fine but less spectacular than that of the leading *crus*, so it is a good second-tier Pomerol. The '78, '79, '81, '82, '83, '85, '86, '88, '89, '90, '94 and '95 are all successful here – these are beautifully made and consistent wines.

Château Lafleur

Owners: Sylvie and Jacques Guinaudeau. 4·6ha. 2,400 cases. Mer 50%, CF 50%. Second label: Les Pensées de Lafleur.

This minute but superb property is situated on the gravelly high plateau, with some of the precious clay soils found at the best *crus* making up its vineyards. It is next to La Fleur-Pétrus but its subsoils differ considerably, La Fleur-Pétrus having none of the clay deposits.

In 1985 the Guinaudeaus assumed responsibility, running the property for Mlle Robin, and have further enhanced the already great reputation of this *cru*. Unfortunately, with so little wine produced, it is rare as well as expensive.

The style is all opulent charm and great finesse and it has a lovely bouquet, but recent vintages have been slower to mature.

Château Lafleur Gazin

Owner: Mme Delfour. Administrator: Éts J-P Moueix. 7·8ha. 3,500 cases. Mer 80%, CF 20%.

A property on the northeastern limits of the plateau next to Gazin. Here the predominantly gravelly soil is mixed with sand.

This *cru* has come into prominence since Éts J-P Moueix became *fermiers* here in 1976. It is run with the meticulous care associated with the Moueix team under Christian Moueix and his oenologist Jean-Claude Berrouet.

The wine is rich and quite powerful with an underlying firmness. A serious wine worth following.

Château Lagrange

Owner: Éts J-P Moueix. 8ha. 4,000 cases. Mer 95%, CF 5%.

Another Moueix property on the gravelly high plateau. Some new wood is used for the cask maturation. The wines seem to have a certain originality of flavour, a breeding allied to charm and structure, which marks them as fine wines.

The vintages of the '80s and '90s are all impressive. Château Lagrange is a good second-tier Pomerol.

Château Latour à Pomerol

Owner: Mme Lily Lacoste. Administrator: Éts J-P Moueix. 8ha. 3,900 cases. Mer 80%, CF 20%.

This fine property lies on the gravelly high plateau northwest of the church. Its owner is also co-proprietor of Pétrus, and it is managed and distributed by Éts J-P Moueix. Cask maturation is in 25 per cent new oak. In the past there were inconsistencies and fine bottles were interspersed with disappointments, but the property improved noticeably throughout the 1970s. More recently the wines have been marked by a wonderful perfume and a delectable beauty of flavour, power and finesse.

There is now a clear similarity of style with La Fleur-Pétrus, and with the '83 I even thought Latour the better wine. The wines since '85 have been wonderfully concentrated and impressive. Now indisputably among Pomerol's leading *crus*, as well as being one of the best value for money.

Château Mazeyres

Owner: Caisse de Retraite de la Soc Générale. Administrator: Alain Moueix. 18ha. 9,000 cases. Mer 80%, CF 20%.

This property lies on the recent gravel and sand of the lower plateau north of Libourne and at the western extremity of the appellation. 30 per cent new oak is now used. Much progress has been made here since the pension fund of the Société Générale bought it in 1988. The wines are now more concentrated without having lost their attractive style.

Château Moulinet

Owner: SC du Château. Administrator: Armand Moueix. 18ha. 10,000 cases. Mer 60%, CS 30%, CF 10%.

This relatively large property lies beyond the Libourne-Périgueux road on the gravelly sandy soils of the middle plateau and is one of Armand Moueix's well-run properties. A third of the wood used for maturation is new. The wines are scented and charming. A pleasant, widely distributed wine.

Château Nenin

Owner: J-H Delon. 25ha. 10,800 cases. Mer 70%, CF 20%, CS 10%.

One of the largest and best-known Pomerol properties. It lies on lower ground northwest of the high plateau, on sandy gravelly soils.

This important and once-famous *cru* had been an habitual under-performer until Jean-Hubert Delon from Léoville-Las Cases bought it in 1997. In spite of some improvements in 1992-3, the wines had remained disappointing. The fact that '97 was much better than '96 showed what was possible, while '98 is really impressive. Now Nenin should soon re-establish its position as one of Pomerol's leading *crus*.

Château Petit-Village

Owner: AXA-Millésimes. Administrator: J-M Cazes. 11ha. 4,000 cases. Mer 82%, CF 9%, CS 9%.

A finely placed vineyard on the high plateau, with gravelly clay soils, close to La Conseillante and St-Émilion. Previous owners, the Prats family (*see* Cos-d'Estournel), sold to AXA in 1989. One problem has been that after the '56 frost the vineyard was largely replanted – with too much Cabernet Sauvignon. This has now been corrected and the wines are improving. A minimum of 50 per cent new wood is used, according to the year.

The style is closest to that of La Conseillance, especially since '78. The wines have a lovely aroma and are rich and deep, firm-centred with a lovely flavour and great breed.

On this form Petit-Village is back in its rightful place among the leading *crus*.

Château Pétrus

Owners: Mme L P Lacoste and J-P Moueix. Administrator:
Christian Moueix. 11·4ha. 5,000 cases. Mer 95%, CF 5%.

Fifty years ago Pétrus was unknown outside a small circle of
wine-lovers in Bordeaux, but it has become one of the region's
great names. Unfortunately it is more talked about than drunk,
due to its price and rarity.

This is the world's greatest Merlot wine and shows what can
be done with this grape when conditions are right. There is an
unctuous and almost chewy quality of richness and power which
has some similarity with that of Cheval-Blanc, but Pétrus tends to
be more concentrated, firmer and slower to develop. The complexity and nuances of flavour that develop with age are
astonishing. Vintages such as '67 and '71 could be enjoyed when
only seven to ten years old, but then go on to surprise one with
their further development; great years such as '64 are still flexing
their muscles. Of vintages still drinking, '71 is remarkable if con-
troversial; '73 and '76 are also good; '75, '78, '79 and '81 are all
great and '82 is acquiring legendary status and prices to match.
The '83 is not far behind, '85 has a lovely ripe supple character,
but without the concentration of its two fine predecessors; '86 is
enormously concentrated and tannic, a great *vin de garde*. The
'88, '89 and '90 are all massive, slow-developing wines. Then after
a great '95 and fine '96; '98 is one of the greats. Every wine-lover
should find a way of experiencing Pétrus.

Le Pin

Owner: Thienpont family. 1·9ha. 900 cases. Mer 88%, CF 12%.

The wines of this tiny property have developed great prestige
since the Thienpont family took over in 1979. They are attractive
wines, almost Californian in style, and are sold at high prices,
now in excess of Pétrus in some instances. While excellent wine,
it lacks the complexity and depth of the leading *crus*.

Château Plince

Owner: Moureau family. 8·3ha. 3,700 cases.
Mer 68%, CF 24%, CS 8%.

A good lesser *cru* situated on the sandy soils in the southwest of
Pomerol behind Nenin. A small proportion of new oak is used for
the cask maturation. This property has long had the reputation
for producing deliciously fruity, supple wines. The marvellous '47
remained fresh and opulent for over 30 years. Good wines are
now being made here, and they are excellent value for a *cru* on
the sand. This one is making the most of its high potential.

Château La Pointe

Owner: Bernard d'Arfeuille. 23ha. 11,500 cases.
Mer 75%, CF 25%. Second label: La Pointe Riffat.

This large well-known property is on the sandy, gravelly soils of
the middle plateau opposite Nenin, though on slightly lower
ground. The wines are widely distributed by the *négociants*
d'Arfeuille in Libourne. For the maturation 35 per cent new wood

is used. A retrospective tasting in 1983 confirmed my suspicions that this wine is not as good as it used to be. Mostly they seem only moderate, if charming, lightweights.

A certain lightness, allied to finesse and stylishness, has long been the mark of La Pointe, but it always had a certain balance and flair which somehow seems missing now. The '89, '95 and '98 are richer and more powerful exceptions.

Château Prieurs de la Commanderie

Owner: Clément Fayat. 3·5ha. 1,700 cases.
Mer 80%, CF and CS 20%.

Situated on Pomerol's middle terrace, this *cru* is an amalgamation of several small plots formed in 1984 by Clément Fayat. A new *cuvier* and *chai* have been built, incorporating the most modern winemaking equipment – including automatically temperature-cooled *cuves*. With its limited track record, these wines which are rich-textured and marked by oak appear to be steadily improving with every vintage.

Clos René

Owner: Pierre Lasserre. 12ha. 6,000 cases.
Mer 70%, CF 20%, Mal 10%.
Other label: Château Moulinet-Lasserre.

This is a wonderfully perfumed, dense, rich, plummy Pomerol which seldom disappoints. The '82 has a smell of prunes and an incredibly dense, rich but supple flavour; the superb '83 is more tannic and alcoholic than this and the '85 has the richness and charm of its year. The '86 is exceptional, with intense fruit and a lovely smell of damsons, yet is tannic. The '89, '90 and '95 are also excellent vintages. This is a good second-tier Pomerol. For fiscal and family reasons, a part of the crop is sold as Château Moulinet-Lasserre. The wines are the same – this is not a second label, but an alternative one.

Château La Rose Figeac

Owner: Despagne-Rapin family. 5ha. 2,000 cases.
Mer 90%, CF 10%.

This small vineyard is close to the St-Émilion–Pomerol border, and the wine is made and kept at Château Maison Blanche, the proprietor's main property.

In the best years, such as '90, 100 per cent new oak is used, and the wine is concentrated with dense chunky fruit and splendid depth and power. The '93 on the other hand, only had 80 per cent new oak, and was rich and solid for the year. These are fine, attractive, well-made wines.

Château Rouget

Owner: Labruyère family. 16ha. 6,250 cases.
Mer 85%, CF 15%.

This is an interesting property on sandy and gravelly soils, with some clay, at the northern limit of the high plateau. The wine is traditionally made and 70 per cent of the wood used for the cask maturation is new. The present owners took over in 1992 and have undertaken a lot of work in the *chai*.

This wine takes time to develop. Even in a ripe flattering vintage like '79 the Rouget has a dense, austere nose and is quite powerful with lots of fat. The '95 suggests that the wines in future will be more polished.

Château de Sales

Owner: GFA du Château de Sales – Héritiers de Laage.
Administrator: Bruno de Lambert. 47·5ha. 22,500 cases.
Mer 70%, CF 15%, CS 15%.
Second label: Château Chantalouette.

This is the largest property in Pomerol by a comfortable margin and lies on sandy soils with some recent gravel, in the northwest corner of the appellation near the Libourne–Perigord road. It has belonged to the same family for almost 400 years; Henri de Lambert's wife is a de Laage. Their son Bruno is an oenologist.

The property has an impressive 17th- and 18th- century château, set in a park. Wines are alternated between vats and used casks for maturation. There was a noticeable improvement in quality here from 1970 onwards. Wines are now scented, rich, plummy and powerful with a pleasant stylishness, and develop quite quickly. Good reliable Pomerol at a reasonable price.

Château du Tailhas

Owner: GFA du Tailhas. Administrator: Luc Nébout. 10·5ha.
4,900 cases. Mer 70%, CF 15%, CS 15%.

This property is on sandy soils in the extreme southwest corner of the appellation and near to Figeac, just the other side of the stream which is also called Tailhas. Fifty per cent new wood is used for the cask maturation. This is well-made and well-reputed second-tier Pomerol. The wines have a full colour, a highlighted bouquet which is most attractive, and lots of young fruit with that slightly earthy taste that occurs in some growths in Pomerol where there are iron deposits in the subsoil. There is now a pleasing degree of consistency.

Château Taillefer

Owner: Bernard Moueix. Administrator: Bernard Moueix.
11·5ha. 5,800 cases. Mer 50%, CF 30%, CS 15%, Mal 5%.

An attractive 19th-century château and park dominate this *cru*: one of the largest in Pomerol. It produces some light-bodied, fruity wines from its modern winery. The wines are elegant and quite fine.

Château Trotanoy

Owner: Éts J-P Moueix. 7·2ha. 3,600 cases. Mer 90%, CF 10%.

This leading *cru* is on gravel and clay soils at the western edge of the high plateau. Apart from being one of the most illustrious jewels in the Moueix crown, it is also the home of Jean-Jacques Moueix, nephew of the legendary Jean-Pierre Moueix. Of course the care of this *cru* stands high among the priorities for Christian

Moueix and his oenologist Jean-Claude Berrouet. A proportion of 50 per cent new wood is used for the cask maturation.

The reputation of Trotanoy is now higher than ever before, as can be seen from the prices collectors are prepared to pay for its mature vintages at auction. The style of the wine is for me more reminiscent of Pétrus than any other Pomerol, with its dense colour, rich spicy enveloping bouquet, and opulent fleshy body that develops an enchanting flavour of exceptional length. Great and often exceptional vintages were the '75, '78, '79, '81, '82, '83, '85, '86, '88, '89, '90, '95, '97 and '98.

Vieux Château Certan

Owner: Héritiers Georges Thienpont. 13·6ha. 5,000 cases.
Mer 60%, CF 30%, CS 10%. Second label: Clos de la Gravette.
Until the rise of Pétrus, this fine *cru* was long regarded as the leading *cru* in Pomerol. It is splendidly placed on the high plateau, with sandy clay mixed with its gravel. Pétrus, La Conseillante and L'Évangile are neighbours, with Cheval-Blanc not far away. The small but aristocratic 17th-century château is the only one of note among these leading Pomerol *crus*. Until the end of the 18th century the estate was actually much larger. It has belonged to the Belgian Thienponts since 1924 and Léon Thienpont ran the property from 1943 until his death in 1985. He has been succeeded by his son Alexandre, who had the useful experience of working at La Gaffelière from 1982 until this time. The *chai* and *cuvier* were enlarged and modernised in the early 1970s, though wooden vats were kept. A third of the wood used for the maturation is new.

This is a wine of marked individuality: perfumed, less dense in colour than other leading Pomerols, compact and firm on the palate, with a complexity, finesse and flavour that set it apart. It lacks the opulence of Trotanoy, and while it has something of the structure of La Conseillante, it lacks its unctuousness. Harmony, 'race' and finesse are the great hallmarks here. The '78, '79 and '81 are classic wines; the '82 with its great richness and '83 with its unusual power are two exceptional vintages and the '85 has all the seductive charm one would hope for from this *cru* in this year. The '86 has great power and concentration and is also an exceptional wine; '88 is a classic; '89 has an amazing overripe opulence; '90 a beautifully silky finish; '93 and '94 were successful and '95 and '98 exceptional. Evolution tends to be slow; the '71 is still at its peak and the '80 needs longer keeping than most from this year. For individuality this is still one of the best Pomerols.

Château Vray-Croix-de-Gay

Owner: Baronne Guichard. 3·7ha. 1,800 cases.
Mer 55%, CF 40%, CS 5%.
This small *cru* is on gravelly soils on the edge of the high plateau near Le Gay and Domaine de l'Église. Its owner also has the excellent Château Siaurac in Lalande de Pomerol. In style the wines are closest to those of Le Gay, powerful and densely textured, needing time to show their worth. They have been inconsistent but improved recently.

Lalande de Pomerol

This appellation of growing importance covers about 1,100 hectares of vines, of which roughly 60 per cent are in the commune of Lalande and 40 per cent in that of Néac. In Lalande the vineyards are on relatively low-lying recent gravel and sand terraces. However in Néac there is a high plateau with those *crus* facing south towards Pomerol being on good gravel. The best wines are close in quality to lesser Pomerols, with less power and tannin; developing quickly, but attractive, with finesse and style.

Château des Annereaux
Owner: Vignobles Jean Milhade. 18ha. 9,000 cases.
Mer 70%, CF 30%.
A good *cru* on the gravel and sandy soils of the lower plateau. Very elegant, attractive wines, sometimes inclined to be dilute, but spicy and delicious in good vintages. Fifty per cent new oak is now used.

Château de Bel-Air
Owner: Jean-Pierre Musset. 15ha. 7,500 cases.
Mer 70%, CF 15%, Mal 10%, CS 5%.
This well-reputed *cru* is on the gravel and sand of the middle plateau, opposite Moulinet (Pomerol). It has long been considered one of the appellation's leading *crus*. These are delicious fruity wines for early drinking.

Château La Croix-St-André
Owner: Carayon family. 16·5ha. 8,300 cases.
Mer 80%, CS 10%, CF 10%.
Second label: Château La Croix-St-Louis.
One of the best *crus* in Néac, where the soil closely resembles that on the plateau of Pomerol. The vineyards and vinification are followed with meticulous attention to detail. Old vines, careful selection and the use of 25 per cent new oak completes the picture. I found the '90 had an oaky spicy background which however did not hide the lovely ripe fruit.

Château La Croix des Moines
Owner: Jean-Louis Trocard. 8ha. 4,400 cases.
Mer 80%, CS 10%, CF 10%.
At this property on the gravel plateau of Lalande, 40 per cent new oak is used. I found the '90 scented with delicious up-front fruit, lacking structure perhaps, but hedonistic for early drinking.

La Fleur de Boüard
Owner: de Boüard de Laforest family. 17ha. 8,000 cases. Mer 70%, CF 30%. Second wine: Château La Fleur St-Georges.
When Hubert and Corinne de Boüard de Laforest of L'Angelus bought this well-sited property in Néac from AGF in '98, they decided to personalise the wine, keeping the château name for the second wine. Copybook wines had been made here under AGF since '94, but the '98 shows a real step up.

Château Grand Ormeau

Owner: Jean-Claude Beton. 11·5ha. 6,300 cases. Mer 65%,
CS 10%, CF 25%. Second label: Chevalier d'Haurange.

One of the leading *crus* of the appellation, situated in the highest part of Lalande. At a blind tasting of '90s in November 1996 it was outstanding with delicious hedonistic fruit, great ripeness and opulence, but also with depth and harmony, the epitome of fine Merlot-based wine. Fifty per cent new oak is used.

Château Haut-Chaigneau

Owner: André Chatonnet. 21ha. 5,000 cases.
Mer 70%, CF 15%, CS 15%. Second wine: Château La Croix
Chaigneau.

A good *cru* in the commune of Néac. Rich, plummy and attractive wines are made. Consistently good wines have been made here since André Chatonnet bought this old established property. There is now a cuvée prestige. However, I found the '95 very extracted with bitter tannins. The normal '96 was preferable, although also of a rather extracted style. But see also Château La Sergue.

Château Haut-Chatain

Owner: Héritiers Rivière. Administrator: Martine Rivière-
Junquas. 10·8ha. 6,000 cases. Mer 80%, CS 10%, CF 10%.

This *cru* in Néac has passed from daughter to daughter since the family acquired it in 1912. The Rivière currently in charge is also an oenologist.

The '90 has scented ripe fruit, a lovely supple, opulent flavour and delicious silky texture: this is ripe fruit perfectly vinified.

Châteaux Les Hauts-Conseillants and Les Hauts-Tuileries

Owners: Pierre and Monique Baurotte. 10ha. 4,500 cases.
Mer 70%, CF 20%, CS 10%.

This good *cru* is in Néac. 'Les Hauts-Conseillants' is used for *vente-direct* in France, 'Hauts-Tuileries' for exports. One third of the wood for the cask-maturation is new. The wines are well made and have a marvellous opulent, perfumed bouquet and a seductively silky texture with good concentration worthy of a Pomerol. The present owners also have Château Bonalgue in Pomerol.

Château Moncets

Owner: Louis-Gabriel de Jerphanion. 18·6ha. 8,900 cases.
Second label: Château Gardour. Mer 60%, CF 30%, CS 10%.

An excellent *cru* on gravel and sand at the edge of the plateau in the best southern part of Néac. The wines are bottled in Libourne by Éts J-P Moueix. They are rich and velvety in texture with style and breed, placing them in the category of good lesser Pomerols.

Château Sergant

Owner: Vignobles de Jean Milhade. 18ha. 8,500 cases.
Mer 70%, CS 20%, CF 10%.

This excellent *cru* is on the gravelly plateau of Lalande and was the creation of the present owners. Wonderfully opulent hedonistic wines with deliciously succulent fruit for early drinking.

Château Le Sergue
Owner: Pascal Chatonnet. 5ha. 1,250 cases.
Mer 85%, CS 10%, CS 5%.
Pascal Chatonnet is the oenologist son of André and Jeannine Chatonnet of Château Haut-Chaigneau. This *cru* is, in fact, made from a selection of different plots within the Haut-Chaigneau vineyard. After some trials in '94 and '95, '96 was the first vintage to be released. 80 per cent new oak was used. I found the '96 had ripe fruity highlights and vanillin with a very seductive supple texture, lovely fruit quality and rich, well integrated tannins. This was a very polished performance worthy of a Cru Classé St-Emilion or a good *cru* of Pomerol, and far superior to the Haut-Chaigneau. But has this simply ripped the heart out of it?

Château Siaurac
Owner: Baronne Guichard. 33ha. 8,000 cases.
Mer 60%, CF 35%, CS 5%.
This important *cru* is situated to the south of Néac, on gravel and sand at the edge of the plateau. One of the best-known *crus* in the appellation, consistently producing most attractive firm, fruity wines.

Château Tournefeuille
Owner: Sautarel family. 16ha. 8,900 cases.
Mer 75%, CF 15%, CS 10%.
One of Néac's leading *crus*, on the high slopes of gravel and strata of clay which form the banks of the Barbanne overlooking Pomerol. The de Belleyme map of 1765 shows that vines were already planted here at that time, when much of Pomerol was still under cereal crops. Thirty per cent new oak is used. The '90 has a good tannic backing for its attractively succulent ripe fruit.

Château de Viaud
Owner: Soc CEH. 19ha. 10,000 cases. Mer 85%, CF 10%, CS 5%.
This is one of the oldest vineyards in the Lalande commune, appearing as it does on the Bellorme map of 1785. This is fine wine of great charm, the '90 is rich and concentrated with more tannic structure than many wines in this appellation.

Fronsac
In the early 18th and 19th centuries, Fronsac was the most reputed of the Libournais wines, fetching higher prices than those of St-Émilion. After a long period of obscurity, it is slowly re-emerging as a quality region. There are about 1,100 hectares of vines divided between the appellations of Canon-Fronsac (27 per cent of the area) and Fronsac (73 per cent). These vineyards, like

those of the St-Émilion *côtes* are wines of the plateau and *côtes*, only more spectacularly so. The vineyards of Canon-Fronsac are on a *plateau calcaire* and on outcrops and *côtes* of sandstone, while those of Fronsac are mostly on a *plateau calcaire* covered with red soils similar to those of St-Christophe-des-Bardes.

The vineyards in Fronsac tend to be small, but there are some lovely buildings, such as the châteaux at La Rivière and La Dauphine. Merlot now dominates, but Cabernet Sauvignon also has an important place in some of the best vineyards. There has been a tendency to use too much old wood and keep the wines in cask too long, and many château-bottled wines have looked rustic, but things are improving. With Éts J-P Moueix taking an increasing interest, better quality should have led to better prices and a wider interest, so there could be a brighter future for Fronsac.

Château Cardeneau

Owner: Jean-Noël Hervé. 14ha. 6,000 cases.
Mer 65%, CF 20%, CS 10%, Mal 5%.
A *cru* showing much promise. The vineyard was replanted in the early 1980s and yields wines that are notably tannic, yet fruity in character, both on the nose and the palate. From such young vines these are qualities that bode well for an excellent future.

Château de Carles

Owner: Antoine Chastenet de Castaing. 20ha. 5,800 cases.
Mer 65%, CF 30%, Mal 5%.
The emperor Charlemagne is said to have camped here en route to Spain, and it is to this visit that Château de Carles owes its name. Its 15th-century château is especially attractive. The wines have not been particularly impressive but, as the J-P Moueix empire is now taking an interest in the property, they will be worth watching.

Château Dalem

Owner: Michel Rullier. 14·5ha. 7,500 cases.
Mer 70%, CF 20%, CS 10%.
An important property on the *côte*, just out of Saillans to the southeast, producing perfumed wines with real charm. They develop soft, ripe, fruity flavours when young, but last well: while the '78 was already pleasing when four years old, '64, '67 and '70 were still full of fruit and not drying up at all. Impressive wines were made in the '80s, and in the '90s there is more flesh and youthful charm. All the wine is château-bottled.

Château de la Dauphine

Owner: Éts J-P Moueix. 8ha. 4,000 cases. Mer 85%, CF 15%.
One of the best-known Fronsac *crus*, on the lower *côte* west of the town. The wines here at la Dauphine are well made. Twenty per cent new wood is used, and the wines are bottled at the right time. This all leads to delicious fruity wines, with character, that can be drunk young.

Château Fontenil

Owner: Michel Rolland. 7ha. 3,500 cases.
Mer 86%, CS 14%.
Fontenil is in the commune of Saillans; it comprises plots from several different growers which were amalgamated by Michel Rolland to create this *cru* in 1986. A winemaker with an excellent reputation, Michel Rolland's makes distinctly new-wave, intense, oaky wines at this property.

Château Gagnard

Owner: Mme Bouyge-Barthe. 10ha. 5,000 cases.
Mer 50%, CS 25%, CF 25%.
Wines from this *cru*, on the sandstone terrace north of Fronsac, are classics in the Fronsac style and have attractive perfumed fruit, sound structure and good breed. Also sold under the La Croix-Bertrand label.

Château Jeandeman

Owner: M Roy-Trocard. 25ha. 13,000 cases.
Mer 80%, Cab 20%.
This is the largest vineyard in Fronsac, and is on the *plateau calcaire* with red soil in the commune of St-Aignan. The wines are distinctly perfumed and have a delicious fruitiness on the palate that makes them drinkable after three to four years.

Château Mayne-Vieil

Owner: Sèze family. 26ha. 16,500 cases. Mer 90%, CF 10%.
An important and well-distributed *cru*. The vineyard is on sand and clay producing attractive wines with a rich middle flavour, good structure and character, very drinkable in three to four years.

Château Moulin Haut-Laroque

Owner: Jean-Noël Hervé. 14ha. 6,000 cases.
Mer 65%, CF 20%, CS 10%, Mal 5%.
This important Fronsac *cru* is on the *plateau calcaire* and *côte* southwest of Saillans. Wines are perfumed with more power and structure than many straight Fronsacs, and are slower to develop (four to five years) than some. Tannin and fruit are well matched.

Château Moulin-Haut-Villars

Owner: Mme Brigitte Gaudrie. 4ha. 2,000 cases.
Mer 70%, CF 30%.
The recent adoption of new oak for maturing these wines has changed their character considerably. Once light-bodied and pleasantly young-drinking, they are at present somewhat overpowered by tannins.

Château Plain-Point

Owner: Denis Ardon. 30ha. 16,000 cases.
Mer 80%, CF 10%, CS 10%.

Once an important mediaeval fortress, the ancient château overlooks the property and much of the surrounding Fronsac
countryside. Its vineyards are on the chalky soils of the *plateau
calcaire* and have recently been considerably expanded. There is
certainly the potential for these wines to do well.

Château Puyguilhem

Owner: Janine Mothes. 10ha. 6,000 cases.
Mer 60%, Cab 30%, Mal 10%.

A *cru* in Saillans with vineyards on the *côte* and on the limestone
plateau. The wines have a tendency to be tannic, but the high
proportion of Merlot in the blend can soften this harshness in
good vintages.

Château La Rivière

Owner: M Leprince. 47ha. 22,000 cases.
Mer 60%, CS 17%, CF 13%, Mal 10%.

A grand château, superbly sited and complete with huge underground cellars. The vineyard is on the *plateau calcaire* and *côte*. A
proportion of 30 to 40 per cent new wood is used, and the wines
are powerful and tannic and age well. The '82, '83 and '87 were
the best vintages of the '80s. Since '95 the new owner has brought
extra depth and richness to the wines.

Château Rouet

Owner: Patrick Danglade. 11ha. 5,500 cases. Mer 65%, CF 35%.

Situated on the edge of the plateau in St-Germain-la-Rivière, this
cru has a superb view over the surrounding countryside. Patrick
Danglade works hard to promote both his own wines and those of
the region. Unfortunately, the samples I have seen do not seem
to live up to their generally good reputation.

Château La Valade

Owner: Bernard Roux. 15ha. 9,000 cases.
Mer 70%, CF and CS 30%.

This *cru* is on the *plateau calcaire* and *côte* of the commune of
Fronsac. The wines are perfumed and vigorous, well balanced
with lots of character and quite fine.

Château La Vieille Cure

Owner: The Old Parsonage (C Ferenbach, P Sachs, B Soulan).
18ha. 8,000 cases. Mer 80%, CF 15%, CS 5%.
Second label Château Courtreau.

A *cru* with a bright future. La Vieille Cure is well situated: its vineyards on the *plateau calcaire* and *côte* produce some luscious
Merlot-based wines, full of varietal character.

   An American syndicate took over in 1986, and since then
the winery has been thoroughly modernised. Winemaking
is now controlled by Michel Rolland of Château Le Bon-Pasteur,
and new oak casks are used for the maturation. Excellent
wines with real breed and concentrated fruit flavours have been
made in the '90s.

Château Villars

Owner: Jean-Claude Gaudrie. 28ha. 11,500 cases.
Mer 60%, CF 30%, CS 10%.

This *cru* is in the commune of Saillans, on the *plateau calcaire* and *côte*. For the maturation a third of the wood used is new. The wines have a lot of fruit but tend to be rather soft and develop quickly (over about three years).

CANON-FRONSAC

The appellation Canon-Fronsac, or Côtes de Canon-Fronsac, is a small island of about 300 hectares in the middle of the Fronsac appellation consisting of parts of the communes of Fronsac and St-Michel-de-Fronsac. Although the outstanding *crus* are in Canon-Fronsac rather than Fronsac, the two areas can in practice be treated as one appellation.

Château Barrabaque

Owner: Noël Père & Fils. 9ha. 5,000 cases.
Mer 70%, CF 20%, CS 10%.

This property is on Fronsac's mid-*côte* and produces wines which have shown dramatic improvement over recent vintages. Fine fruit flavours and plenty of structure have been achieved at Château Barrabaque in the '90s. These are improving wines, of some originality.

Château Canon

Owner: Christian Moueix. Administrator: J-P Moueix. 1·4ha.
700 cases. Mer 100%.

The '95 and '98 were both stunning vintages from this property, full of the breed and style expected from a *cru* such as this, on one of Fronsac's best sites. It was the Moueix family's first château in this appellation, and their wines are well made and realising their full potential.

Château Canon

Owner: Mlle Henriette Horeau. 10ha. 5,000 cases.
Mer 90%, CF 5%, CS 5%.

Château Canon is one of the leading properties in this appellation. It has an extensive history, dating back to the early 1700s, and once belonged to the Fontémoing family. All the wines are marketed by the Libourne firm of *négociants* Horeau-Beylot.

Château Canon-de-Brem

Owner: Éts J-P Moueix. 4·7ha. 2,400 cases.
Mer 65%, CF 35%.

This is one of the best known and best reputed of all Fronsac properties. The wines have remarkable concentrations of fruit and flavour, and are rich and supple with great style and character. This really reveals what the appellation is capable of. The wines need four to five years ageing to show at their best, and will keep well. The property was bought by Éts J-P Moueix in 1985.

Château Canon-Moueix (formerly **Pichelèbre**)
Owner: J-P Moueix. 4·1ha. 2,000 cases. Mer 90%, CF 10%.
This property belonged to the de Brem family of Canon-de-Brem fame until sold by them to J-P Moueix in 1985. The wines under the de Brems were full of character, powerful, and long-keeping. The first Moueix vintage, '85, was rich and deep-flavoured, softer and more generous early than Canon-de-Brem and the style has been maintained.

The vineyard is on the *côte* and must now be reckoned among the leading *crus* of the appellation.

Château Capet-Bégaud
Owner: Alain Roux. 4ha. 2,800 cases.
Mer 80%, CS and CF 20%.
The '82 vintage from this château was particularly outstanding, with rich, ripe fruit flavours, balanced by a good tannic background. The '85 was similar in style but slightly mellower.

Château Cassagne-Haut-Canon
Owner: Jean-Jacques Dubois. 13ha. 6,500 cases.
Mer 70%, CF 25%, CS 5%. Second label: La Truffière.
This château also produces wines under the label La Truffière, a name derived from the truffle oaks growing on the property. After some appealing voluptuous wines at the end of the '80s, recent vintages seem over-concentrated and rather charmless.

Château Coustolle
Owner: Alain Roux. 20ha. 9,600 cases. Mer 60%, CF 30%,
CS and Mal 10%. Second label: Château Grand Cafour.
A fine *cru* on the *côte* north of Fronsac. For the maturation 20 per cent new wood is used, and the result is a wine of concentration and richness which holds well and develops character and some distinction.

Château La Croix Canon
Owner: J-P Moueix. 4ha. 5,000 cases.
Mer 70%, CF 25%, CS 5%.
Until 1993 this was Château Bodet, one of the best placed vineyards in the appellation, on a steep slope above La Dauphine. Then Moueix acquired it and renamed it Château Charlemagne. The '94 and '95 vintages were sold under this name. Now, in response to protests from Burgundy, the name has changed again. The wines combine structure with richness of fruit. Christian Moueix believes this to be the finest site in Canon-Fronsac, so watch this space!

Château la Fleur-Cailleau
Owner: Paul Barre, 3·6ha. 1,900 cases. Mer 90%, CF 10%.
Some highly individual and quite delightful wines are produced at this small property. A distinctive bouquet of wild cherries, rich tannins and elegant fruit flavours is noticeable in good vintages. Certainly a wine to look out for.

Château La Fleur-Canon

Owner: A de Coninck. 7ha. 4,000 cases.
Mer 90%, CF and CS 10%.

A small *cru* in the commune of St-Michel, making some pleasantly fruity wines which are unusual in that they mature quickly, drinking earlier than those of their neighbours.

Château du Gazin

Owner: Henri Robert, 30ha. 18,000 cases.
Mer 60%, old vines 28%, CS 6%, CF 2%, Mal 4%.

This is the appellation's largest property and is situated on the limestone plateau of St-Michel. Its wines look to have a promising future, they are beautifully scented, firm but with plenty of breed and elegance.

Château Grand-Renouil

Owner: J-F and M Ponty. 5ha. 2,500 cases. Mer 70%, CF 30%.

Another *cru* in the commune of St-Michel. This property is situated on the *côte* and produces some attractive wines that are certainly worth looking out for.

Château Haut-Mazeris

Owner: Mme Ubald-Bocquet. 6ha. 3,600 cases.
Mer 60%, CF 20%, CS 20%.

Haut-Mazeris is on the *plateau calcaire* in the St-Michel commune. Its wines are assertive with consistent balance and quality.

Château Junayme

Owner: Héritiers de Coninck. Administrator: René de Coninck.
16ha. 10,000 cases.
Mer 80%, CF 15%, CS 5%.

This well-known *cru* is on the *côte* of Canon. Its wines are less powerful than the best *crus* today in Canon-Fronsac, but they have a wide following.

Château Mausse

Owner: Guy Janoueix. 10ha. 5,000 cases.
Mer 50%, CS 25%, CF 25%.

A good *cru* on the *plateau calcaire* northeast of St-Michel. This property produces perfumed wines with richness and concentration which develop pleasing suppleness after four to five years.

Château Mazeris

Owner: Christian de Cournuaud. 15ha. 7,000 cases.
Mer 80%, CF 10%, CS 10%.

This *cru* is one of the best in its appellation. Its wines have marked individuality, as was recognised by *négociants* J-P Moueix, who bought the property's entire crop in '85. There is a possibility of expanding the vineyard to 20 hectares. The wines produced here have a great richness and concentration of flavour. This is one of the rising stars of the area.

Château Mazeris-Bellevue

Owner: Jacques Bussier. 9ha. 5,500 cases.
Mer 45%, CS 40%, CF 15%.

A fine *cru* situated on the *plateau calcaire* and *côte*. Unusually, the Cabernet Sauvignon is in the ascendancy here, and the result is a wine of distinguished, fine flavour with lots of character and style.

Château La Roche-Gaby

Owner: Marie-Madeleine Fronin. 9ha. 5,000 cases.
Mer 80%, CF 20%.

A fine old *cru* on the *côte* and *plateau calcaire* northwest of Fronsac. The wines are rich and powerful with lots of extract, needing time to develop, and can keep well. The '62 was still delicious when 20 years old. It was formerly known as Gaby and belonged to the Kermoal family with a history going back 300 years.

Château Toumalin

Owner: Bernard d'Arfeuille. 8ha. 4,000 cases.
Mer 75%, CF 25%.

This *cru* is on the *côte* above the valley of the River Isle north of Fronsac, and belongs to the well-known Libourne *négociants* who also own La Pointe (Pomerol) and La Serre (St-Émilion). They are lovely vivid, fruity wines with the necessary balance to be enjoyed young.

Château Vincent

Owner: Mme François Roux. 10·5ha. 5,600 cases AC Canon Fronsac, 3,000 cases AC Fronsac (under the name Château Tertre de Canon). Mer 85%, CF 15%.

Rather confusingly the Fronsac is the part of the vineyard that carries the name Tertre de Canon, rather than the Canon-Fronsac part. These are well-made wines that see no wood. I have sometimes found myself preferring the more robust Tertre de Canon to the Vincent. The '91 Tertre was a great success here, from frost-free vines; much better than the '92.

Château Vray-Canon-Boyer

Owner: Coninck family. 8·5ha. 4,000 cases.
Mer 90%, CS 5%, CF 5%.

This excellently situated *cru* produces wines with elegance and finesse, and which also mature successfully. The '96 is particularly good.

Minor Appellations

The following section covers some of the appellations that do not belong the major league of Bordeaux regions but nevertheless produce many wines worth investigating. Wines from these appellations tend to mature earlier than the Grands Crus of the well-known appellations, which makes them useful commercially. Among them are wines of great charm and personality that it would be a pity to overlook.

CÔTES DE BOURG

The attractive, hilly and often wooded countryside of the Côtes de Bourg has seen something of a revival in the past decade. There are now over 3,500 hectares of vines, this area having shown an increase of 17 per cent in a decade.

The soils are mostly of limestone and clay, and gravel and clay on a limestone subsoil. The traditional *encépagement* was a third each of Cabernet Sauvignon, Merlot and Malbec (still to be found at Château Guerry), but in most properties the role of the Malbec has been reduced and that of the Merlot increased. This factor, together with the inability today of many owners to afford casks for maturation, has meant that something of the distinctively rich fruitiness of the Bourg has inevitably been lost.

But good and attractive wines are being made here in increasing quantities and as the demand for good, reasonably priced red Bordeaux grows, Bourg should prosper.

Château de Barbé
Owner: Richard family. 64ha. 38,000 cases.
Mer 70%, CF and CS 25%, Mal 5%.
This is one of the region's largest, finest and best-reputed properties. There is no wood-ageing here and the wines are light-textured, fruity and charming with some 'race', for drinking after two to four years.

Château Brulesécaille
Owners: Jacques Rodet and Martine Recapet. 19ha.
10,500 cases. Mer 50%, CS 25%, CF 20%, Mal 5%.
This good property in the commune of Tauriac produces robust earthy wines with plenty of fruit and character which age well. The excellent Brulesécaille '88 was still improving after five years.

Château Guerry
Owner: SC du Château Guerry. Administrator: Bertrand de Rivoyre. 22ha. 13,000 cases. Mer 45%, CS 30%, Mal 25%.
This *cru* shows the kind of quality that Bourg is capable of. There are two distinctive features: Malbec is retained as a major variety, and this is one of the last remaining *crus* in Bourg where all the wines are matured in cask. The result is a wine which combines richness and suppleness, power and finesse. Distribution is exclusively through GVG group.

Château Guionne
Owner: Richard Porcher. 14ha. 9,300 cases.
Mer 50%, CF and CS 45%, Mal 5%.
This *cru* is all château-bottled and produces fruity, attractive and quite elegant wines.

Château Mendoce
Owner: Philippe Darricarrère. 14ha. 6,000 cases.
Mer 70%, CS 25%, CF 5%, PV 5%.

This is one of the best known and best reputed wines in this region. There is a fine château, parts of which date from the 15th century. The wines are supple with some richness, and mature rapidly.

Château Peychaud
Owner: Jacques and Bernard Germain. 29ha. 17,000 cases.
CS 60%, Mer 30%, Mal 5%.
This large and well-known property was acquired by the current owners in 1971. The château has a good reputation for supple, pleasing wines.

Château Roc de Cambes
Owner: François Mitjavile. 9·6ha. 3,000 cases.
Mer 35%, CF 35%, Mal 30%.
The same principles of low yields, old vines, late harvesting and meticulous winemaking apply here as at the proprietor's more famous Tertre-Rôteboeuf in St-Émilion. The wine is rich, succulent and marvellously attractive; but do not expect to pay Côte de Bourg prices. This commands the price of a St-Émilion Grand Cru Classé – when you can find it!

Château Rousset
Owner: M et Mme Teisseire.
Administrator: Gérard Teisseire. 23ha. 13,000 cases.
Mer 47%, CS 38%, Mal 10%, CF 5%.
Situated in the commune of Samonac, this is certainly one of the best *crus* of Bourg. The wines have richness and length of flavour which place them above the general run of wines from this area.

Château Tour-de-Tourteau
Owner: GAEC Chagnaud Père & Fils. 17ha. 11,000 cases.
Mer 60%, CF and CS 35%, Mal 5%
This excellent *cru* was once part of Rousset. All the wines are château-bottled and distributed by Calvet and Éts de Rivoyre & Diprovin-Louis Dubroca. The wines are unusually rich and powerful, even pungent, making delicious drinking when three to four years old.

PREMIÈRES CÔTES DE BLAYE
This region forms the northward extension of the Côtes de Bourg. Although it is larger than the Bourg, the parts suited to the vine are smaller. The area of vineyards has, however, more than doubled over the last 20 years, now covering over 4,000 hectares. The output consists predominantly of red wine with only a small and unimportant production of white. The soil here is of limestone and clay and the Merlot is more predominant than in Bourg. The prices achieved are often no more than for Bordeaux Supérieur, and some of the growers take advantage of the higher permitted yields for the lesser appellation and declare their wines as Bordeaux Supérieur instead of Premières Côtes de Blaye. This is a good source of fruity, easy-to-drink red Bordeaux.

Château Bourdieu

Owner: Jean Kléber Michaud. 33ha. Red: 15,000 cases.
Mer 50%, CS 40%, CF 10%.
White: 5,000 cases. Sém 80%, Sauv and Col 20%.

A well known and well-reputed *cru*, unusual in its high proportion of Cabernet Sauvignon and in using wood maturation. The result is a wine above average in character and quality.

Château Charron

Owner: Vignobles Germain. 22ha. Red: 13,000 cases. Mer 80%, CS 20%. White: 4ha. 2,500 cases. Sém 70%, Sauv 30%.

This is a well-reputed *cru* that uses wood maturation and some new oak. The result is a wine with more colour and richness than average.

Château L'Escadre

Owner: GFA L'Escadre. Administrator: Jean-Marie Carreau.
32ha. 13,000 cases. Mer 70%, CS 20%, Mal 10%.
Second label: Château la Croix St-Pierre.

This good *cru* in the commune of Cars has acquired an excellent reputation for consistency over the last two decades. Some wood maturation is used, and the wines are charmingly fruity and stylish.

Château Segonzac

Owner: J and C Marmet-Champion. 30ha. 20,000 cases.
Mer 60%, CS 25%, CF 10%, Mal 5%.

This *cru* in the commune of St-Genès-de-Blaye produces fruity, light, supple wines for early drinking.

ENTRE-DEUX-MERS

This huge area is the largest source of good dry white wines in Bordeaux. There are now 2,590 hectares benefiting from the AC (including the small Haut-Benauge AC), considerably more than there were 15 years ago. This is a region of large estates with mechanical harvesting now widely used and cool fermentation as the rule. Much good red wine is also made, but this is entitled only to the appellation Bordeaux or Bordeaux Supérieur.

Château Bonnet

Owner: André Lurton.
Red: 73ha. 44,000 cases. CS 67%, Mer 27%, CF 6%.
White: 40ha. 26,000 cases. Sém 50%, Sauv 30%, Musc 20%.
Rosé: 1,000 cases. Second label: Le Colombey.

One of the most impressive properties in Entre-Deux-Mers, with an elegant 18th-century château and enormous vineyard. It is in Grézillac, due south of St-Émilion. The *chai* and *cuvier* are as well equipped as André Lurton's prestigious Graves properties. The white wine is cold-fermented at 16–18°C (61–64°F), and some of the red is matured in cask and sold in special numbered bottles. With its interesting mixture of *cépages*, the white wine is perfumed and full of elegant, fruity flavours. This is one of the best-value and most dependable dry white wines to be found on French restaurant lists. The red grapes are mechanically harvested, and the red wines are thoroughly attractive with quite a pronounced character.

Château Fondarzac

Owner: J-C Barthe. White: 34ha (Sauv, Sém, Musc). Red: 29ha.
This *cru* has been owned since the 17th century by the Barthe family whose winemaking skills have manifested themselves in more recent generations. Jean-Claude Barthe has shown himself to be a particularly talented oenologist. The wines have a delicious bouquet and plenty of fruit.

Château Fongrave

Owner: Pierre Perromat.
Red: 40ha. 22,000 cases. CS 60%, Mer 40%.
White: 13ha. 7,000 cases. Sém 60%, Sauv 40%.
Second label (for red wines): Château de La Sablière-Fongrave.
This *cru* at Gornac is run by Pierre Perromat, who also owns Château d'Arche and was president of the INAO for many years. The property has been in his family since the 1600s and produces some attractively scented wines, both red and white.

Château Jonqueyres

Owner: Éts G A M Audy. Administrator: Jean-Michel Arcaute.
Red: 38ha. 23,000 cases. Mer 75%, CS 25%.
White: 1·7ha. 200 cases.
This property at St-Germain-du-Puch in the northern Entre-Deux-Mers has benefited from the winemaking capabilities of Jean-Michel Arcaute, seen to spectacular effect at Château Clinet (*see* page 198). Look out especially for the Vieilles Vignes selection.

Château Launay

Owner: Rémy Grèffier.
Red: 18ha. 10,000 cases. Mer 63%, CS 20%, CF 17%.
White: 45ha. 25,000 cases. Sém 40%, Musc 33%, Sauv 27%.
Second labels: White: Châteaux Dubory, Braidoire, La Vaillante. Red: Châteaux Haut-Castenet, Haut-Courgeaux.
This large property is at Soussac, on the road between Pellegrue and Sauveterre in the eastern Entre-Deux-Mers. All the wine is château-bottled. The wines are well reputed.

Château Moulin-de-Launay

Owners: Claude and Bernard Greffier. White: 75ha. 44,000 cases. Sém 40%, Sauv 30%, Musc 20%, Ugni Blanc 10%.
Red: 1ha. 400 cases. CF 50%, Mer 50%.
Second labels: Châteaux Tertre-de-Launay, Plessis, La Vigerie, de Tuilerie.
This large property at Soussac in eastern Entre-Deux-Mers between Pellegrue and Sauveterre was entirely consecrated to the production of white wines – fruity, with elegance and length – until the planting of a hectare of red in 1992.

Château de la Rose

Owner: Jean Faure. White: 9ha. 6,000 cases.
Red: 7.7ha. 5,000 cases.

This property in the north of the region is small compared with most in Entre-Deux-Mers. The wines produced are extremely attractive with a charming bouquet and with floweriness and fruit on the palate.

Château de Sours

Owner: Esmé Johnstone.
Red: 27ha. 12,500 cases. Mer 80%, CS 15%, CF 5%.
White: 13ha. 3,800 cases, Sém 75%, Musc, Sauv and Mer Blanc 25%. Second label: (red) Domaine de Sours.

The owner is an Englishman who has come to Bordeaux after a career spanning banking in Hong Kong and retailing wine in the UK and California. The property is at St-Quentin de Baron between Branne and Créon in north central Entre-Deux-Mers. The soil is gravel and clay on limestone, and there are limestone *caves* under the property, now used for cask maturation.

The red wine is made with the assistance of Michel Rolland (*see* Le Bon-Pasteur, page 196) and is aged for 15 months in new and second-year casks. The resulting wine is attractive for drinking when around three years old, but it will also keep and improve.

The white wine (sold as Bordeaux AC, not Entre-Deux-Mers) is made with the help of David Lowe (formerly of Rothbury in Australia's Hunter Valley) and has a pleasing middle richness combined with fruit and elegance. There is also a delicious rosé made by the *saignée* method, with free-run juice taken from the vats after 12–18 hours' skin contact.

Not surprisingly these wines have rapidly made a name for themselves.

Château Thieuley

Owner: Francis Courselle.
Red: 20ha, 8,300 cases. Mer 70%, CF 20%, CS 10%.
White: 20,000 cases. Sauv 60%, Sém 35%, Musc 5%.

The proprietor here is a professor of viticulture. The property is at La Sauve near Créon in western Entre-Deux-Mers. The white wines have a most attractive fruit, without exaggerated acidity, and are light and fresh.

Château Tour de Mirambeau

Owner: Francis Courselle.
Red: 29ha. 19,500 cases. Mer 68%, CF 18%, CS 14%.
White: 81ha. 54,000 cases. Sauv 64%, Sém 36%.

A large property near Branne producing large quantities of consistently reliable wines: the white is particularly successful and the red fresh and fruity for early drinking. The Bordeaux Blanc Cuvée Passion is a selection from the oldest vines, harvested by hand and then fermented in new wood. The other wines are mechanically harvested.

Château de Toutigeac

Owner: Philippe Mazeau.

Red: 38ha: 25,000 cases. CS 50%, Mer 50%.

White: 2ha. 1,300 cases, Sém 50%, Sauv 25%, Musc 25%.

One of the best-known properties to use the sub-appellation Entre-Deux-Mers-Haut-Benauge. The appellation can be used only for white wines. Both red and white wines here are well reputed and all are château-bottled.

PREMIÈRES CÔTES DE BORDEAUX

This attractive area runs from the suburbs of Bordeaux southwards down the right bank of the Garonne to the sweet wine regions of Loupiac and Ste-Croix-du-Mont. It produces moderately sweet white wines and fruity, vivacious reds for early drinking. Fifteen years ago there was a slightly greater vineyard area devoted to white than to red wine production, but today the situation is reversed and the red vineyards have increased by over 50 per cent over the past decade to 2,868 hectares, while those covered by white vines have decreased to 800 hectares. The best whites in the south of the area carry the superior AC Cadillac, but the idea has not really caught on. The real future of the region seems to rest more with its pleasant red wines.

Château Birot

Owner: Fournier-Casteja family.

Red: 10ha. 4,000 cases. Mer 52%, CF 25%, CS 23%.

White: 10ha. 2,800 cases. Sém 58%, Sauv 35%, Musc 7%.

This *cru* in the commune of Béguey is best known for its fresh, fruity whites, with well-balanced acidity, sweetness and elegance. It is now run by Fournier, formally of Château Canon.

Château Brethous

Owner: Denise Verdier. 13ha.

Mer 45%, CF 25%, CS 20%, Mal 10%.

This good *cru* at Camblanes produces wines that are deliciously fruity and scented. They drink well when two to three years old, but can still be fresh and delicious after eight years.

Château Carsin

Owner: Juha Berglund.

Red: 11ha. 5,500 cases. Mer 60%, CF 30%, CS 10%.

White: 24ha. 11,500 cases. Sém 65%, Sauv 20%, Sauv Gris 15%.

An interesting property at Rions with an international flavour. The owner is Finnish; the winemaker, Mandy Jones, an Australian who worked previously at Château de Landiras under Peter Vinding-Diers. In addition to the vineyard belonging to the château, a further 20 hectares of pure Sémillon are leased.

The white wines have had a great success in England for several years, as well as in Juha Berglund's native Finland. The Cuvée Prestige is fermented in cask with *bâttonage*, (a stirring up of the lees before the first racking). The normal quality is fermented in stainless steel and then spends about three months in different types of oak. The attention to detail is meticulous. The normal white has zesty lemon-like fruit and excellent acidity, the Cuvée Prestige is perfumed with oaky notes, a broader, richer flavour with clear wood influence and a distinctly New World feel to it. The '96 is outstanding. Also look out for the L'Etiquette Grise, sold without the appellation or vintage, made from the rare Sauvignon Gris, it is a real surprise. The reds are clean and fruity and need a year or two to develop.

Château Cayla

Owner: Patric Doche. 24ha.
Red: 14·5ha. 6,500 cases. CS 34%, CF 33%, Mer 33%.
White: 6·7ha. 1,500 cases. Sém 75%, Sauv 25%.
Since 1985, this property at Rions has been transformed by the present owner. The reds have varied fruit and are delicious when three years old; the whites are rotated through ten per cent new oak after a cool fermentation and pre-fermentation skin contact.

Domaine de Chastelet

Owner: Jean Estansan.
8ha. 5,000 cases. Mer 50%, CS 45%, CF 5%.
A *cru* at Quinsac producing wine that has solid fruit with plenty of charm. It needs three to five years to achieve harmony.

Château Fayau

Owner: Jean Médeville & Fils. 36ha.
Red: 26ha. 12,000 cases. CS 40%, Mer 35%, CF 25%.
White: 10ha. 4,000 cases. Sém 50%, Sauv 40%, Musc 10%.
This excellent *cru* in Cadillac is carefully run by the Médeville family who make a particularly good sweet white Cadillac, with fruit and style, that ages well.

Château Le Gardera, Château Laurétan, Château Tanesse

Owner: Domaines Cordier.
For many years Domaines Cordier have run these adjoining properties in the Premières Côtes as a single production centre, producing several different appellations. Since 1983 the production of Château Laurétan has ceased, and this has been changed into a brand, Laurétan Rouge and Laurétan Blanc, with the simple Bordeaux appellation. The other two châteaux are as follows:

Château Le Gardera: *25ha. Red (AC Bordeaux Supérieur): 11,5000 cases. Mer 60%, CS 40%.*
Le Gardera now produces an attractive, light-bodied Merlot-dominated red wine.

Château Tanesse: *Red (AC Premières Côtes de Bordeaux): 35ha. 12,000 cases. CS 55%, Mer 35%, CF 10%. White (AC Bordeaux Blanc): 20ha. 12,000 cases. Sauv 85%, Sém 15%.*
Tanesse makes a more Cabernet-dominated red wine together with a flowery, fresh, Sauvignon-style white.

Château du Grand Mouëys

Owner: SCA Les Trois Colines (Reidermeister & Ulrichs).
Administrator: Carstin Bömers. Red: 50ha. Mer 50%, CS 25%,
CF 25%. White: 21ha. 10,000 cases. Sém 67%, Sauv 33%.

Since the important Bremen house of Reidermeister & Ulrichs
bought this large property at Capian in 1989 there has been considerable investment in the vineyard, cellar and château.

Ten hectares of the red wine vineyard are currently used
to make Bordeaux Clairet, the red wine is matured for between
five and ten months in cask, depending on the year. A part of
the white wine is fermented in new barrels, the rest in stainless
steel. Attractive white wines are already being made here,
although the red wines are taking a little longer. This is clearly a
property to watch.

Château de Haux

Owners: Jorgensen brothers.
Red: 22ha. 13,000 cases. Mer 42%, CS 40%, CF 18%.
White: 7ha. Sém 64%, Sauv 30%, Musc 6%.

In 1985 two brothers, wine merchants from Denmark, bought this
property at Haux and have rapidly transformed it. Their red wine
is rich and solid with attractive fruit and definite character, the
white is exceptionally attractive, with long-flavoured, crisp fruit.

Château Lagarosse

Owner: M Ottari. Administrator: G Laurencin. 32ha.
Red: 26·7ha. 16,000 cases. Mer 80%, CS and CF 20%.
White: 5·9ha. 2,200 cases. Sém 80%, Sauv 20%.

This property at Tabanac was bought in 1987 by a Japanese
importer of agricultural machinery. The red wines have intense
fruit, a rich, solid flavour and a suggestion of liquorice. The whites
have a big broad flavour with lots of fruit and character. In '96 and
'97 excellent Cadillac was made.

Château Laroche-Bel-Air

Owner: Martine Palau. 25ha.
Red: Mer 55%, CS and CF 40%, Mal 5%.
White: Sém 80%, Sauv 20%.

This *cru* at Baurech produces stylish, fruity but quite tannic wines
that need four to five years' maturation before being ready. They
are matured in cask. The wine matured in vat is softer, but also
robust and can be drunk earlier. It is labelled as Château Laroche.
The same labelling differences are used for the white wines to
distinguish those vinified in cask from those vinified in vat.

Château Laurétan *See page 225.*

Château Nenine

Owner: Francis Fouquet. 25ha. CF 45%, Mer 35%, CS 20%.
This vineyard at Baurech is the retirement home and hobby of a
man who spent his career as a *négociant* at Borie-Manoux and
Gilbey de Loudenne.

Monsieur Fouquet believes the Cabernet Franc is ideally suited to the particular *terroir* of his vineyard, and makes charmingly fruity, scented wines that are ideal for early drinking.

Château de Pic
Owner: François Masson Regnault.
Red: 28ha, 18,500 cases. CS 50%, Mer 45%, CF 5%.
White: 2·5ha. 1,100 cases. Sém 75%, Sauv 20%, Musc 5%.
This property is at Le Tourne, just outside Langoiran. Since the present owners took over in 1975, extensive improvements have been made. There is a basic wine matured in vat, delicious to drink soon after bottling, and a Cuvée Tradition aged in cask, which has more structure and depth of fruit.

Château Plaisance
Owner: Patrick Bayle. Red: 23ha. 12,000 cases. Mer 50%,
CS 35%, CF 15%.
White: 1·5ha. 600 cases. Sém 100%.
Patrick Bayle left a business career to run this property at Capian in 1985. His wines have a rich, berry-like fruit that needs three or four years to mature. There is also a cask-fermented white wine.

Château de Plassan
Owner: Jean Brianceau.
Red: 20ha. 9,000 cases. Mer 50%, CS and CF 45%, Mal 5%.
White: 15ha. 6,000 cases. Sém 50%, Sauv 40%, Musc 10%.
Second label: Château Lamothe.
This fine property at Tabanac has one of the region's rare Palladium buildings, with château and *chai* forming a harmonious whole. The reds are concentrated and solid but with good fruit, serious wines needing time. There is an attractive white wine vinified in vat and bottled in the spring and a Cuvée Special which is vinified in cask but made only in selected vintages.

Château Puy Bardens
Owner: Yves Lamiable. 17ha. 10,500 cases.
Mer 50%, CS 45%, CF 5%.
A good *cru* at Cambes, commanding fine views over the Garonne and the vineyards of Graves from its hilly position. Two qualities are made, one matured in vat, is perfumed, with structure and personality, while the Cuvée Prestige is matured in cask and has plenty of fruit and substance. A distinctly fine wine.

Château Reynon
Owner: Denis and Florence Dubourdieu-David.
Red: 15ha. 9,000 cases. Mer 65%, CS 30%, CF 5%.
White: 20ha. 11,000 cases. Sauv 85%, Sém 10%, Musc 5%.
Second labels: Le Second de Rey (for both red and white),
Le Second de Reynon.
This well-known and well-distributed *cru* is the most important property in the commune of Béguey, near to Cadillac. The soil is gravelly with calcareous clay. Here an excellent red wine

is made, possessing the almost startling fruitiness which characterises the area. It is aged in cask after a long maceration. The deliciously floral fruity white wines have justly won a considerable reputation. They are vinified and aged in vat. In '96 a Cadillac was made for the first time. One could have mistaken it for a Barsac, it was so fine.

Château Tanesse *See* page 225.

STE-CROIX-DU-MONT

The two appellations of Ste-Croix-du-Mont and Loupiac are situated on some spectacular hillsides and the plateau, just across the Garonne from Sauternes and Barsac, affording a splendid panorama of the whole Graves-Sauternes region. They also provide the best sweet wines outside Sauternes. In fact the best properties are able to make wines which can be better than the lesser Sauternes, given grapes properly affected by noble rot. They tend to be lighter and less rich than Sauternes, but are fruity and long-lived. The cooperative at Ste-Croix-du-Mont produces wines of a good standard. The area under vine is 460 hectares.

Château Coulac
Owner: Gérard Despujols. 16ha. 4,000 cases.
Sem 80%, Sauv 10%, Musc 10%.
The Despujols family produce very dependable and quite rich wines which mature well.

Château Loubens
Owner: Arnaud de Sèze. 4,500 cases.
Red: 6ha. 2,500 cases. Mer 45%, CS 40%, CF 15%.
White: 15ha. 5,000 cases. Sém 95%, Sauv 5%. Second labels: Château Terfort, Fleuron Blanc de Château Loubens.
This has long been one of the best *crus* of the appellation. The sweet wines have an elegant fruit and freshness about them and are well made with well-balanced sweetness. The vineyard is finely placed at the top of the *côte*. There is an attractive dry wine, sold under the name of Fleuron Blanc, and another sweet wine, Château Terfort, which also maintains an excellent standard.

Château du Pavillon
Owner: Viviane and Alain Fertal. 7.6ha. 2,500 cases.
Sem 85%, Sauv 15%.
Very elegant botrytised wines of real class are being made here and at the owners' Loupiac vineyards of Les Roques.

Château La Rame
Owner: Yves Armand. 20ha. 4,000 cases.
Sem 75%, Sauv 25%.
One of the most attractive and consistent wines being made in the '90s in Ste-Croix du Mont. Elegant fruit flavours and Barsac-like breed.

LOUPIAC

Apart from the fact that they lie in different communes, there is no useful distinction to be made between the Loupiac appellation and that of its neighbour, Ste-Croix-du-Mont. Loupiac has just over 400 hectares under vine.

Château du Cros

Owner: Michel Boyer. 38.5ha. 2,500 cases.
Sem 70%, Sauv 20%, Musc 10%.

A superbly sited historic property with links to Richard the Lionheart in 1196. The wines have quite rich fruit with lemony acidity and are elegant and attractive.

Château Loupiac-Gaudiet

Owner: Marc Ducau.
White: 25ha. 8,900 cases. Sém 80%, Sauv 20%.

This has been one of Loupiac's best and most consistent wines for many years. The wines are mostly aged in vat. They have delicacy and finesse with a fruity sweetness, and age well.

Château Les Roques

Owner: Viviane and Alain Fertal.
See Château du Pavillon (Ste-Croix-du-Mont).

Château de Ricaud

Owner: SC Garreau-Ricard. Administrator: Alain Thienot.
55ha. Red: 12,000 cases. CS 50%, Mer 50%.
White: 20ha. 10,000 cases. Sém 80%, Sauv 15%, Musc 5%.

This is the most famous *cru* in Loupiac, and many of the historic vintages (such as '29 and '47) are still superb. Unfortunately in the last years of the previous ownership the property was neglected and run down, but since the new owners from Champagne took over in 1980 there has been steady progress. The Loupiac is finely perfumed with finesse, real elegance and richness. Some new wood is now used for the maturation.

Fine examples were made in '81, '82 and '83 but the real breakthrough came with a gloriously botrytized '86 which could well pass for a good Barsac. There is a rather traditional Sémillon-dominated dry white with the Bordeaux AC, and a fruity, attractive red wine which has the Premières Côtes AC in the best years ('81 and '82) and otherwise the Bordeaux Supérieur AC. Again these wines are matured in cask. The property has rapidly regained its former reputation.

CÔTES DE CASTILLON

This region lies between the St-Émilionnais and the boundary of the Gironde and Dordogne departments, and used to be categorised as 'St-Émilionnais' before the appellations came into force. It produces some of the best Bordeaux Supérieur, with body and some character, much of it from a good *cave coopérative*. With 2,832 hectares of vines, the area under vine has more than doubled since 1974.

The following châteaux among others, are worth looking out for: d'Aiguilhe (acquired in 1998 by Stephan von Neipperg of Canon la-Gaffelière), de Belcier, Cap de Faugères, La Clarière-Laithwaite, Castegens (also sold as Fontenay), Chante-Grive, de Clotte, L'Estang, Haut-Tuquet, Lardit, Moulin-Rouge, Pitray, Puycarpin, Rocher-Bellevue, Roquevieille, Ste-Colombe, Thibaud-Bellevue, La Treille-des-Girondiers.

CÔTES DE FRANCS

This small appellation to the north of Castillon has gained a reputation in excess of its size (only 450 hectares) due to the pioneering work of the Thienpont family at Château Puygueraud, where superb red wines are being made. Other wines to look out for are Châteaux de Francs, Laclaverie and La Prade.

Additional Châteaux

This alphabetical listing is a directory of some 220 châteaux that are not profiled in Part I of the book. It aims to give as broad and useful a selection as possible within the limits of the space available.

Where possible, the following details are given, and in the corresponding order: château name, appellation, classification (if any), owner (*see* page 5 for types of company), size of vineyard in hectares, colour of wine (R or W for red or white), and the average number of cases produced annually. If a star appears after the name it means that the wine concerned is above average and worth investigating.

The appellations and classifications are abbreviated as follows.

Appellation	Abbreviation
Barsac	Bars
Blaye	Bl
Bourg	Bg
Bordeaux	Bord
Bordeaux Supérieur	Bord Sup
Canon-Fronsac	C-Fron
Cérons	Cér
Côtes de Castillon	Cast
Entre-Deux-Mers	E-D-M
Fronsac	Fron
Graves	Gr
Haut-Médoc	H-Méd
Lalande de Pomerol	L de Pom
Listrac	List
Loupiac	Loup
Lussac-St-Émilion	L-St-Ém
Margaux	Marg
Médoc	Méd
Moulis	Moul

Pauillac   Pau
Pomerol   Pom
Premières Côtes de Bordeaux   Prem Côtes
Ste-Croix-du-Mont   Ste-Cr
St-Émilion   St-Ém
St-Estèphe   St-Est
St-Julien   St-Jul
Sauternes   Saut

Classification	**Abbreviation**
Cru Bourgeois	CB
Grand Cru	GC
Cru Grand Bourgeois	CGB
Cru Bourgeois Supérieur	CBS

Balac H-Méd, CB, L Touchais, 15ha, R8,000

Barbé* Bl, Carreau, 30ha, R5,000, W5,000

La Barde Bg, A Darricarrère, 17ha, R11,600

Bel-Air Ste-Cr, M Méric, 10ha, W4,000

Belle-Rose Pau, CB 1932, Bernard Jugla, 7ha, R4,000

Bellevue* Méd, CB, Yves Lassalle et Fils, 23ha, R14,500

Bigaroux* St-Ém, GC, Dizier, 15ha, R7,000

Le Boscq* Méd, CB 1932, Claude Lapalu, 27ha, R15,500

du Bouilh Bord Sup, Comte P de Feuilhade de Chauvin, 48ha, R22,000, W1,000

Bournac* Méd, B Secret, 13ha, R8,000

du Bousquet Bg, Castel Frères, 62ha, R36,000

Bouteilley, Dom de Prem Côtes, J Guillot, 37ha, R22,000

Brame-les-Tours St-Est, P de Padirac, 8ha, R4,000

des Brousteras Méd, SCF du château, 25ha, R15,000

de Caillavet* Prem Côtes, SC, 71ha, R30,000, W8,900

le Caillou Pom, A Giraud, 7ha, R3,500

de Calvimont* Gr, J Perromat, 12ha, W4,000, R2,000

de Camarsac* E-D-M, L & B Lurton, 58ha, R33,000, W500

Canet* E-D-M, B Large, 38ha, R8,000, W8,000

Carcanieux* Méd, CB 1978, SC, 36·7ha, R18,000

du Cartillon* H-Méd, CB 1932, Vignobles R Giraud, 46ha, R23,000

de Cérons* Cér, J Perromat, 12ha, W3,000

Le Châtelet St-Ém, H & P Berjal, 5ha, R2,400

Civrac* Bg, J-P Jaubert, 20ha, R6,000

La Commanderie Pom, F & Mlle M H Dé, 5·6ha, R3,500

de la Commanderie L de Pom, Dr H-R Lafon, 22ha, R11,000

de Courteillac E-D-M, Stephane Assés, 17ha, R5,500, W700

Crabitey* Gr, SC, 25·5ha, R13,000, W2,000

de la Croix Millorit Bg, GAEC Jaubert, 22ha, R10,000

de Cugat E-D-M, B Meyer, 48ha, R27,000, W4,500

Doms* Gr, Vignobles Parage, 7ha, R6,500, W3,500

Falfas Bg, Éts Riveaux-Beychade, 17ha, R9,500

Faubernet* Prem Côtes, Adrien Dufis, 25ha, R15,000

Ferrand* Pom, Gasparoux & Fils, 15ha, R7,000

Florimond-la Brede Bl, L Marinier, 24·5ha, R10,000, W2,000

Fonchereau E-D-M, Mme Georges Vinot-Postry, 28ha, R15,000, W2,000

Fonrazade St-Ém, GC, G Balotte, 13ha, R6,500

Fort-de-Vauban H-Méd, A Noleau, 8·6ha, R4,500

Franc-Maillet* Pom, G Arpin, 5·6ha, R3,000

La France E-D-M, La France Assurances, 60ha, R33,000, W6,500

Franquet-Grand-Poujeaux* Moul, CB, P Lambert, 8·5ha, R3,000

de Fronsac Fron, Seurin, 8ha, R4,000

Gaillard St-Ém, GC, J-J Nouvel, 20ha, R12,000

Le Gay E-D-M, R Maison, 20ha, R8,500, W2,000

Gazin-Rocquencourt Gr, P Michotte, 13·5ha, R6,500

de Goélane E-D-M, SC, 73ha, R33,000, W2,000

Gombaude-Guillot* Pom, GFA, 7ha, R2,500

Gontier Bl, D Levrand, 20ha, R11,000

La Grâce-Dieu* St-Ém, GC, M Pauty, 13ha, R6,500

Grand-Duroc-Milon Pau, CB 1932, Bernard Jugla, 6ha, R2,200

Le Grand-Enclos du Ch Cérons Cér, Lataste, 6ha, W1,000

Grand-Jour Bg, SCEA, 40ha, R25,000

Grand-Monteil Bord Sup, Jean Techenet, 113ha, R65,000, W8,500

Grand-Moulin H-Méd, R Gonzalvez, SC, 18ha, R11,000

de Grand-Puch E-D-M, Société Viticole, 90ha, R50,000

Grate-Cap Pom, G & M Janoueix, 10ha, R5,000

du Grava* Prem Côtes, SCI de la Rive Droite, 45ha, R30,000

de la Grave* Bg, R & P Y Bassereau, 40ha, R21,000

Gravelines Prem Côtes, Dubourg, 10ha, W25,000, R8,500

Graville-Lacoste* Gr, Hervé Doubourdieu, 8ha, W3,500

Grimonac Prem Côtes, P Yung, 25ha, R13,000

Grolet Bl, Bömes family, 28ha, R15,000

Gros-Moulin Bg, J Arzeller, 28ha, R16,000

Gueyrot St-Ém, de la Tour du Fayet, 8ha, R4,000

Guibon E-D-M, A Lurton, 35ha, W11,000, R5,000

Haut-Breton-Larigaudière Marg, CB 1932, SCEA, 13ha, R7,000

Haut-Brignon Prem Côtes, 54ha, R31,000

Haut-Lavallade* St-Ém, J-P Chagneau, 12ha, R6,000

Haut-Lignan* Méd, Castet family, 11ha, R7,000

Haut-Macô Bg, Mallet Frères, 37ha, R20,000

Haut-Maillat Pom, J-P Estager, 5ha, R2,520

Haut Ségottes St-Ém, GC, D André, 9ha, R5,000

Houbanon Méd, CB 1978, SC, 13ha, R6,500

Hourtin-Ducasse* H-Méd, CB, M Marengo, 25ha, R13,000

Jacques-Blanc St-Ém, GFA, 18·8ha, R10,000

des Jaubertes* Gr, Marquis de Pontac, 31ha, R8,500, W2,000

Jean-Gervais Gr, Counilh & Fils, 39ha, R12,000, W7,500

Jean-Voisin St-Ém, GC, SC Chassagnoux, 14ha, R7,500

du Juge*, Bord Sup, (Cadillac), P Dupleich, 28ha, W10,000, R6,000

du Juge Prem Côtes, (Haux), J Mèdeville, 28ha, R9,000, W3,000

Le Jurat St-Ém, GC, SCA Haut Corbin, 6ha, R3,500

Justa* Prem Côtes, M Mas, 19ha, R10,000, W2,400

Laborde L de Pom, J-M Trocard, 20ha, R8,500

Puy-Blanquet* St-Ém, GC, R Jacquet, 23ha, R10,000

Puyblanquet-Carille St-Ém, GC, J-F Carille, 12ha, R7,000

Quentin St-Ém, GC, SC, 30ha, R1,800

de Ramondon Prem Côtes, Mme van Pé, 25ha, R14,00, W9,000

du Raux H-Méd, SCI, 15ha, R8,500

Raymond, E-D-M, Baron R de Montesquieu, 27ha, R28,000

de Respide Gr, Vignobles Bonnet, 40ha, R18,000, W8,000

Reynier* E-D-M, D Lurton, 75ha, R35,000, W9,000

Richelieu Fron, Y Viaud, 12·9ha, R7,500

La Rivalerie Bl, Gillibert Chauvin, 34ha, R17,500, W1,000

La Roche Prem Côtes, P Dumas, 15ha, R10,000

du Rocher St-Ém, GC, Baron de Montfort, 15ha, R7,000

La-Rose-Côte-de-Rol St-Ém, GC, Y Mirande, 9ha, R4,000

La Rose Pourret* St-Ém, GC, B Warion, 8ha, R4,000

Roumieu* Bars, Mme Craveia-Goyaud, 16ha, W3,500

Roumieu Saut, CB, R Bernadet, 20ha, W2,000

Roumieu-Lacoste* Saut, Hervé Dubourdieu, 12ha, W3,000

St-Christoly Méd, CB 1932, Hervé Héraud, 24ha, R16,500

St-Paul H-Méd, SC, 20ha, R10,000

Ségur H-Méd, CGB 1932, M Grazioli, 36·8ha, R24,500

Sémeillan Mazeau List, CBS 1932, SC, 17ha, R8,000

Senailhac* E-D-M, Magnat, 55ha, R25,000, W1,500

Senilhac* H-Méd, CB 1932, P & F Grassin, 20·5ha, R11,500

Simon Bars, CB, J Dufour, 17ha, W4,500

Suau Prem Côtes, M Aldebert, 49ha, R30,000

du Tasta* Prem Côtes, P Perret, 13ha, R6,500

Tayac Bg, P Saturny, 30ha, R16,000, W300

Templiers, Clos des L de Pom, Vignobles Meyer, 11ha, R6,000

de Terrefort-Quancard Bord Sup, Quancard family, 65·7ha, R37,000, W1,300

de Thau Bg, Vignobles Schweitzer, 27ha, R15,000

Timberlay* Bord Sup, R Giraud, 130ha, R55,000, W11,000

La Tour Blanche Méd, CB 1932, Vignobles d'Aquitaine, 27ha, R12,500

La Tour-Pibran Pau, CB 1932, SARL, 9ha, R5,500

La Tour-Prignac Méd, CB 1932, SC, 140ha, R44,000

La Tour-Puymirand E-D-M, Degueil, 33ha, R15,500 W3,000

Tour-du-Roc H-Méd, CB 1932, Philippe Robert, 12ha, R6,000

La Tour-St-Joseph* H-Méd, CB, M & C Quancard, 13ha, R5,000

Tour-St-Pierre St-Ém, GC, J Goudineau, 10ha, R5,000

La Tour-Seran Méd, CB 1932, SCEA, 18ha, R10,000

des Troischardons Marg, C, Y & A Chardon, 2·7ha R1,500

Le Tuquet* Gr, P Ragon, 50ha, R7,500, W7,500

de Tustal E-D-M, Comte d'Armaillé, 43ha, W11,000, R7,500

Videau Prem Côtes, SARL Benito, 25·9ha, R15,000, W1,500

La Vieille France Gr, M Dugoua, 23·5ha, R10,500, W2,500

du Vieux-Moulin Loup, Mme Perromat-Dauné, 18ha, W4,000

Vieux-Robin Méd, CB, D & M Roba, 16·8ha, R10,500

La Violette Pom, Vignobles S Dumas, 4·5ha, R2,000

Virou Bl, SCEA, 62ha R41,000

Vrai-Canon-Bouché C-Fron, Roux, 13ha, R6,500

Index

Alphabetisation ignores au, de, des, du, la, le and les.
Château and Domaines (abbreviated to Ch and Dom respectively) appear under their individual names. Wine names in italics are those of second or other labels.